"This book is a "Masterp
source of inspiration to a
soul, taking them on a journey of inner ...
'Angel of Light'."

—Lisa S. Marzi,
Poet/Writer, Scotland, United Kingdom

"Just as God sent the dove with the olive branch to Noah as a testimonial for him to keep his faith about finding land, He has sent us "Olive" with her signs of faith. Truth always resonates to the soul, and her story is soulful!"

—Grace Grella,
Professional Intuitive, and Host of her own award-winning
Cable Television Show, New York, USA

"*Secrets of My Soul* is a heartfelt book sharing experiences of what it is to be in communion with the Divine. Olive's innocence and angelic nature shines through as she shares the part of her life of feeling what it is to be with the truth of all that is."

—Sheila Unique,
Energy Coach, Author, *Quick Shifts*, Saskatchewan, Canada

"Olive is a true gift! Her stories of divine intervention are touching. The love she and her husband share is inspiring! What a moving read."

—Michelle Fox,
Author of the Forthcoming Book, *The Graceful Divorce*, Colorado, USA

"I've always been skeptical about angels but reading just a few pages of this book had me believing! This is a memoir that will capture your attention and your heart over and over again."

—Jade Hanson,
Independent Business Consultant, California, USA

"These are extraordinary tales...unique and fascinating encounters with the Creator. These tales reflect more than one faithful woman's accounts but also reflect the closeness of God to His people."

—Amani Hamdan, Ph.D.,
Author, *Muslim Women Speak: A tapestry of lives and dreams*, Al-Khobar,
Saudi Arabia

"I felt the unfolding of Olive's spiritual journey in each word. The loving care she has taken with each experience and her reverence for the process is so moving, I cried. She is undeniably powerful yet her stories reflect a genuine, humble heart."

—RHONDA PATRICK-SISON,
Master Intuitive Coach, Psychic Channel &
Holistic HR Consultant, Illinois, USA

"Rich with warmth, compassion and life, Olive invites us on an amazing spiritual journey, with personal stories of profound truth. A book to be cherished that will stir and comfort its readers."

—TERESA BROWN,
Intuitive/Medium, Author,
Discovering The Power of Ceremony, Florida, USA

"The spiritual stories shared in this book, give us inspiration to know that there is life after death and our loved ones are waiting for us. The stories will touch and inspire you."

—VANESSA TALBOT,
Author, *Extraordinary Beings, Success Creation and Life Optimize, Extraordinary YOU...The Art of Living a Lusciously Spiritual, Vibrant Life*, New South Wales, Australia

"Olive so eloquently captures the essence of angels around us, and inspires a feeling of security and love that is always with us."

—LAURIE JOSLIN,
President, Unlimited Coaching Solutions Inc., New York, USA

"Olive's story comes from her heart and true life experiences. For anyone desiring to learn more about Guardian Angels and the uplifting support they provide, this book is a must read."

—CHERYL A. RAINEY LMFT, PH.D.,
Marriage and Family Therapist, Florida, USA

Secrets Of My Soul

A memoir of extraordinary true stories, of a spiritual journey,
which made me know the truth about life, death and the Other Side.

*Olive shares her inner most secrets and tells the
world the answers to the mysteries of life.*

OLIVE NEIL NOSEWORTHY

BALBOA.
PRESS
A DIVISION OF HAY HOUSE

Balboa Press books may be ordered through booksellers or by contacting:

Balboa Press
A Division of Hay House
1663 Liberty Drive
Bloomington, IN 47403
www.balboapress.com
1-(877) 407-4847

Cover photo by Klik Photography, St. John's, NL Canada.

ISBN: 978-1-4525-7672-5 (sc)
ISBN: 978-1-4525-7674-9 (hc)
ISBN: 978-1-4525-7673-2 (e)

Library of Congress Control Number: 2013911101

Printed in the United States of America.

Balboa Press rev. date: 09/05/2013

To My Darling Husband

Dave, you truly understand the meaning of love; it is therefore with great pride and privilege that I dedicate this book to you. While we have traveled this Earth together as husband and wife, you have been my soul mate, true friend, loving and devoted father to our children, and a dear and loving husband to me. You have chosen to make the commitment to remain by my side and to cherish me for all eternity. Your resolute determination to continue to love me through the years, offers an inspiration to me that lights my way while completing my travels on this home we call Earth.

My husband, Dave

To My Adorable Katie

Until one has loved an animal,
a part of one's soul remains unawakened.

Anatole France
A Book of Miracles

To my darling baby girl, my dog Katie, who gives me
unconditional love each day. The joy you bring to my life is
immeasurable and will always be treasured, deep within my
soul, for I realize now you have always been with me over the
years, and because you love me so much, you keep coming
back to me, and I know that you have never truly left me.

My dog, Katie

In Loving Memory

To a dear and loving father, my dad, Ralph Neil, who gave me many gifts of love during his lifetime here on Earth. He was my dad until his time came to return home to Heaven, and even though he is now on the Other Side, he visits me quite often. He lets me know he still loves me very much, and that he is always there for me, especially during the difficult times. He has let me know that he will never abandon me nor let me down, and that he watches over me each day, until it is my time to join him, and that he still remains my dad.

My dad and I on my wedding day

Table of Contents

Foreword

When Ol, as I like to call her, asked me to write the foreword to her book, *Secrets of My Soul*, I was excited. I met Ol a few years ago when God planned for us to meet. We found love and Heaven in each other's company. We have shared good times; we have prayed together and narrated accounts demonstrating God's role in our lives and confirming our belief in the Holy Spirit. In addition, we both believe in the angels that accompany us in the difficult moments in our lives.

The remarkable events that are included in this book, Ol has shared with me. I have empathized with her and yet I have envied her at the same time. I empathized with her because it was not easy to undergo her experiences, and I also envy her because it is a real privilege to experience the metaphysical and to transgress the boundaries between the two worlds—the here and the hereafter.

In a problematic, unmerciful world in which hatred is dominant and peace and love are scarce, Ol and I have developed a bond of faith. Our faith in God's existence and in God's mercy and love to us as His people, made Ol and I stronger in facing challenges and overcoming the grueling times in our lives.

As you begin the journey of reading these captivating stories, I urge you to think of God as your savior, to pray to Him, and to embrace the love of God every moment in your life.

Dr. Amani Hamdan

Preface

As people living here on Earth, we have many unanswered questions. We have a deep, soul-searching need that requires answers. Everyone needs to know the true meaning of living life here on Earth, and to know the truth of all that is. And so, the time has come for the veil of secrecy to be lifted.

Once I reveal my secrets to you, it is then you will understand my desire to reveal my innermost secrets of my soul, and by sharing the secrets of my soul, you can follow a spiritual path to discover the secrets of your soul. Thus, the title of my aspiring book, *Secrets of My Soul,* is born.

The stories I describe are factual and real life events that happened, and all the people written about in this book are real people; however, in order to protect the privacy of certain individuals, I have disguised the names and identifying characteristics of these people.

Acknowledgments

The journey of spiritual awareness while traveling this Earth is truly a miraculous experience, and for me, I never would have accomplished my spiritual goals without my loved ones by my side.

First, I wish to extend my profound gratitude to my lovingly Heavenly Father who waits for me back Home. He has allowed me to come to this Earth, to travel purposefully down His path towards greater knowledge and spiritual awareness, and to serve Him and others.

I wish to thank my Guardian Angel, Gabriel, who used to watch over me from a distance, but who is now with me each day, providing me with guidance, direction, protection, wisdom and love. I humbly thank him also for providing clarity and purpose for my life lessons, and for helping me to do God's work by writing this book.

I also wish to thank my seven Guardian Angels, including Gabriel, who appeared to me while I was living in Saudi Arabia. They continue to be with me on this journey and aid me in my spiritual accomplishments.

My gratitude is extended to my two Guardian Souls, Aunt Mildred and Uncle Edward, who have traveled back Home and who took turns every three days to lovingly guide, protect and love me each minute of every day, before my Guardian Angel took over, and who are now watching over me from a distance.

A very special thank you to my dad, Ralph Neil, for being such a devoted father to me and for his never ending guidance and love, and who still shows his devotion to me even though he has returned to the Other Side. He has been and still is the "great teacher" in my life.

My warmest thank you to my Uncle Stan for his continued love and support, and for helping me to begin to understand the spiritual truths of life.

I wish to thank two of the most beautiful, devoted, and loving souls who share this time on Earth with me, my children, for their everlasting love.

Finally, yet importantly, I wish to acknowledge my husband. Blessed by his love, I am incredibly grateful to him, for he has always encouraged me to be a free soul and to follow my dreams. He inspires me each day as I walk in God's path of righteousness and love.

Introduction

Somewhere ages and ages hence;
Two roads diverged in a wood, and I,
I took the one less traveled by,
And that has made all the difference.

Robert Frost
The Road Not Taken

Encountering spiritual struggles is not new to me, especially as a child who grew up knowing she was different, in a world where she always felt she did not fit in. There were many reasons for feeling this way, however, one of the main reasons is that I considered myself a "doubting Thomas." Thomas was one of the twelve disciples of Jesus but he was not with the others when Jesus appeared to them, after Jesus was crucified on the cross. Thomas did not believe the others when they told him that Jesus was alive. He needed proof. He told the other disciples unless he saw the wounds of the nails in Jesus' hands, and he could place his finger in the puncture of the nails, and place his hand on Jesus' side, he would not believe. I too would not believe what others told me was the truth, even when one of the others was my own father. It did not matter. I needed proof.

I always had doubt and yearned for the truth. However, exactly what was the truth? Many people had their thoughts and opinions but much to my surprise, I always found them to be conflicting and confusing. I was always a curious child and knew I had to learn more. I absorbed information like a sponge and conversed with anyone who was willing to share his or her thoughts with me. I had an unquenchable thirst for spiritual knowledge, which was never satisfied.

As a child, I had a typical religious upbringing while living in a Christian family, receiving the standard religious education from my parents, school, Sunday school and church. I attended church service every Sunday morning and every Sunday evening, while also attending Sunday school in the afternoon. As I grew older, I became a member of the Junior Church Choir and later a member of the Senior Church Choir. I also became a Sunday School Teacher, which lasted for approximately four years. We always celebrated the major Protestant Christian holidays and therefore I was exposed to all the Christian traditions. Our Christian faith taught me there is a loving God and we should live our lives according to the teachings of His Beloved Son, Jesus Christ, who came to this Earth many years ago.

I learned about religion in a historical context but could never understand why there were so many different religions in the world. I also found it surprising that many religions of the world did not believe in the God that my family and I believed to be the one and only Creator! If this was not surprising enough, what really shocked me was that there were many different Christian religions! How could this be? If we are all Christians and believe in the same loving God, and follow the teachings of our God from the same book, the Holy Bible, then why did we follow different rules? None of this made any sense to me.

I had a strong interest in trying to understand why people of the Roman Catholic religion were Christians, and yet were segregated from the rest of us Christians, who called ourselves Protestants. If this was not confusing enough for me, I then learned that there were Christians who are Protestants but who also have different religions from our Protestant religion, Anglican! They too attended different churches, their children went to different schools, and they kept mostly to themselves.

However, the following information is what really devastated me. I learned that in Ireland, where many of our Newfoundland ancestors came from, there are two main Christian faiths. One is the Roman Catholic faith and the other is the Protestant faith. The people of these two different Christian religions of Ireland, consider themselves so different the Irish War of Independence resulted, and the country of Ireland was divided into what is now known as the Republic of Ireland and Northern Ireland. This information was far too hurtful for a young child to comprehend. I was beginning to feel that I was living in a world that was gone mad. I decided at a very young age that I was not very keen about all of these different, organized religions.

As I grew older and learned more, I became more and more curious. The more I learned, the more I doubted. I began to realize that I was of the Anglican Christian faith, because my parents were of this faith. They were of this faith because of their parents and so on and so on. Religious teachings and beliefs are passed down from family to family and from generation to generation. In addition, this was not just true for my family; it was true for every family! I quickly came to the realization that this was true for all religions of the world: the Jewish faith, the Muslim faith, the Christian faith, all of them, passed down their beliefs from one generation to the next! My new understanding made me realize, that people tend to believe and accept the truth according to what the people from their own families and ancestry believe to be true.

Later in my life, I changed my religion to that of the United Church because this was the religion of my new husband, and I felt we all should be of the same faith as a family, especially if my husband and I planned to have children. The United Church is a Protestant Christian religion and similar to the Anglican faith to which I was accustomed. However, even though I was a member of this organized Christian religion, I felt I was not completely serving God, if there was a God. I was now convinced more than ever that organized religion can and does complicate the truth between the person and God.

I was also very disturbed by the different situations revealed to me over time as I grew into a young adult, for example, the starving children of the world. How could this be when there are so many with so much? How people could be so blind and look the other way was beyond my understanding. Then there were the wars fought in the name of freedom and justice. Sons and daughters were sent off to fight in wars, which many did not believe in, and were forced into killing in order to save their own life or the life of a fellow soldier. Many times over the years, I recall feeling such despair. One particular time, I was visiting my friend

Renu and I voiced my concerns. She said to me, "Olive, you can't change the world." I felt hopeless. I was suffering a lot of emotional and spiritual pain, and if I were to survive, I knew I had to know if there was a loving God. I knew I had to carve out my own spiritual identity and I had to search for the truth, and search I did.

I remained a "doubting Thomas" for many years; however, over time my spiritual life started to unfold, and little by little, the truth started to unravel. I was well into my late twenties before the pieces of the puzzle started to fall into place. The ability to "feel" and "see" the truth was amazing! I started to do a lot of reflecting and much to my astonishment; I began to see a pattern. There were even signs from God. Signs that were obvious, yet I had been completely blind to them for many years. I call them Soul Signs.

Most of my life I considered life experiences to be a coincidence. I now know that there is no such thing as coincidence or luck. Everything is planned and orchestrated. Everything has a purpose. My life here on Earth has a purpose. I know now after all these years why I always had such a passionate interest in pursuing the truth. Believing and knowing are not the same. I do not believe what is supposed to be true, I *know* what is true.

PART 1

MY EARLY YEARS

CHAPTER 1

In The Beginning

Your children are not your children.
They are the sons and daughters of Life's longing for itself.
They come through you but not from you,
And though they are with you yet they belong not to you.

Kahlil Gibran
The Prophet

Raised in an upper-middle class family in a small town called Spaniard's Bay, in the province of Newfoundland and Labrador in eastern Canada, I lived a life that most people would consider Heaven on Earth. Spaniard's Bay is a beautiful small town and very picturesque, and one of the great features of this town is that it is in a bay, and thus surrounded by the Atlantic Ocean, and our house was situated directly across the road from the ocean, so I had access to the beach. As a child, I felt I had everything I needed, at least in the physical sense.

I remember my friend's mother, Minnie Gardiner, telling me about the day I was born. Jocelyn was one of my closest friends, and she lived across the road from my house. Mrs. Gardiner would begin the story by telling me that she remembered the day very vividly. Dr. Drover, after being summoned, had arrived at my house carrying his large, black, leather medical bag. Everyone in the surrounding area knew that Dr. Drover had arrived, and there would be news of a newborn baby soon. It was always so exciting to wait for the arrival of a dear and precious baby, and it was even more exciting to wonder if it was going to be a boy or a girl. There were already two girls in my family, so maybe this time it would be a boy.

On September 16, the doctor left the house, and the news was out. It was a beautiful baby girl! My parents had anxiously waited for the arrival of their child, and now they had another precious daughter. They had hoped that this time it would be a boy, but now that their baby had arrived, all that mattered was that she was healthy. When I questioned Mrs. Gardiner about my mode of transportation, she told me that Dr. Drover carried me to our house in his big, black medical bag! My curiosity was satisfied.

The house where I was born and lived as a child

I had everything I wanted and more. Financially, we were well off and consequently I was never in need. I was showered with material gifts and much love. I had many friends and my childhood was full of fun, laughter and play. I had a wonderful childhood filled with precious memories; for I was given a childhood that most people only read about in storybooks.

As a child growing up in my small town by the sea

My life was complete, but for some strange reason, I felt an emptiness; and it was an emptiness that I could not explain. I felt I did not belong and did not fit in. I felt like a stranger in a foreign land and I did not know why I had these feelings. I had always felt different, and I even looked and acted different. There was no physical resemblance to any other family member, not even extended family. As the years went by, I became somewhat accustomed to hearing my parents making comments, as they tried to figure out which family member I looked or acted like. The only conclusion they could come up with was that both my grandmothers were small-framed and petite women. Other than that, nothing else made any sense.

As I grew older, I questioned in my mind if it was possible that I had been mixed up in the nursery room while in the hospital. I knew this was possible because I had heard stories of mothers who were given the wrong baby; however, I quickly dismissed this from my mind because I remembered that I had been born at home. Then the thought came to me that it was quite possible that I was adopted. However, if this was the case, why were my parents always trying to figure out who in the family I looked or acted like? None of this made any sense to me.

As the time went by, I knew I had to search for the truth, and search I did. However, in the end, the truth revealed the same story as Mrs. Gardiner had told me, except for the mode of transportation in Dr. Drover's big, black medical bag!

Left with the unknown, the alienation I felt at times was almost unbearable. Many times in desperation I sought out places in nature; I would sit in the corner of our garden or I would sit on a huge rock on the seashore, gaze out into the distant waters and pray, hoping someone would hear my prayers and take me back home to where I belonged. I had a lingering homesickness that I could not explain. I suffered in private and was left with the emptiness of the unknown, searching for the truth.

CHAPTER 2

Love Is No Stranger

A good idea is to give love,
then you will feel love.

Marshall Stewart Ball
Kiss of God

From my earliest childhood memories, I can always remember being in the presence of loving souls. I was very fortunate to have been exposed to a loving family environment whose teachings of love were taken seriously. At a very young age, I can remember knowing that love is a gift from God, that love represents God, and that to know God, you have to love God as well as others, including yourself. In addition, if you do not love God, you do not love yourself, and therefore you are not capable of loving others.

I was the middle child of five daughters, two older and two younger. I was the youngest for ten years and was supposed to have been the last child. However, little did my mother and father know that God had other plans, and so two other baby girls were born. I did not have any brothers and I considered this to be to my advantage. My father worked outside of our town and came home only on the weekends. Those were special times for me because on Saturdays, I would spend time with my dad. My father grew his own vegetables, and I remember the most enjoyable part for me was when it was harvest time. I loved it when it was time for my father to have the soil tilled and the rows of soil opened up, and the potatoes were exposed. I helped pick the potatoes from the ground with my dad and learned from watching and helping. During the week, I had my mom. I also knew how to make bread, do laundry, iron clothes and clean the house; however, I learned very quickly that I did not like to house clean. I never had to do any work; I helped if I chose. My mother and two older sisters did the housework; but even then, they did not do it all the time because my mother usually had a housekeeper come to our house.

I experienced love not only from my immediate family but also from my extended family. I found every uncle and aunt to be loving and kind. However, there are certain ones I feel a stronger bond with than others. Uncle Stan is my mother's brother, and he was always so caring and loving. It was not until after his death that I came to understand the close bond, which exists between us. Then there was my Uncle Abel, whom I loved dearly and I always loved to be in his company. I never knew until after he had died why I loved him so much and why there was such a special bond of love between us.

Uncle Allan and his first wife, Aunt Lucy, showed me much affection and love and as a little girl, I remember how they would buy me special gifts and do things for me to show how special they believed me to be. One of my most cherished gifts is a small cup and saucer Aunt Lucy gave me during one of my summer visits. I also remember that Aunt Lucy would always make me Caramel Square Cookies because she knew I loved them so much. On one occasion while visiting Uncle Allan and Aunt Lucy in Corner Brook, I recall wanting some sweet pickled baby onion, which I love. There was none in the house so Uncle Allan went out to buy some. He was gone for such a long time because he had difficulty finding just the right onions that I liked. He had to shop all over town until he finally found them.

Visiting Corner Brook

Then there was Uncle Doug and Aunt Flo. Uncle Doug is my father's brother and his wife is Flo. I always felt so much love from them. It was not until I had gotten older, that I found out they wanted to adopt me.

Uncle Bernard was also very loving and kind. Uncle Bernard was married to my father's sister, my Aunt Evelyn. One year, when they visited from New York, they took my oldest sister back with them for a vacation. She was only eleven years old at the time. I remember them telling me that they would take me also, except I was too young. It would be another time.

Uncle Ted I loved and I knew he loved me. He is my father's brother. Uncle Ted always sent special gifts at Christmas time. My first year in nursing school, he sent me money for Christmas and I bought a silver Bulova watch, which I have to this day. When I got married, he sent me a large sum of money for my wedding gift, and I bought a hostess cart. It is now many years later and my hostess cart is still in my dining room. When I was in high school, Uncle Ted offered me a gift that most girls only dream about when they are young. He sent me brochures and information about the University of Waterloo, Ontario. He offered to pay for my post-secondary education and for me to attend the University of Waterloo with my cousin, his daughter Joan, who was a student at this university. He told me I could choose any program of study that I wished. I could have chosen medicine, nursing, business, or any program that interested me.

I even experienced love also from our neighbors. Because Spaniard's Bay is just a small community, we knew our neighbors very well. Our neighbor, William (Bill) Hedderson, he is Mr. Hedderson to me, lived directly across the road from our house and was the principal of our school. He has a daughter Dawn, who was around my age and we were very close friends. Mr. Hedderson knew my father was away from home working during the week, so he made sure I had a car ride to and from school every day. Some mornings I would be running late but, it did not matter; he showed much patience and love and would park his car in front of our house and wait for me to come out.

Another neighbor I found to be very loving and kind is Shirley Gosse, Mrs. Gosse to me. She also has a daughter around my age, Karen, and we were very close friends. I practically lived at their house. I felt as though I was one of them. I remember Mr. and Mrs. Gosse going on vacation one year to Nassau, the Bahamas. After a couple of weeks, Mrs. Gosse returned with gifts for both Karen and me. The gifts she gave me were more than material gifts because she gave me the identical gifts she brought her own daughter! I learned two very important lessons that day. I learned that this lady was very loving and generous, and displayed her love for me by showing no difference between her daughter and me. I also learned that love does not coexist with jealousy. It occurred to me that Karen could have easily been upset because of jealousy; however, she wasn't. Another year the same thing happened. Mr. and Mrs. Gosse took a vacation to London, England. Again, upon their return, there were gifts for both Karen and me. Once again, the gifts were identical. One of the gifts we were given were identical black, patent leather shoes. Oh, how we loved those shoes!

Karen and I wearing our identical black, patent leather shoes

Even though there was so much love in my life, I was not blind to the fact that not everyone or everything is perfect in this world. I started to recognize danger and experienced loss and pain at a very young age. It all began one day after I had just started school. I was only five years old and I noticed someone following me while walking home alone. He was much older than I was and maybe in his late teens or early twenties. At first I did not really think too much of it. However, the next day, there he was again, waiting outside the school on the other side, and once I started walking, he started walking, and the faster I walked, the faster he walked, and the faster I ran, the faster he ran. I started to experience fear like I had never known.

When I arrived home, I was so out of breath, I could hardly speak, but somehow I managed to tell my mother about the stranger who was waiting outside the school, and who was following me home. From that day onward, my grandfather walked me to school every morning, and was always outside every afternoon, waiting to walk me home. From the very first day my grandfather was by my side, this stranger disappeared.

My grandfather and I

I knew the feeling of fear and I was about to experience it again. My father was a very friendly man and it did not matter to him if a person was rich or poor. He had friends from all over our small town and from faraway places as well. There was one person in our town that was very poor, and he was so poor that his house was not painted and it looked old and run down. He himself looked very scary, having a long beard and, long, dirty looking hair and an old coat that was tattered and torn. He was always kind and friendly and I had no reason to be afraid of this man, except for the way he looked; and even though I knew my father was friends with him, it did not seem to console me much.

One particular Saturday afternoon, I opened the kitchen door to walk out into our back porch, at exactly the same time Mr. Billy Neil opened our back door to enter! I screamed at the top of my lungs and started to cry hysterically, all the while crouching down in the corner behind the door. My father came running and quickly grabbed me in his arms, and I clung on to my dad's neck for dear life, sobbing all the while. He took me inside into the kitchen and sat down with me on his lap, all the while trying to calm me down and apologizing to his dear friend, Mr. Neil. My dad offered his friend a chair and they both started talking, and not only did they talk to one another but they both also talked to me. It was at that moment that I came to appreciate the kindness and loving nature of this man and that I had nothing to fear.

After experiencing fear, I later experienced loss. One of my best friends, Jocelyn Gardiner, moved away because her father had accepted another position of work outside our province. It was a sad time for me. We promised we would write letters to one another and would always remain friends. In the beginning, I received one letter with a photo of her, with her mother and sister, celebrating her birthday; however, after that, no matter how many cards or letters I sent, I did not get any in return. I felt heart broken. We were such good friends, how could this happen? She too had sent me many letters. She too was heartbroken and did not understand how I could not answer her letters, and it was not until many years later we both learned the truth.

Mr. Humphries was an elderly man who walked to the post office each day and picked up the mail for all the neighbours in the area. Therefore, any cards, letters or parcels that our family wanted mailed, we would deliver them to his house. If there were any mail for us, he would give it to us each day. As a small child, I remember many times going to his house to pick up our mail. However, it was not until after his death, much to the shock of all the people in our town, bags and bags of mail were found in his shed! Years after my dear friend Jocelyn had moved away and we were much older; we received our letters of love from long ago. Our hearts were mended, and the mystery finally solved!

As a young child, I also experienced loss through death. Looking back, I do not think I fully understood what was happening, for all I remember was hearing that one of the students in our school had taken quite sick and would not get better. The doctor told her mom and dad that she had leukemia. It was about six months later that my friends and I were told, she had died. I asked my mother what this meant, and she told me that she had to go to Heaven. Go to Heaven, what did this mean? Why would she have to go away? Was anyone to go with her? I had so many questions that even my parents found it difficult to give me answers, and so I asked my older sisters, but they did not seem to have the answers either.

I heard people say that she was waking at her house, and so my friend and I wanted to go and visit her. It is as clear as though it happened yesterday. We knocked on the door and a woman answered, and we asked if we could see our friend. She just nodded her head. As we entered and were taken into the front room of the house, lying in a casket, very still, and not moving or speaking, was our friend from school. I remember no one spoke, and all I could hear were sobs and cries from the other people present. It was unbearable and I did not understand. All I knew was that our friend had to go away, to where I really did not know, for no one could really tell me where Heaven was, except to point upward to the sky!

It was a few years later, growing up in my small town by the sea, that I experienced sadness and grief once again. The news was out that a teenager had committed suicide! What was this? I did not know. What happened? My questions were answered very quickly as the devastating news flew around town worse than a windstorm. This was a student from my school but much older than me, for he was a teenager. I remembered him so well because he was the only one in our school who could play the piano with such excellence, yet he had never taken piano lessons, nor did he have a piano in his house! I did have a piano in my house because my dad bought it for me so I could take piano lessons, however, I could not play the piano as exceptional as he did, even though my music teacher had awarded me first place in a piano competition.

Playing the piano during a musical concert

The rumor around town was that this child was so intelligent, he was always one step ahead of the teachers; for what the teachers were teaching in the daytime, this child had already learned. He was so smart that he could teach the teachers. He was brilliant! Yet, here is the news that he is now dead! He had gone missing, and was found later hanging from a tree!

A couple of years later, I experienced fear once again and this time the fear was far greater than I could have ever imagined. My dad worked in Argentia, a small town in our province, and only came home on weekends, and to look out the window and see my father's car stop in front of our house during the middle of the week, was very unusual. And not only was that out of the ordinary, but also the fact that my dad was not driving his car, but instead, my Uncle Stan was.

Immediately both my mother and I jumped to the conclusion that my father had been in a car accident because the front of his car was damaged. The fear that swept over me was massive! The thought of my dad seriously injured sent shock waves throughout my body. As my Uncle Stan assists my father out of the passenger seat of the car and escorts him to the front steps of our house, it is plain to see that my dad finds it extremely difficult to walk. My dad is bent over and stumbling; as though he is drunk. But how could this be? My dad only drank alcohol on Saturday evenings while watching the hockey game on television, and then it would only be a couple of beer. And he would occasionally have a drink of Scotch whiskey, and then it was just usually during special times, such as Christmas. However, here is my dad finding it difficult to walk and his speech is slurred.

My mother and I quickly run to assist my uncle to get my dad up the steps to our house and as we do, my Uncle Stan tells us that my dad is very sick. He explains to my mother that he was the one driving my father's car, because my dad was not well enough to drive it himself, and that it was him who was involved in the car accident while driving my dad home.

After many visits to medical specialists and numerous medical tests later, the conclusion was that a diagnosis could not be made. All the doctors were completely baffled. My dad presented signs and symptoms that could not be explained. He could not walk properly and had to be assisted, and his body was bent over and he appeared much older than his age. His eyesight was affected and he did not have peripheral vision because both his pupils were fixed and not moving. It seemed as though he had some type of neurological damage, however, there was nothing conclusive. The doctors explains to my mother that there is nothing that can be done, and their only recommendation is to have my father transferred to Montreal, Quebec, to see a specialist there. She is informed that there is only one other known case similar to my dad's and that this patient resides in the United States. They never did tell my mother if that person survived the illness.

After many sleepless nights, many tears, and many prayers to our Heavenly Father, my mother and father decide it would be best for my dad to accept the recommendation of the doctors. He would go to Montreal, even though it would be extremely costly. However, little did my parents know that there was an angel living in our small town. Mark

Gosse, more commonly known as skipper Mark, a next door neighbor, visits my dad and offers him an extraordinary gift. He tells my dad, he doesn't know my father's financial status and that it doesn't matter one way or the other; however, he would like to pay for all expenses for my dad to travel to Montreal. He wants him to see the medical specialist there, and if need be, to remain there for any treatment that is required, in order for him to get well.

As it turns out, my father's signs and symptoms gradually disappeared, making the trip to Montreal not necessary. However, the gracious gift of generosity that Mr. Gosse offered my dad that day is one that will remain with all of us for all eternity.

My life turned upside down; one day, I am so happy playing with my friends and having fun; and the next day I hear some terrible news. Is this what life is really like? I found it extremely difficult to understand living life. Did anything make any real sense? As the years went by, I still felt safe and loved, no matter what was happening outside of my home. I still had my dad who came home on the weekends and made me baked eggs for breakfast and my mom during the week, who made custard and pies. In addition, I had my friends. I have so many wonderful memories playing with my friends, and I remember even playing with the Ouija Board, trying to contact spirits! I remember all too well the first time the Ouija Board moved, without any help from us. As it started to move, we screamed so loud I think the neighbours heard us! That was the first and last time we ever played with the Ouija Board!

Then I started high school, and another tragedy unfolded. It was Christmas time and we heard the news about one of the students in my class who was accidently killed. His parents had given him a motorcycle for Christmas. He was riding it in his backyard, hit a patch of ice, had fallen and hit his head. The impact of the news did not fully register with me until the day we returned to school after Christmas break and his seat was empty! The sadness and sorrow that swept over our classroom lasted for months!

As other people lived their lives, I lived mine. I learned over time that my life was so very different from many others walking this Earth. Living life was not easy, at least for many. In addition, why I was living the storybook life, I did not know. However, the one thing that I did know was that my mom and dad loved me very much and they would never intentionally say or do anything to hurt me. They were there for me no matter what, and we laughed, played and did many fun things together. I have many fond and loving memories of my mother and father, as a child growing up.

One such memory was the year I graduated from high school and my parents took my two younger sisters and me on a vacation. During our travels I visited New York City! My father's brother, my Uncle Bert, who lived in White Plains, New York, took my father and me to the Big Apple! We did all the sightseeing tours, including visiting the Empire State Building, which at the time, was the tallest building in the world! Uncle Bert also took us to a very posh restaurant called "The Riverboat" for lunch. As we entered, we had to walk down a flight of winding stairs, which took us to a room with round tables draped in white tablecloths, donned with sparkling glasses and silverware. The waiters were dressed in tuxedos and brought our meals out on plates covered with silver dome covers. While we ate our lunch, a violinist played. Everything was so glamorous and elegant! That day I spent with my dad and my Uncle Bert was one of the most cherished memories of my childhood. I later visited Cape Cod and the city of Boston with my family and had the holiday of a lifetime, especially for a young girl of only sixteen!

The glamor of the big city life came to an end, as well as our fabulous vacation; however, I had no problem leaving and going back to where love was no stranger to me, to my small town by the sea.

CHAPTER 3

You Will Know It Is Him

When you have been touched
by the eternal truths of the spiritual dimension,
you cannot possibly go back to the old way of living.

James Van Praagh
Ghosts Among Us

As I grew into young adulthood, I left my loving and secure home with my family and friends of my small hometown, and entered a nursing program in the capital city of our province, St. John's. In the fall of the year, September to be precise, I entered the Grace General Hospital School for Nursing. My two older sisters attended and graduated from this same school and so it just seemed destined for me to follow my sisters' footsteps. This was an exciting time in my life and I was meeting many new friends; however, it was also a very frightening time because I was finding that not all people were kind, considerate and loving. It did not take very long before I had a drastic awakening.

My new home in the nurses' residence was room 628. Little did I know at the time that this room number has great spiritual significance for me, and it was not until many years later that I came to understand the true meaning of this number in my life. I am in the nurse's residence, room 628, and a loving voice was speaking to me! I immediately recognized the loving voice to be that of a female, and she was saying to me, "You will know it is him."

In amazement, I quickly turned my head to see who was talking. There was no one in the room! At least no one that I was able to see, so I frantically asked, "Who are you?"

"I am your Guardian Soul."

"I have a Guardian Soul?" I questioned with a surprise tone of voice.

"You most certainly do."

"And what is a Guardian Soul?"

"I have been assigned to watch over you and to protect and keep you safe on your journey of life."

"You are to protect me and keep me safe?"

"Yes, my dear."

"Am I in danger?" I frantically ask.

"No, you are not in any danger. Please do not be alarmed."

"And when do you do this?"

"I do this all the time. This is my spiritual work. I am to watch over you during your lifetime while you live here on Earth, or until such time someone else takes my place; for you have been given two Guardian Souls to watch over you."

"I do?"

"Yes, you do."

"Who told you to do this?"

I now heard this female voice give a chuckle as she answered, "My dear, the One and only."

"The One and only, who is this?"

"You already know."

"I already know; I don't know any such thing!"

Again, I heard the female voice chuckle. "You must not forget who you are."

I was speechless. I finally broke the silence. "Why can't I see you?"

The loving female voice replied, "You can, you just think that you can't."

Again, I was speechless.

The loving voice continued. "I have been sent to give you a soul message."

"What do you mean by a soul message?"

"A soul message is a message from the Other Side; the spirit world."

I felt complete awe, as I sat in my bed clutching my blanket, trying to make sense of everything. There was only silence, as I found I was once again speechless. I was finally able to utter the words, "The Other Side; the spirit world?"

"Yes. Please do not be distressed. There is no reason for you to feel this way. You are very familiar with the spirit world, for this is where you belong."

I tried to let the words I was hearing sink into my brain. The tears streamed down my face and finally I cried out, "This is where I belong?"

"Yes, my dear. You have always known this and this is why you have always felt you didn't belong on Earth."

I found myself clutching my blanket closer to me as I cried tears of joy, with the knowledge of why I had always felt I did not belong here on Earth! Now it was all making sense to me. I did not belong here! This was not my home! Earth was not my real home! As I wiped away my tears with my blanket, I finally asked, "Are you still here?"

The response I received had an exceptional loving tone. "I am still here. I will never leave you alone."

As I tried to gain my composure, I asked, "You said you have a soul message for me; is the message that I don't belong here on Earth?"

"Knowing that you don't belong here on Earth is a soul message, but this is not the soul message I came to give you."

"What is this soul message that you are supposed to give me?"

"The soul message is that you will know it is him."

"I will know it is him. What do you mean by this? Am I supposed to meet someone?"

"Yes, my dear. This man has been waiting for you. It is all planned for you; you just have to follow."

I was awestruck because I did not fully understand what this loving voice was telling me. Was I hearing correctly? I am supposed to meet a special man! I had dated some great guys but the magic was not there and I would always end up walking away, and it had gotten to the point where I began to think that there was something wrong with me. Finally, I asked, "Who is this special man that I am going to meet?"

"You will know this in time."

"When will I meet this man?"

"In time, my dear, all in good time you will have your answers."

I was lost for words.

The loving voice continued to speak. "The special man that you will meet will become your husband. As I said, it is all planned, you just have to follow."

I just have to follow. I did not know if I could do this. Before I can ask my next question, I received the answer.

The loving female voice responded, "Yes, you can do this."

"You knew what I was thinking?" I swiftly asked.

"Yes. I can hear your thoughts."

"You can actually hear my thoughts?" I questioned in complete astonishment.

"Yes. Others can also hear your thoughts. And you are able to hear ours."

"I can?"

"Yes."

"But I know I am not able to hear other people's thoughts."

"You only think you cannot. In time, my dear, you will know that I speak the truth. In the meantime, as I said, your life is planned for you and all you need to do is follow."

"Do you mean my whole life is planned out for me?"

"Yes, your whole life."

I felt I was embarking on a major soul lesson; if my whole life had a plan, then this must mean that everyone else had his or her life planned out also. Once again, the loving female voice answered my question before I was able to ask it.

"Yes, everyone living on the Earth plane has his or her life planned out for them."

"This is amazing!"

The loving voice laughed. "And don't become impatient; for delays are not denials."

"Delays are not denials? What does this mean?"

"It means there may be what seem like denials to you but in time, it will all happen. And God has granted you two children to love, one boy and one girl."

There was silence, for once again I found myself unable to speak. I was going to have a baby boy and a baby girl. This was what I had always wanted: two children; a boy and a girl; and I wanted the boy to come first. I wondered was that the way it was going to be.

"You will have a boy and a girl, and the boy will come first. They are waiting to be born. It is all planned, and it will all come in good time."

"Is it really all planned?"

"It most certainly is all planned; all you have to do is follow."

"Okay."

"This special man you will meet will give you special signs."

"What kind of special signs?"

"The special signs this man will give you are spiritual signs or soul signs."

In complete wonder, I asked, "Spiritual signs or soul signs; what are these?"

"Spiritual signs or soul signs are signs from those of us in the spiritual world, presented to you by your Guardian Souls, your Guardian Angels, or some other soul that is connected to you while you are living in the physical world. Soul signs can come in many different forms, for example, a particular word, thought, sound, smell, color or object which can suddenly present itself or just pop into your mind, and this is because it has been infused into your mind."

I sat on my bed in complete bewilderment. I was trying desperately to grasp all this information; however, I was starting to find it overwhelming. "What do you mean infused into my mind?"

"When I say infused into your mind, I am referring to information that is placed into your thoughts or mind, which we refer to as infused knowledge. This means there can be many times that a soul from the spiritual world will provide you with information for your benefit. The special man you are to meet will do this. He will give you spiritual signs because these spiritual signs will be infused into his mind at the time in order for you to recognize him."

"This is absolutely incredible!"

"If you think so, but this is only because you are using your mind and not realizing who you really are and where you come from."

"And just who am I?"

"You are one of us."

"One of you; what does this mean?"

"It means you are a child from the higher realms of our Heavenly Father. You are a loving child of our One and only, our Creator."

"Are you saying that there really is a God?"

"Yes, my dear, there most certainly is a God."

I sat in complete silence, unable to continue because I found this information to be completely overpowering. The tears were streaming down my face as I clutched my blanket and retrieved the end of it to wipe away my tears. I had been searching my whole life to find the truth as to whether there really is a God, and I was now being told that there is indeed a God. Before I was able to ask my next question, this loving voice spoke again.

"There is one and only one Creator and this Creator is God, and God is all-loving, all-powerful and all-knowing. He is all-loving, meaning that He represents love. He is all-powerful because He has power over all there is, and He is all-knowing because He knows everything that is."

At this point, I found I was so overcome I was sobbing. The tears were flowing down my face like water flowing down a stream. I needed tissues but I was afraid to move, so again I wiped my tears with my blanket.

The loving voice continued. "Please do not become so emotional. You already know all of this; it is just that you are allowing yourself to become too grounded in the physical world."

I tried my best to control my emotions so I could concentrate on the loving voice and everything she was saying to me. I was finally able to calm down. I questioned, "I already know all of this?"

"Yes, you most certainly do."

"And what do you mean when you say I am allowing myself to become too grounded in the physical world?"

"You must remember the real you. You are not of this physical world. You have only been granted a short time to live here on Earth and then you will return to your real home."

"I must remember the real me?"

"Yes, my dear. You are not a physical being; you are a spiritual being. You are a spiritual being living inside a physical body during your journey of life."

24

I felt my mind was racing, as I promptly asked, "I am a spiritual being? What does this mean?"

"You are a spiritual being because you are a soul. Your soul living inside your physical body can be compared to a driver of a vehicle, for example, a car; the car is the physical body, and the driver inside the car is you."

"Okay, this makes much more sense to me."

"And this is why it is of the utmost importance for each person on this Earth to honor his or her physical body; for each of you is a child of God, given the gift of the physical body in order for you to live on the Earth plane. It is therefore important to honor your soul by physically presenting yourself each day, at your best. Every day you should provide rest, nutrients, water, exercise and you should wash and dress to maintain your physical body to be the best it can be, for in order to care for your soul, you must care for your physical body. If the physical body is not cared for with respect, it will break down and sickness will result."

"Oh my, I know this to be so true because of my nursing background."

"Yes, my dear, I know. The soul signs I have mentioned earlier can be very vivid; however, if you are not spiritually aware, you may easily dismiss this important spiritual information which is being presented to you."

"I didn't know this."

She responded with a chuckle. "You do know this. It is just that you have at many times made a point to ignore these soul signs by pushing them out of your mind and to continue to focus on the physical world around you."

"I am so sorry. I truly didn't realize I was doing this."

"I understand. This is why I have come to you today to speak with you. At times, I have tried to be persistent and have embedded the soul sign in your mind or have done it while you are in a dream state."

"You are able to give me information when I am sleeping?"

"Yes, my dear. While you are sleeping, you sometimes dream and in this dream state, a soul sign is given to you to help you find a creative solution to an issue that you are experiencing, and therefore can be an effective method for a resolution. However, if you choose not to become spiritually aware, unfortunately you are choosing to ignore vital information that is of utmost importance to you and for your spiritual health and growth. Consequently, you may have to deal with negative or hateful emotions from others, followed by negative and hateful behaviors. It is very important for you to understand that dreams are just one way that souls on the Other Side try to communicate to you important and vital information for your well-being and benefit."

I found myself once again unable to utter one word, as I sat and listened intently to this loving being, that I was unable to see, as she continued to speak so eloquently, and with such wisdom.

"The soul signs which I have been trying to deliver to you can come in many different forms, such as birds, for example, a robin red breast, a blue jay, or a crow. Feathers, ladybugs, butterflies, songs, phrases, and scents, such as a familiar perfume or the smell of a cigar or a particular flower, such as a rose, and of course, numbers are also soul signs. You have unique spiritual numbers, my dear."

"I do?" I exclaimed.

"Yes, you most certainly do."

"A soul sign can represent who you are as a soul. You have a special spiritual number that represents you as a soul."

"And just what is my special spiritual number?"

"You already know this."

"I do?"

"Yes, you do. I wish to continue to tell you about these spiritual signs which you must become aware of." After a brief pause, she said, "Spiritual signs or soul signs can also let you know that you are following your chosen life plan while living on the Earth plane, and soul signs can also let you know that you are not alone, and that you are being guided and directed at all times."

"At all times?" I questioned in complete awe.

"Yes, at all times. As I said before you are never alone."

"What does this mean? You mean there is always someone with me?"

"Yes, this is correct. There is always someone with you and you are never alone."

"I am actually never alone?" I exclaimed.

"This is correct, my dear. As I said earlier, you have two Guardian Souls to watch over you at all times."

I was in deep thought and trying to understand what the words imply.

The loving voice continued. "Soul signs can also represent a message to you; however, it is up to you to interpret the message."

"And the message that I am to interpret is that I will know the man I am going to marry because he is going to give me a specific soul sign?"

"Yes, this is correct. But remember I told you he is going to give you more than one sign so you must be aware. You will meet him when the time is right and he will give you these special soul signs. You will recognize him because he will not call you by your name Olive, but he will have his own unique name for you. One of the soul signs is that he will call you by this particular name. You will also recognize him because during your first meeting with him, he will also do something exceptional. This soul sign you will recognize immediately because it will be so out of character and out of the ordinary. I will now leave you alone with your thoughts."

"You are leaving me?" I anxiously questioned.

"Yes, I am for now, but you are still not alone."

My mind was racing as if it was dancing to music and as the music played louder and louder, my mind danced faster and faster. Finally, I took a deep breath and told myself I needed to relax. First, I was going to try to get my brain around the fact that I had just been speaking to someone in my room that I was unable to see, yet I knew she was with me. Not only was she with me, but she also gave me astonishing information. "Oh, my gosh!" I screamed aloud. The information hit me like a ton of bricks. I was soon going to meet the man I was supposed to marry! This was hard to believe!

I have always believed that females look for men who are similar to their fathers; that is, if they have a loving father, and I knew this was true for me. I love my dad so much and have always admired him for the man that he is. I realized that I have always searched for someone like him. Now, I was to meet a special man that I was to marry and wondered if he would be anything like my father.

27

Then finally, one evening, I met the man of my dreams, or so I thought. My roommate set up a blind date for me with one of her friends she had gone to school with. She thought we would be a great match. We hit it off instantly and dated for a couple of years. I loved him and I knew he loved me but over time, we parted ways. In the end, he told me he loved me and that he was in love with me, but he also told me that he knew I loved him, but I was not in love with him. I found this difficult to understand and to come to grips with what his words truly implied. I knew I loved him, but he was saying I was not in love with him. I was shocked because I did not know there was a difference. My heart was broken and I did not know how to mend it. After many tears and much sorrow, I learned a very valuable life lesson and yes, there is a difference between loving and being in love with someone.

In the months that followed, I waited anxiously once again to meet the new man who was supposed to come into my life. I thought I had met him but it seemed that I was wrong. I remember my Guardian Soul telling me that this specific person would call me by a special name, I guess sort of like a nickname, and so whenever I met someone new, I waited to see if he would call me by a different name. This went on for the longest time until finally one evening, my friends and I visited one of our favorite dance bars called the Circle Lounge. We loved this place; the music was always fantastic and it was a great way to meet new friends. As I sat with the girls enjoying the music, I felt a tap on my left shoulder. I looked up, and much to my surprise, it was the same man that I had noticed earlier sitting at the bar. He had the most beautiful smile and he asked, "Would you like to dance?"

I smiled back and graciously replied, "Yes, I would."

He helped me move back my chair from the table and escorted me to the dance floor. The music was fast and we were enjoying our dance together. After the music stopped, I was about to leave the dance floor, but before I did, this stranger looked into my eyes so lovingly and, much to my surprise, he bent down and kissed me on the forehead! Wow! This was different. I was taken aback by the behavior from this person I had just met; and actually, I had not really met him because I did not even know his name.

The music started again. He held me in his arms, and we were dancing a waltz. Once again, the music stopped and I was about to walk back to my table but I was stopped. He held my hand and asked, "What is your name?"

I replied, "Olive."

I remember he gave me the most beautiful smile and said, "Such a beautiful name." We remained on the dance floor for the remainder of the evening, and when it was time for me to leave with my girlfriends, he looked at me and said, "Thank you, Ol."

A couple of months later, I was a young graduate from the Grace General Hospital School of Nursing; and a couple of years after my graduation, I was a young bride with many dreams. My relationship moved so quickly with this new man in my life that we arranged our wedding day, even though there were many obstacles placed before us. On April 28, I walked down the aisle of the Holy Redeemer Church, in my small town by the sea, with my father by my side. Waiting at the altar for me was my soon-to-be husband, the man that was brought into my life by the plans of my loving female visitor years earlier.

My graduation from nursing school

My new husband made a home for us where love, understanding, and mutual respect were shown every day. My adult life was no different from my childhood years except now I was finding hate in the world, and it was rampant! My life had really done a somersault!

I was now a "doubting Thomas" more than ever! In addition, I was more determined to search for the truth and to find God, if there was a God! The loving voice, who said she was my Guardian Soul, told me there was a God, but I still did not truly know. I made a commitment to myself that I would never stop searching for the truth for I needed proof.

PART 2

MY MIDDLE YEARS

CHAPTER 4

The Time Is Not Right

To every thing there is a season,
and a time to every purpose under heaven:

The Holy Bible: Ecclesiastes 3:1
King James Version

All memories are stored in the soul. Memories are not only of this lifetime but also of all our past-lifetimes, as well as our time spent on the Other Side. As I look back on my life, I can very easily recall having such soul memories. As a small child, I had the greatest desire to sing and dance, but not any particular dance, it had to be ballet. I had never taken singing lessons or ballet lessons but I felt I did not need to, for it all seemed so familiar to me. Many times as a small child, I would take the broom handle, or the handle of a knife, and pretend it was my microphone and I would sing to my heart's delight with my mother as my audience. I also recall having a deep desire to attend ballet classes, and my mother said I could; but in the end, I couldn't because there were none offered in the area where I lived. Instead, I had my own ballet classes, practising whenever I could with my friend Lorraine. Those were such fun times, etched in my memory forever.

As time moved by, I learned that soul memories come to us in the most surprising of times. One such time can be during a life crisis, when raw emotions trigger soul memories, and this certainly seems to be what happened to me.

It is evening time and I am on the phone with my sister who tells me that our Uncle Abel in Corner Brook has died. I am lost for words and I feel so deeply saddened. I loved Uncle Abel dearly and I know I will miss him. However, I also know he lived a good life and a long life, because he was over ninety years old. My sister asks if I intend to go to Corner Brook to attend the funeral. I tell her no. I know I would be given only one day off for bereavement leave from my place of employment, and therefore I did not have enough time to travel to Corner Brook, attend the funeral, and travel back home. Hanging up the phone, I tell my husband my sad news. He also had a loving relationship with this uncle, and so he has the same reaction as me.

Upon reflection, I realize this is not the first time I have received such a telephone call. Other relatives had died in the past, including aunts and uncles. Blessed with a loving family, I have been close to all my aunts and uncles, even the aunts and uncles by marriage, and Uncle Abel was no exception. He too was an uncle by marriage, and yet we loved each other dearly. He was always so loving, enthusiastic and full of life. He was a joy to be around and always had a smile. Just being in his presence was enough to bring joy to my soul. I loved Uncle Abel very much, but then I love all my other aunts and uncles, so why am I feeling so different about the death of this uncle? I know my feelings are not the same feelings I experienced in the past with the deaths of other relatives. These feelings are strange, and what is most peculiar is the fact that I am unable to cry. If I could cry maybe, I would feel much better. The tears will not come, and consequently I spend an uneasy and restless night.

The next morning, I get up at my normal time and get ready for work, intending to go about my day as usual. However, it seems an impossible task. The deep sadness inside of me is unexplainable. After a lot of consideration, I do not feel it is disrespectful not to go to Corner Brook and attend the wake and funeral, because time is not on my side. I drive to the college, where I am a nursing instructor, and prepare for my 9:00 A.M. class. While lecturing, tears fill my eyes for no apparent reason and I know I am losing control. The tears stream down my face as I quickly exit the classroom and literally run down the corridor! I rush to the staff bathroom and lock myself inside. Once inside I cry uncontrollably, and I have no idea why.

A short time later, one of the other instructors knocks on the door, and asks if I am okay. I opened the door, and explained as best I could, that I have no idea what had come over me. I tried to calm down and get my composure, but to no avail. I am finally able to tell her of the news I had received the evening before, and that I had been unable to cry at the time, so I guess I am making up for lost time. I tried to make light of my situation but it was not working, because I felt so emotionally drained. I decided it is best for me to go home. My colleagues wanted to get someone to drive me home, but I tell them I would be fine to drive. I left work and went straight home, and spent the remainder of my day sobbing, and not knowing why I was so emotionally distraught over the news of my uncle's death. This was a complete mystery to me.

Later in the evening, I realized I would have to travel to Corner Brook to see my uncle one last time, and to attend his funeral. I arranged to take time off from work using my annual leave; however, this was not necessary because my supervisor, much to my disbelief, granted me extended bereavement leave.

My oldest sister and my youngest sister and I, along with our Uncle Stan, make the necessary travel arrangements. My oldest sister decided to travel by car with our uncle to Corner Brook because she does not want Uncle Stan travelling by himself for the eight-hour drive. Therefore, my youngest sister and I travel by plane and arrive much earlier, giving us the time to check into our hotel, the Glynmill Inn, unpack and settle in and wait for our sister to join us.

Sometime later, our sister arrives at the hotel and after she freshens up, we go to the funeral home. Much to our surprise, when we arrive, there is no one there. As I approach the coffin and look at my uncle lying there, I instantly break down into sobs of uncontrollable tears. Shortly after, with the help of my sisters, I leave and return to our hotel. Finally, back at our hotel, my sisters ask me why I had become so emotional. The only answer that came to me was that I found it very upsetting that our uncle was in the funeral home by himself. At the time, little did I know that this was not the true reason.

The following day, we return to the funeral home for the funeral service. It is very crowded for all the family and close friends are present. As the minister starts the service, once again, I feel myself crying uncontrollably, and again, why I am so upset is beyond my understanding. I look around at the others, and especially at my two sisters, who are standing next to me, to see if they are as emotional as I am, but they are not. In fact, what really startles me is that not even my uncle's own daughters are as distressed as what I am. I can see that they are grieving but not to the extent that I am displaying. How can this be? What is happening to me? None of this makes any sense.

With the help of my sisters, I manage to calm down to the best of my ability as we leave the funeral home and proceed to the gravesite for the remainder of the service. Standing at the gravesite, I find myself to be in the same disturbed, emotional state. The tears turn into sobs and not for the life of me do I understand why. The service finally ends, and as I walk away from the graveside, my cousin, Edgar, walks beside me. He looks at me with an expression of bewilderment on his face. "You seem to be taking this really hard." Without giving it any thought, my response is immediate. "He didn't know how much he was loved." As I walk away, my only thoughts are that I know that I was visibly troubled at the funeral home, during the funeral service and now at the gravesite, and I do not know why. I keep walking in complete confusion and an unbearable grief that I am unable to explain, not even to myself.

The weeks following my uncle's death are far from pleasant because I still have this awful burden of sorrow that I just cannot seem to shake. A friend of mine tells me of a lady, who lives not too far from me, who is supposed to be able to contact loved ones who have died. I just feel so confused and desperately need some kind of explanation as to these bizarre feelings and behaviors I have been experiencing since my uncle's death. I need an explanation, and if there is someone out there who can help me in any way, I am willing to meet with this person.

I have the name and the telephone number and I call and make an appointment. She is able to see me in the afternoon at 2 P.M. As I am driving, I feel very anxious. I have never gone to such a person who claims to be able to make contact with loved ones who have deceased. I know it is going to be quite an experience, if this person can truly make contact and of course, I know that I will be able to ascertain as to whether or not this lady is genuine and is able to do this kind of thing.

In addition, not just do this kind of thing, but to make the claim that we do not really die! There is no such thing as death, only death of the body!

I ring the doorbell and a very pleasant, petite woman greets me at the door. She invites me to come in and introduces herself as Beth. She says, "You sounded really anxious on the phone to meet with me."

"Yes, I am anxious, there have been things happening to me that I can't explain, and I am hoping that you are able to get some answers for me."

"Well, we will see." She offers to take my coat and then she escorts me to her kitchen. "I was just about to have some tea. Would you like a tea or coffee?"

"I would love a cup of tea, thank you," I reply.

While she is preparing the tea, she asks, "Who do you want to contact?"

"I recently had a death in the family and I would like to contact my uncle."

"Oh, that's interesting. I thought you would want to make contact with a female because there is a female here with us now. She is standing next to you."

Astounded by this remark, I reply, "You can actually see a female standing next to me?"

"Yes, I most certainly can. She is taller than you are and she is wearing a style of dress of former years. Her hair is pinned in the old-fashioned hairstyle, so this tells me she died some time ago. You see, they usually look like they did during their last time here on Earth."

"This is all quite new to me."

"Do you have any idea who this lady is that is with us?"

"No, I'm afraid I don't. Maybe she's not really here because of me," I respond quickly.

With this, Beth gives a chuckle. "Oh, she is definitely here to be with you because she came with you."

"She came with me?"

"Yes, when I opened the door, she was standing next to you. And as you entered, she entered."

"Beth, I have to say, I find all of this quite fascinating."

Beth responds with a smile, offers me my cup of tea and then she escorts me down the stairs to a small room decorated with a small table and two chairs on opposite sides of the table. She gestures to me to sit in the chair to the right as we enter the room while she takes the chair opposite to me. As I am sitting in this tiny room with Beth, she states, "There is a gentleman here with us now. He is not speaking and he is standing behind the veil."

"What do you mean he is standing behind the veil?"

"There is a separation between the spiritual world and the physical world; it's like a thin sheet of plastic. I call it the veil because I can see through it and so I can see who is standing behind."

"Oh!" I exclaim.

"Yes. Sometimes the spirits pierce the veil and sometimes they don't. This time the spirits who are here have not come over. They are standing behind the veil."

"What do you mean by, they?"

"The female who was with us here, has crossed over and is no longer in the room with us but instead she is behind the veil, standing next to this gentleman. I don't know who this male is but I do know he looks just like Joey Smallwood."

With this comment, I let out a gasp. Tears are now filling my eyes. As I take a tissue from the tissue box sitting on the small table to wipe away my tears, Beth asks, "Do you know who this gentleman is?"

I nod my head yes. I am unable to reply because I have become too emotional.

Beth patiently waits for me to calm myself before she continues. "Are you ready?"

"Yes I am. Are they still here?"

"Yes."

As I am finally able to control my emotions, I explain to Beth why she thinks the man she sees looks like Joey Smallwood. As Beth is well aware, Joey Smallwood was the premier of our province, Newfoundland and Labrador, for over twenty years, and is therefore, very well known throughout the province. Anyone can attest that Mr. Smallwood is a unique looking individual. Some people say that we are all supposed to have "a double," and if this is true, Mr. Smallwood had a double and his name is Abel W. Stratton; my uncle Abel! Uncle Abel resembled the premier of our province so much that many times when he was out in public, people would mistakenly think he was the Honorable Joseph R. Smallwood, the premier of the province. So now, here I am sitting with Beth who is telling me she has a man present who looks like Joey Smallwood. I reaffirm Beth's comment and say, "Beth, I have no doubt in my mind that the person you are seeing is indeed my Uncle Abel."

Beth chuckles and declares, "Well, I know that Joey Smallwood is still alive and therefore I know it is not him."

"Yes, Mr. Smallwood is still living."

"I don't know who the lady is that came with you and is now standing next to him. Do you think it is his wife?"

"No, it can't be his wife because my aunt is still living."

"Well, it has to be someone that he knows otherwise she would not be here with him. She is now speaking. Your husband does not believe in the spirit world. Is this true?"

"Beth, she must know my husband."

"It certainly seems that way." After a short pause, Beth asks again, "Is what she is saying about your husband true, Olive?"

"Yes it is, and this is one of the problems that we have. I believe in the spirit world; well, actually, I do not just believe, I know there is a spirit world. I have proof. And I am unable to talk to my husband about these matters because he doesn't believe at all and therefore he has no interest in discussing such topics with me."

"You say you have been given proof. What do you mean by this?"

"Some years ago, I had someone come to me and speak to me about the spirit world. I could not see who was speaking to me but I knew it was a female voice, and she told me many things. Actually, Beth, I have never told anyone about this. You are the first person. I have always kept this to myself."

"I am happy you are comfortable to share such a remarkable visit with me."

As I smile, I say, "You make it very easy for me to speak of such things because I can tell that you truly do understand."

As Beth laughs, she comments, "I most certainly do understand, Olive. I have had many such visits myself."

"It is all quite intriguing, don't you think?"

Again, Beth laughs as she answers, "It certainly is intriguing. You got that right."

My thoughts now go back to my husband. "Beth, I find that most people in this world are like my husband. I find there are not many true believers. Some people call themselves religious and say they believe, but when it comes right down to it, they still do not really believe. I also realize that people can be religious and not spiritual and therefore have very little understanding."

"I totally agree with you, Olive. Your Uncle Abel is speaking now. Your Aunt Mildred is your Guardian Soul. He must be referring to the woman who is with him. Who is Aunt Mildred?"

Astonished by this remark, I say, "Wow!" There is now silence between us because I need time for my mind to comprehend such a revelation. My thoughts take me back many years earlier, when I was in my room in the nurses' residence and awakened by a loving, female voice who was talking to me. It instantly occurs to me that the loving, female voice was my Aunt Mildred! Beth is very patient with me. She waits for my answer to her question. I blurt out, "Beth, I just had the most amazing thought. If you are telling me that my Aunt Mildred is my Guardian Soul, then it must have been Aunt Mildred who visited me so many years ago when I was a nursing student while living in the residence. Can you ask Uncle Abel if this is true?"

"I don't have to ask Olive because your Uncle Abel just confirmed that it was indeed your Aunt Mildred who visited you during that time. She has always been your Guardian Soul, from the very beginning, the very first day that you were born."

My only response is one of bewilderment. "Oh, Beth!"

"Well, I'm somewhat confused. How can your Aunt Mildred be your Guardian Soul if she was living here on Earth? And who is Aunt Mildred?"

"Aunt Mildred is my grandmother's sister who died at a very young age. Beth, she died before I was born."

"Oh, of course, now it makes sense to me."

"Beth, when you asked me earlier if the lady with Uncle Abel was his wife and I said no, that's because I was forgetting that my uncle was married twice. My Aunt Mildred was married to my Uncle Abel. She was his first wife."

"Well, this makes perfect sense now because in the beginning we didn't know who this lady was that came with you, but now we know she is your aunt. She is now speaking. She was at the funeral home when you and your two sisters visited. There was no one else present, only just the three of you. Is this right?"

"Yes, this is true!"

"Why would there be just the three of you at the funeral home and no one else? That's a bit weird, isn't it?" Beth exclaims.

"Yes, actually when I think about it, it was weird but that's exactly what happened. As we walked into the funeral parlor where Uncle Abel was, we were startled to see that we were the only ones there. So what you are being told by Aunt Mildred is correct."

"And why weren't there any family members or other visitors at the funeral home?"

"Because it wasn't visiting hours, and we didn't know this before we left the hotel."

"Oh, okay, now I understand."

"We didn't stay long. I do remember though I found it upsetting that Uncle Abel was there by himself. I realize now that this is normal. I was just so emotionally troubled; I wasn't in my right frame of mind."

"Your Aunt Mildred expresses she was standing beside you at the end of the casket."

With this comment, a flood of memories come racing back in my mind. The tears are starting to trickle down my cheeks as I grab another tissue. "Beth, all my memories are so vivid."

"Take your time, I'm in no rush."

"Thank you, Beth. I truly appreciate your understanding."

"Your uncle and aunt can see how emotional you are. They are looking at you with such concern and love."

"Beth, can you ask Uncle Abel why I was so upset after his death and why I was so upset during his wake and funeral?"

"I don't have to ask him, Olive, because he has heard your questions. He has put his right hand up with the palm of his hand facing me in a gesture that means stop, and he states the time is not right."

"The time is not right? What does he mean by that?"

"He answers again that the time is not right."

"When will the time be right?"

"He says not now."

"I would like to know why I reacted so strongly to his death; for I know all too well that my reactions were far from normal, considering he is an uncle."

"He is now stepping back, Olive, and your Aunt Mildred is standing in front of him. It seems you are not going to get your answers at this time, at least not from your Uncle Abel."

"Oh, okay. So Uncle Abel is standing the farthest away?"

"Yes. Your Aunt Mildred says your life was built up around someone whose way was either his way or no way; you had to do your best; you grew into this. Is this true?"

I chuckle as I answer Beth. "I know Aunt Mildred is talking about my dad. My father is a firm believer in education and hard work. He believes that if you are going to do something, do it right the first time."

"Your Aunt Mildred states that in the future, regardless of any project you take on, it is going to work out. All you have to do is ask for it. You will get great publicity and you are going to be successful."

"Everything you are telling me, Beth, is absolutely amazing!"

"Your Aunt Mildred is speaking again. You are starting to feel bored and tired but you should not allow yourself to get down. Look at this time as a needed rest because something big is coming, and you have a lot more to do."

"She is right, Beth. I do feel tired more than usual and I feel bored."

"She declares she knows that there are times you feel like you want to go away by yourself and think things through. This is okay. If you do this, you will emerge with greater understanding."

I dry my tears again. "Beth, this is all so true. There are times I feel like going off into the woods and staying in a cabin by myself. Sometimes I feel as though I need some downtime and to just be alone."

"Your Aunt Mildred declares that you are an old soul and therefore very wise."

"I've heard that phrase used different times throughout my life but what does this mean?"

"Well, I also have heard that saying many times, Olive, and my belief is that an old soul is someone who is very wise, like your aunt said. Oh, your Aunt Mildred is shaking her head yes, so I must be right. She is speaking again. An old soul is someone who is very spiritual and who has a deep understanding of all things and is wise beyond her physical years, such as Olive. You came to Earth this time, as in other times, to help others. You want to bring about positive change and to make the world a better place. Deep down, you know your soul purpose."

"What is my soul purpose?"

"Your soul purpose is to serve others and to foster their spiritual growth by teaching and helping them to learn."

"How will I do this?"

"Her comment is that you will know all in time. You get strength from your mind. You plan things out and it is your mind that is the best thing you have going for you; it is your mind that gives you strength."

"Well, Beth, I know that physically I am not very strong. As you can see, I have a petite body frame. And yes, I guess I would have to agree that my real strength does come from my mind."

"And she says you have great integrity."

"Yes, I do have great integrity, and this is one of the reasons I find it so difficult living here."

"What do you mean by that?"

"I mean that most people that I come in contact with are just the opposite. I find many people are very dishonest and have no problem telling lies and being deceitful."

"Well, you know what is written in the Holy Bible about those people you are referring to. I'm pretty sure in John, Chapter 8, Verse 44, it states: *Ye are of your father the devil, and the lusts of your father ye will do. He was a murderer from the beginning, and abode not in the truth, because there is no truth in him. When he speaketh a lie, he speaketh of his own: for he is a liar, and the father of it.*"

"Yes Beth, I'm familiar with this quote. The devil is known as the father of lies."

"Well, I do understand now when you say you find it difficult living here because you mean it is difficult for you to be around those kinds of people who tell lies, and this is because you are such an honest person yourself."

"Yes, Beth, you got it right."

"You are very wise, Olive."

Now Beth has me laughing. "Well, I'm not only wise but according to Aunt Mildred, I am also an old soul and my mind is my strength."

"Yes, this is what she said. Regarding spirituality, you haven't reached how high you can go. You can go much higher, you can go really high; all you have to do is put your mind to it."

"She is saying this?"

"Yes, she is."

"I am really alarmed by this comment."

"Why?"

"Well, because I'm not sure what she means."

"I guess she means you don't know who you really are and what you are capable of doing. And she is nodding her head yes, so I am right."

As I ponder Beth's comment, I reply, "Well, now I am more confused. What do you mean I don't know who I really am?"

"She knows that many times throughout your life, you have felt as though you were lost. There are many times when you experience loneliness, even when there are many people around you."

As the tears start to fill my eyes again, I respond, "Beth, she really seems to know me so well."

"You are from a higher level on the Other Side and you have evolved to a level of spiritual awareness that most souls living on the Earth plane do not understand. Because of this, there are many times that you feel no one understands you."

"Oh my, Beth, this is so true!"

"Because of your spiritual awareness and spiritual knowledge, you don't have anyone in your circle of family and friends with whom to share such a depth of understanding. She understands that there are times that you find it very frustrating because no one seems to really understand you, and there are times when you feel you don't really understand yourself."

"Yes, this is also true."

"This is the reason why some times you feel so alone and feel you are carrying such a heavy burden."

I feel the tears well in my eyes again because the words I am hearing are having such a profound impact on me. I am lost for words.

"She says that every person living on the Earth plane has the potential to become spiritually aware; for spiritual awareness brings understanding of who the soul really is and his or her purpose for being here and this new knowledge is life changing. The soul needs perfection by obtaining more knowledge; for the more knowledge obtained, the more the soul will learn and grow. A piece of gold is only a lump until it is perfected into a beautiful piece of jewellery, and a diamond in the rough becomes beautiful and brilliant only after it has been perfected. Thus it is with the soul."

"Is she talking about me, Beth?"

"Yes, she is but I guess she is also talking about everyone. She says you have to perfect by honoring your soul and God by obtaining knowledge, and therefore knowing the truth. Knowledge provides wisdom which in turn speaks the truth and this truth will give you power to set your soul free; for knowing the truth, your soul will experience the feeling of becoming a free soul, and consequently will elevate yourself to a higher spiritual level, closer to God, when you return to the Other Side."

"So I am to become more spiritually aware?"

"Yes, Olive, this is the message. Those who have chosen to become spiritually aware have accepted complete responsibility for their lifetime on the Earth plane. They look at their life with new meaning."

"How do I become more spiritually aware?"

"She states each soul walking this journey of life will meet many challenges; however, these challenges are not problems but instead are opportunities for learning."

"What does she mean by challenges?"

"I'm not sure. She says you need to have challenges in your life. When you understand this, you will recognize life's problems as opportunities for learning and growing spiritually."

"Oh my, Beth, is she really saying that we are supposed to have problems in life?"

"She is nodding her head yes, Olive."

I am now staring at Beth in disbelief. "Who would ever think that problems in life are necessary?"

"I sure would never have thought this!"

"No, and me either."

"She says that you must realize that living life here on the Earth plane is about experiencing problems. Each soul on this Earth is born to experience problems; however, it is how you choose to deal with each problem is your challenge, and this is why life problems can be considered challenges."

"Okay, Beth, I understand."

"There is one very important lesson to learn while you live here on the Earth plane, and that is life problems are inevitable. Also, remember that problems should be seen as opportunities for learning. You all have problems to face, eventually, one way or another. In fact, one of the main reasons you came here to live on the Earth plane at this time is to encounter problems. These problems are gifts to you."

"Beth, I find it difficult to believe that life problems are gifts."

"You're not the only one. I don't know if I would ever consider problems as gifts, especially the problems I've encountered in my lifetime."

"I know exactly what you mean, Beth."

"Well, your Aunt Mildred is definitely not agreeing with us because she declares that she knows it may seem very strange to you that you should consider life problems to be gifts, but that's exactly what they are, and they truly are gifts from God."

"Beth, I really have to give this a lot of thought, don't you?"

With a chuckle, Beth replies, "You got that right! She says your problems are your own and unique to you and only you. Life problems are thought-out plans to help you learn, develop and advance."

"It sounds as though she is saying that not only are we supposed to have problems in life but that these problems are planned for us. Is this what it is she is saying?"

"She's nodding her head yes again, Olive."

"Beth, did you ever think in your wildest dreams that your problems are just for you?"

"No, never in my wildest dreams, but all of this is going to make me think twice from now on. She is speaking again. Because your life problems are specifically for you, it is very important for you to take responsibility for all the people and circumstances in your life. You need to have problems in your life in order to learn and grow spiritually. When you understand this, you will no longer see your problems as problems, but instead you will recognize life's problems as opportunities for learning and growing spiritually; for it is absolutely necessary for you to grow spiritually, otherwise your time spent on the Earth plane will be considered a waste of time."

"I have to say I'm finding this extremely difficult to believe."

"You're not the only one. She says when you encounter a difficult person or a difficult situation, don't see the person or the situation as a problem but instead see the person or the situation as an opportunity for learning; for with learning comes knowledge, and with knowledge comes a solution for greatness."

"I have to say, Beth, I am really finding it difficult to understand what Aunt Mildred is saying to me. It sounds as though I am supposed to embrace hardships in my life, because problems can definitely become hardships. To make matters worse, she is telling me that I am supposed to embrace difficult people in my life. How am I ever going to do this?"

"She states, Olive, this is because you are not allowing yourself to be as spiritually aware, the way that you should be."

"Well, how do I become more spiritually aware?"

"She expresses that while the soul is experiencing these life challenges, remember that tears cleanse the soul and are necessary."

"So she is saying that as people, we should cry when we encounter difficult times, for this is right to do?"

"Yes, but not only is it right to do, it is necessary. One has to know that living life on the Earth plane is going to be difficult at times; however, in the end, the reward will be great."

"Oh Beth, we will be rewarded for all the hardships we have to go through?"

"This is what she said."

"I remember a friend of mine telling me once that often people have to go through a dark forest before one reaches the meadow."

"This is wise thinking."

"Yes, I agree."

"God has bestowed many gifts upon you and you must share your gifts. One of the most loving and beautiful gifts you can give is your smile, for the gifts of caring, affection, and kindness are very precious gifts to offer. When you meet a stranger, you can smile and silently send a blessing of peace, joy and love. Also, pray for others, even strangers; for a prayer said in love has tremendous power. She is telling me that your prayers are very powerful; however, you do not realize the true power that you have."

"Beth, I do pray because this is what I was taught to do as a child. However, I must say, I certainly didn't consider my prayers to be powerful."

"She is speaking again. When you visit a relative or friend always bring a gift. The gift can be a flower from your garden, or a card. A compliment given with sincerity is also a precious gift, so give anything of your choosing, as long as it is given from your soul and given with love."

"This certainly makes a whole lot of sense to me, Beth. She is so right."

"Yes she is, Olive. She now says that in order for you to become more spiritually aware, you must ask questions for only then will you find the answers."

"I have to ask questions, and just who do I ask these questions to?"

"She is laughing, Olive. I think she means ask her the questions. She states you are never alone. You always have a Guardian Soul with you at all times."

"I remember her telling me this many years ago."

"You are already spiritually aware, and not like most souls living on the Earth plane who are not because they have allowed themselves to become too grounded in the physical world. However, if they would allow themselves to become more spiritually aware, the truth will be revealed to them, as it is being revealed to you." Beth pauses and just stares at me.

In turn, I stare right back at her, and ask, "Too grounded, Beth? What does this mean?"

"She answers too grounded in the physical world means people of the Earth plane think all that exists is the physical world and live their lives as though this is all there is, which is far from the truth. Remember, she already told you there is a spirit world."

"Yes, I remember."

"She says that the more you allow yourself to become more spiritually aware, eventually you will experience a spiritual awakening."

"Did she really say a spiritual awakening?"

"Yes, this is what she said."

"Now I'm really getting confused. What is a spiritual awakening?" I question in dismay.

"A spiritual awakening is allowing yourself to become completely spiritually aware and when you do, you will experience different signs. The different signs you may experience are signs such as looking younger than your actual age, looking vibrant and radiant and having a glow about you that people will notice. Man, if becoming spiritually awakened means that I'm going to look younger, then I'm all for this," Beth adds with a laugh.

Beth has me laughing also. "I certainly don't mind looking younger than my age."

"You already look young, Olive."

"Well, that's true. Really, you know, when I think about it, I have always looked younger than my age."

"Your Aunt Mildred expresses you will have dreams that will become more vivid and meaningful, and you will start to have a perception that time is moving by very quickly. You will have increased self-talk, and your sleep patterns will change, for you will find it difficult to sleep and this will last for some time. However, as this subsides, you will then find that you need a lot of sleep, more than your usual amount, and this is because the soul needs to travel to the Other Side while the physical body sleeps; for sleep helps to replenish the soul with energy."

"I don't know about you, Beth, but I am really finding all of this incredible."

"Oh, believe me, I am also finding all of this incredible!"

"And she is telling me that my soul needs sleep because my soul has to travel to the Other Side. What does this mean?"

"Her answer is that it means exactly what it is she is saying."

"Okay."

"Do you tend to sleep a lot, Olive?"

"Well, I do know that I tend to sleep more than most people that I know. Some people tell me they need very little sleep but I am just the opposite. I need a lot of sleep and I have always been like this, even when I was younger."

"She now says that you should not forsake your physical body by either over-eating or under-eating, because you will experience changes in your eating habits. There can be changes in the physical body, such as gaining weight. Be sure to give your physical body the proper daily nutrients and know that most likely you will experience some types of food cravings. This just means your physical body is trying to adjust to the spiritual body. Remember that daily activity is vital; for any substance or activity that is not in harmony with the physical body will do harm to the physical body and the spiritual body, which is the soul. However, do not be overly concerned, my dear, because we know that you will treat your physical body with respect and love, and therefore your physical body will adjust to these new changes."

"Well, all of this makes perfect sense. I have always tried to eat healthy, even though I do treat myself sometimes to some junk food."

"I guess that's not too bad if you only do it sometimes. She is talking again. You have always known that it is important to respect your body."

"Yes, what she is saying is true. I have always been conscious of eating foods low in salt, sugar and fats. As a young wife, I made these changes in my diet and my husband's diet, and now when I think about it, I realize that this wasn't an easy task considering the average diet of Newfoundlanders."

"Gosh, Olive, you are absolutely right. We both know that the traditional foods of Newfoundlanders are high in salt, sugar and fats."

"Yes, and we both know the jiggs dinner with figgy duff, fish and brewis with scrunchions, toutens, lassy bread, and of course pea soup with dough boys are all traditional Newfoundland meals."

"So, are you saying that you don't cook these foods?"

"No, not exactly, what I mean is that I do cook the traditional Newfoundland dishes but I don't cook the foods the old traditional ways. I cook with my own style which means I don't cook with the high salt, high sugar or high fat content of the original recipes."

"Your Aunt Mildred is speaking again. You will start to reflect on your life and in particular, review things you have done in the past. You will have regrets and want to make things right, and with this review you will find yourself become exceptionally emotional and most likely you will find you will do a lot of crying. This review will allow time for you to reflect and you will discover that you wish to break free from old ways of thinking and acting. In addition, you will start to recognize immediately some old issues that keep coming back, and with this recognition, you will learn and make changes."

"I'm already doing this, Beth, and interestingly enough, when I was younger I always told myself that when I got older, I didn't want to have any regrets. So all my life I have always tried to do what is right. However, I know I have made mistakes along the way and I do have some regrets."

"So, what she is saying, Olive, it seems this is already happening to you."

"Yes, Beth, you are right."

"She says you will also have an increase in sensitivity of all your senses, meaning you will become more aware of all things. In addition, with this new awareness, you will start to notice soul signs presented to you for your benefit."

"Beth, this is truly amazing if all of this is going to happen to me!"

With a chuckle, Beth responds, "Yes, and especially the part where you are going to look younger than your age! I sure hope I have a spiritual awakening! I can sure do with some help looking younger."

As I finally stop laughing at Beth, I ask, "When is this spiritual awakening going to happen?"

"Her answer is in time; however, it has already started. You will also have a deeper desire to understand the true meaning of living life."

"Beth, I have been trying to figure out the real meaning of living life here on Earth as far back as I can remember."

"She states she knows this but as time goes by you will come to understand the real meaning of living life on the Earth plane. You will begin to recognize that all life is precious; and with this recognition, you will refuse to kill even an insect. You will also start to feel a spiritual connection to all things, but especially animals because animals, like humans, have a spiritual body which is the soul."

"Beth, animals have souls the same as humans?"

"Yes, Olive, this is what she said and I can see her nodding her head yes. It is very important for you to remember this because there is a lot of cruelty done to animals on the Earth plane and you must help to bring a stop to all of this cruelty to God's Heavenly creatures."

With a deeply saddened heart, I respond, "I know all too well what Aunt Mildred has said about animals abused in this world is so true; for there is too much pain and suffering caused by some humans to innocent animals, but Beth, what is it I have to do?"

"She states in time, my dear, in time you will know all. Because of who you are and who you will become, you will experience feelings of being different."

"I already experience this, Beth. I've had those feelings my whole life."

"Your Aunt Mildred says she knows this but as time goes by, these feelings of being different will increase."

"Okay, I understand."

"She expresses you have feelings of being different than others because you are already from a higher spiritual level and know you are different from most people on the Earth plane."

"Then what she is really saying is that most people living here on Earth are not from the higher spiritual levels. Is this correct?"

"She is nodding her head yes, Olive. Oh! Your Aunt Mildred is showing me jars with black and white beads in the jars. The black beads represent the darkness within a soul and the white beads represent the light within a soul. Darkness represents hate and evil and that light represents love and good."

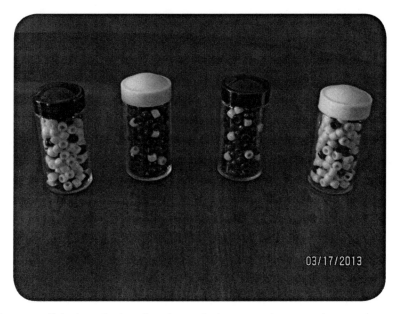

03/17/2013

The jars of black and white beads symbolizing each person living on Earth

Amazingly, as Beth is telling me about the jars of beads, I am able to see these different jars of beads in my mind. "Beth, I completely understand what it is you are describing because I am able to see this in my mind!"

"You can actually see the different jars?"

"Yes Beth, I can."

"Your aunt is speaking again. You will start to feel harmony with the seasons of the Earth plane and the cycles of the sun and the moon."

"I'm not sure I understand, Beth."

"She says that everything is done in perfect timing. The seasons come and go, and then return for another cycle. The same is true for the sun and the moon. The sun rises with each new day and then sets, only to rise again. The ocean waves flow with the ebb of tide. Everything is in harmony, and so must the people of the Earth plane be in harmony also."

"The First Nations People of the Earth have been saying this since the beginning of time, but the so-called white man came and took over the lands and thought the native people of the lands to be ignorant. So, what Aunt Mildred is saying is that the aboriginal people of the lands of the Earth are not the ignorant ones at all."

"She is nodding her head yes, Olive, and she declares you are so wise."

"Well, it just makes perfect sense to me. Everything really has gone full circle."

"Yes, Olive, you are absolutely right. She says you will experience visions, as you have never experienced visions before in this lifetime. You will come to recognize when another soul is in your presence. Even though you may not see the soul with your physical eyes, however, in time, you will use your physical eyes less and your soul eyes more. Because of this, you will experience a change in your vision; however, do not become alarmed for this is all part of the spiritual changes which you will go through and because of these spiritual changes, you will therefore learn spiritual truths very rapidly."

"What are these spiritual truths that I will learn?"

"She answers as you become more spiritually advanced and more spiritually awakened, you will have increased intuitive abilities and will learn spiritual truths."

"I will have increased intuitive abilities; what does this mean?"

"Her answer is that she has already answered this question. You will be able to communicate with souls from the spiritual world."

"I will be able to communicate with souls from the spiritual world? Isn't that what you are doing, Beth?"

Beth chuckles. "Yes, I guess that's what I'm doing now, isn't it. I am able to see your Aunt Mildred and talk with her, even though you can't do this. So it seems you will be able to do what it is I am doing."

"Well, I have to say that this is all mind-boggling to me."

"Your Aunt Mildred states you will have the ability to understand the importance of music. This is all amazing, Olive, don't you think?"

"I most certainly do, Beth!"

"I wonder what she means that you will have the ability to understand the importance of music. Oh Olive, I have your Aunt Mildred laughing. She must think I am funny. She expresses that music is love for the soul and that you will come to understand the real beauty of music and will connect with music from your soul."

"I do believe this because I already love music."

"Yes, but I think she means that you will in time, love and appreciate music even more. Oh, I am right because she is nodding her head yes. You will start to live your life purpose and, in time, know what your true spiritual life purpose is. Everyone has a spiritual life purpose; however, yours is far more advanced than most."

"Why would my life purpose be more advanced than most other people's life purpose? And what does this really mean anyway?"

"It's because you are from a higher spiritual realm and much more advanced, and therefore your life purpose is more advanced."

"So, this seems that most people living here on Earth are not that far advanced spiritually, is this what she is really saying?"

"She is nodding her head yes, Olive."

"Then why is it I am from a higher spiritual realm than most other people here on Earth?"

"Her response is that this is because you have chosen to be from the higher realms on the Other Side."

"Okay, but why wouldn't others want to live on the higher realms on the Other Side?"

"The answer is quite simple. All people on the Earth plane want to reside on the higher realms when they return to the Other Side, but most will not, and this is because they have made the wrong choices in the physical life."

"So am I right to say that what she is really saying is that most people live very selfish lives and do a lot of wrong?"

"She's nodding her head yes, Olive. You will have an increased awareness of coincidences in your life and will realize that there really is no such thing as a coincidence. With this recognition, you will recognize numbers and symbols as part of the spiritual communication. In time, you will come to understand who you really are. You will also recognize all the special abilities you have acquired. With all this new knowledge, you are going to move through personal issues at a very rapid rate and your thirst for more knowledge will increase."

"I'm really glad to hear this, Beth. My whole life I have always had this unquenchable thirst for knowledge. I have always had all kinds of questions about living life here on Earth and because I found it difficult to get answers, at least answers to my satisfaction, I have always found it difficult living here. So if I am going to move through personal issues rapidly and in turn learn more, then this is great."

"Your aunt says you will begin to view the physical world in a completely different way, as well as all the people living in the world. You will recognize people for who they really are and why they have come to the Earth plane."

"Beth, I'm starting to find all of this information to be very overwhelming!"

"Yes, it is a lot of information to take in at one time but it is also really awesome, Olive, and maybe you will be able to tell me why I'm here because for sure as heck, I don't know why I'm here or what it is I am supposed to be doing with my life."

We both laugh as I reply, "Beth, at this stage of the game, I don't even know why I'm here!"

"Olive, we have to stop laughing so we can get everything she is telling you. You will begin to see the world with a completely different understanding, and because of all your changes, you are most likely going to have increased feelings of loneliness. This is because there are few souls living on the Earth plane at this time as advanced as you, and who understand you. You are going to find that you will have to withdraw from certain family and friend relationships and this is because you will find it too difficult to be in their presence; for their energy will start to drain yours, and you therefore will not be able to tolerate their company."

"This is already starting to happen to me, Beth, because there are some people I find extremely difficult to be around. Some people are so negative and are such complainers, and some I have caught telling lies and therefore I know they are not to be trusted. So why would I really associate with such individuals?"

"You shouldn't, Olive, and this is exactly what your Aunt Mildred is saying to you. And it seems by what she has said, you will start to break ties with more people as you learn more and advance higher."

"Yes, this certainly seems what it is she is saying."

"She's nodding her head again, Olive, she agrees with what you just said. This is going to be difficult to do at times because some of these people are in your family. However, please keep in mind that as you move forward, you will come to realize that these same people have the opportunity to change their negative and hateful ways with each new day, and it is their choice to remain the same. Consequently, they have made the choice for you because they will leave you with no other alternative but to distance yourself from them."

"Actually, Beth, I can see this happening."

"And most likely you are going to have a deep longing to return Home; however, know that you have great work to do before your time comes to go back."

"Beth, ask her what great work I have to do?"

"Her response is that it will all be revealed to you in time; however, know that you are preparing for this great spiritual work without even realizing it, for your life has been planned out for you."

"So all I have to do is what?"

"And you're asking me! What do I know? This is all blowing my mind!"

Once again, we are both laughing so hard we find it difficult to control ourselves. Eventually I calm down enough to say to Beth, "I do hope Aunt Mildred has a lot of patience and that she hasn't left."

"No, Olive, she hasn't left. She is still here with us and actually, she is laughing. I think she finds the two of us quite hilarious. She says that the more you advance spiritually, and become spiritually awakened, the more you are going to have soul recognition. Souls will have recognition of you. They will sense your feelings, your love and the innermost workings of your soul. When this starts to happen to you, you will have people recognize you and wonder if they have met you some place before because you look so familiar to them."

"Really?"

"Yes, really. This is what she is saying. People will also recognize you by your name, for you have a very special name. Your name represents love and your light of love will shine so bright that no matter where you go or whom you meet, you will be recognized."

"I find it difficult to believe that my name is special. I really don't consider it to be special."

"Well, this is what she has expressed."

"And how does the name Olive represent love?"

"You got me. She states you are love and therefore you represent God, your Heavenly Father, and consequently you have been given a special name."

"Beth, I absolutely find all of this amazing!"

"And you think it is just you that finds all of this amazing?"

Now we are both laughing again as we just stare at each other in complete awe. After a short pause, I ask, "What else does she have to say to me, Beth?"

"Your Aunt Mildred says in time there will be a new beginning for you; a new beginning where you will be much happier and you will find peace, harmony and balance."

I now feel myself becoming emotional again. There is silence. I am wiping away my tears of joy. I finally break the silence and ask Beth, "When is this going to happen?"

"It is going to happen all in good time."

"In good time, what does this mean?"

"This is what she is saying. You must not despair; it will all come in good time. You must be patient and you must live in the wisdom of uncertainty."

"What does this mean; live in the wisdom of uncertainty?"

"Your Aunt Mildred answers that when your plans don't seem to go the way you had hoped, there is a reason. At the time, the reason is too great for you to conceive or understand. It will unfold and be revealed to you in time."

"Well, Beth, I can think of many times in my life when my plans did not work out the way I had hoped. So, am I to believe that this was all meant to be?"

"She is nodding her head yes, Olive."

"Beth, life is such a mystery!"

"You got that right!" We are now both laughing again. "And she declares that you must accept to live in the wisdom of uncertainty and take each day as it comes."

"Well, I've always heard the saying that you can only live one day at a time. So, I guess this is what she means."

"She's nodding her head yes, Olive. You shouldn't take everything in life so personally; for some things are part of the bigger picture."

"Beth, I can recall so many times throughout my life when I felt so let down, and things didn't work out as I had hoped, and so now I am to understand that this was all for my own good?"

"Yes, Olive, this is certainly my understanding. She expresses that in order to live life to the fullest, you must completely accept God's plan for your life here on the Earth plane, for God's plan is your life plan or soul plan. God has great plans for you and so you must be patient and allow them to unfold. You must put your faith and trust in God. God already knows your intentions. Your Father in Heaven, along with your Guardian Angels and Guardian Souls, will guide you and will orchestrate every detail of your life; for everything is planned for you."

"So, what it is I am hearing is that everything is planned and it all has to happen at a particular time?"

"Well, this is certainly the message that I am getting."

"Yes, Beth, and this is the same message as me."

"Olive, your Aunt Mildred says you are unique and different from everyone else on this Earth plane and there is a reason for you being here. You have chosen to be here and God has agreed to allow you to come to the Earth plane at this time. However, this is true for all souls living here. The righteous and the unrighteous are to live on the Earth plane together until it is time for each one to return to the Other Side of the veil. We all have agreed to live here together in order to fulfill our life purpose."

"Beth, I cannot help but think of one of the great thinkers of all time, Viktor Frankl, a Jewish psychiatrist, imprisoned in a Nazi concentration camp under the evil rule of Adolf Hitler. After his freedom, he wrote a book, *From Death Camp to Existentialism,* which he later titled, *Man's Search for Meaning.* In his book, he writes: *Everyone has his own specific vocation or mission in life... Therein he cannot be replaced, nor can his life be repeated. Thus, everyone's task is as unique as is his specific opportunity to implement it.* So, really what Viktor Frankl said many years ago is exactly what my Aunt Mildred is saying to me now."

"Yes, Olive, I agree with you one hundred percent."

"This is all astonishing!"

"Astonishing is not the word for all of this!" Beth replies with a grin. "She is now speaking again. Your life purpose is different from everyone else living on the Earth plane during this lifetime, because as she explained earlier, your life purpose or soul purpose is to help save the souls of others also. There is one main life purpose for being here and it is the same life purpose for every soul living on the Earth plane. You are all here to learn and to grow spiritually and to move forward, closer to our Heavenly Father. She says, Olive, you are here to save your own soul but because you are so highly advanced, you have been given a great mission; you are also here to save the souls of others."

"What does she mean?"

"She answers when you came here to the Earth plane, you came from the Other Side, your real Home. Each soul comes from a different spiritual level from the Other Side, and ultimately it is each soul's life purpose to move forward or to advance further than the level from which the soul came, and so it is for you."

"I'm flabbergasted by all of this, Beth. What do you make of all of this?"

Beth starts to laugh. "Olive, you're asking me what I make of all of this, are you serious?"

We are now both laughing as I reply, "Yes, Beth, I'm asking you."

"All I know is that I hope all of this is sinking into your brain because if it's not, it sure isn't sinking into mine. Olive, I can see your Aunt Mildred laughing. She must think we're both so funny."

"It's a good thing you are recording all of this, Beth, because there's no way that I would remember everything."

"And there's no way that I would remember all of this either. Thank God for the tape recorder. She is talking again. The secret of peace, harmony and happiness in your life on the Earth plane is to become aware of your spiritual purpose or life purpose, and to commit fully and completely to fulfill it. You will become more spiritually aware when the truth starts to be revealed to you, and you will know the truth by the more knowledge you obtain. You are honoring your soul and God by obtaining knowledge and therefore knowing the truth. Knowledge speaks the truth, and knowledge creates power. The truth will give you power. The truth will set you free. And when you are set free, you will experience the feeling of becoming a free soul because you have chosen to learn the truth; and in doing so, you will elevate yourself to a higher level, closer to God, and in turn will love and serve our One and only Creator."

"Oh Beth, I have been trying to learn the truth all my life."

"She states that you need to choose to dedicate your life and your work to God."

"And how do I do this, Beth?"

"She is not answering. She is just standing there waiting."

"Waiting for what?"

"I don't know. Oh, she is speaking again. Choose to live in God's light of love; for when you walk in God's footsteps and walk His path of love, you will experience a spiritual change and consequently become a free soul, which means you will become carefree and happy and you will experience the gift of peace and serenity. Your soul will radiate with your light of love and you will express it in every aspect of your life for all to see. Once you begin to live your life as the loving expression of God all the time, you will know the true meaning of success while living here on the Earth plane, for love is supreme."

"I definitely believe that love is supreme, don't you, Beth?"

"Yes, Olive, I most certainly do. Oh, she says that many souls do not reach their full potential or life purpose while living on the Earth plane. They allow themselves to live in a negative type of lifestyle and accomplish very little. This is not true for you and they expect you to do great things."

"What great things am I supposed to do?"

"In time it will all be known to you."

"How long do I have to wait to find out, and what do I do in the meantime?"

"Olive, all I know is that you have to be patient."

"Yes, you're right, Beth."

"Olive, she is laughing at us and declares I am right, and she states that you can't hurry the winds."

"I can't hurry the winds, isn't that true?" We are both laughing once again.

"Now she says that in order to complete and fulfill your life purpose, you are given a soul plan while you live in a physical body on the Earth plane. This soul plan or life plan, designed just for you and only you, is unique. Your soul plan is your roadmap for you to follow in order to become the best that you can be in this lifetime. If you do not follow your soul plan, you will not successfully complete your life purpose. However, many times you may choose to not follow your soul plan and this is because you have been given the gift of free will, and therefore you are permitted to make choices."

"I didn't realize that our free will is considered a gift."

"Me neither, Olive, but it makes sense to me. Your Aunt Mildred says your free will allows you to make choices as you travel life's journey while living on the Earth plane. You always have a choice, either to do right or to do wrong. You have complete power to choose in all aspects of your life. Unfortunately, choices that you make may not always be of the highest intent. You are free to choose love from hate, right from wrong, and good from evil."

"Beth, I certainly do understand this."

"Your Aunt Mildred states that a soul who lives by our Heavenly Father's spiritual laws becomes immune to criticism, rejects other souls who are negative, hateful and evil, and fears nothing and no one, feels beneath no one yet feels superior to no one, and has respect for all. Unless you associate with souls of your own spiritual progression, you will never feel comfortable. You will never experience peace, love and harmony the way that you should. Souls who have chosen to not spiritually progress possess negative and hateful characteristics and behaviors. Just being in their presence or associating with a particular soul can bring you feelings of turmoil. If these negative souls refuse to change their ways, then you have to make the choice to dissociate yourself from them. You must protect your soul; for you are not one of them."

"Beth, I truly do understand this because I have come to terms with the fact that there are certain people that I am not able to be around. It is as though I pick up their negative, emotional energy and I can't tolerate such negative feelings."

"Your Aunt Mildred is nodding her head in agreement. She knows what you are saying is true. For example, if your feelings around a particular person are one of pity, you are experiencing negative energy. This type of feeling can be termed emotional blackmail. The medical profession refers to this negative behavior by the individual as that of a hypochondriac. It is a form of attention seeking and it is in the form of negative behavior by the person constantly complaining, especially of sickness. These negative thoughts and feelings will affect you; and it can be in the form of the emotion of pity. Over time, you may move on to other negative emotions and it could be in the form of frustration, and eventually anger. You must not allow yourself to fall into such a trap."

"This makes so much sense to me, Beth."

"I couldn't have said it better myself, Olive." We both giggle as Beth continues. "If you are a soul who chooses unwisely and one who does not choose out of love, you will suffer the consequences. You will always know when you have made the wrong choices; for when you choose to do wrong, you are choosing to walk in evil ways and therefore have veered from your soul plan."

"How will I know this?"

"She answers you will know by your feelings. Your feelings come from your soul, the real you. Your feelings will immediately let you know you are failing. Your feelings will tell you that you have done wrong and that you need to make things right and return to your soul plan."

"Beth, how will I really know what my soul plan or life plan is?"

"Your soul plan is the work you are allotted to do while you live here on the Earth plane."

"Yes, I understand this but what is the work that I am supposed to be doing?"

"Your soul plan is your mission while you live on the Earth plane. Your mission is unique and special just for you, and your soul plan was in place even before you were born during this lifetime. You have agreed to this soul plan, or otherwise you would not be here. Your soul plan is very different and exceptional and is just for you."

"Beth, I can't help but recall a Native American saying by Morning Dove. *Everything on the earth has a purpose, every disease an herb to cure it, and every person a mission.* Wise words, don't you think?"

"Wise words indeed, Olive. She is speaking again. You will begin to see each day unfold with the organized, orchestrated events in your life. And as you walk your soul path on the Earth plane, please do not resist change, but embrace it; for change will allow you to move forward and to follow your chosen path in life."

"Beth, this is all so remarkable!"

Beth quickly responds with a grin. "And you're telling me this as if I don't already know? Olive, your Aunt Mildred is telling me to impress upon you that you must not forget to become more spiritually aware."

"I will not forget."

"Your Aunt Mildred states that each soul incarnates at a different level of spiritual growth, and each one of us needs to go through different experiences living on the Earth plane in order to gain wisdom and expand our spiritual awareness, for the bigger picture of life."

"I think I understand now, Beth. I think she is telling me that I need to go through different experiences in life in order for me to become more spiritually aware. But in order for me to go through the different experiences that is all part of my life plan, or soul plan as my Aunt Mildred calls it, I need to make sure that I make the right choices all the time."

"She is nodding her head yes, Olive. She says that when you become more spiritually aware, you will discover your true self and know who you really are. And you will then have the ability to fulfill any of life's goals and dreams; for the Earth plane is considered the university for the soul and that all souls are here to learn, grow and advance spiritually."

"So, what she is telling me is to just go with the flow of life."

"Yes, Olive, I think this is definitely what she is telling you. I can see her nodding her head yes. She wants you to enjoy each and every moment as you make your travels on the Earth plane."

"Tell Aunt Mildred that I will certainly try and do this. Does she have anything else to say to me?"

"She is smiling and nodding her head no."

"Okay, Beth. Please tell my Aunt Mildred that she has given me a lot to think about."

"Your Uncle Abel is now waving good-bye. He is fading away, going back into the distance and your Aunt Mildred is starting to fade into the distance also. They are both waving good-bye."

I am so overwhelmed and find it difficult to speak but I manage to utter the words, "Good-bye, Uncle Abel, good-bye, Aunt Mildred."

"Olive, I must say this has been one of the most exciting readings I think I have ever done in my life. You were given so much information!"

"I know, isn't this all incredible? Who would ever believe any of this?" We laugh again. As I gather my handbag and start to leave the room, with Beth following behind me, I cannot help but recall my reason for visiting Beth in the first place. "And Beth, the reason why I visited with you is to find out why I was so emotionally upset over the death of my uncle; and I'm still no wiser."

We both laugh as we climb the stairs and Beth sees me to the door, and utters, "The time is not right."

CHAPTER 5

A Visit With My Heavenly Father

...for I have seen God face to face,
and my life is preserved.

The Holy Bible: Genesis 32:30
King James Version

It is December 28, 1993, and little do I know upon awaking this Christmas morning, that this day will become the greatest day of my life, and that my life is about to be changed forever.

It is a wonderful Christmas, or as wonderful as it can possibly be, considering the circumstances. This Christmas is no different from the previous years in our house with our two children, except for the emptiness in our hearts. It was just two months earlier, on October 28, our beloved little dog Tippy died, and I feel I have a huge hole inside of me that has left me inconsolable for she was like a child to me. Now she is gone. I am still mourning my loss and missing her greatly; and no matter what I do or where I go, I think of her. I loved her so much and I always will, even though she is no longer with me. She was a gift from God who gave me unconditional love each day.

I feel so saddened and alone and this unbearable pain and sadness is consuming me, and I know that one of my reasons for feeling this way is that I still do not know if there really is a God. I have been searching for God all my life and I feel I still do not know the truth. I am still a "doubting Thomas," and if something does not change, I know I will feel this way for the remainder of my life. If God is real, I want to know. I yearn to know the truth. I just want to do everything right by God and to walk in His path according to His will; however, in order to do this, I have to know the truth. I need proof. My Guardian Soul, Aunt Mildred, told me that there is a God and I know I should not doubt, but doubt I do.

I think back on that evening in my nurse's residence, room 628, and recall the loving voice. It truly was a gift but it happened many years ago and now I have to question if it really happened at all. I know I should not have these doubts. I remember her telling me that I would never be alone, but I certainly feel alone. I know I have my husband and my children but they are not able to help me because they are dealing with their own sorrow. It just feels so unbearable. She was my baby and now I am left only with her memory, my heart feels torn apart. I remember her coming to me after she died, but was that just my imagination. Through my sobs, I am beginning to realize that I doubt everything that has happened to me in the past, at least everything that no one else was witness to.

I remember being in the family room lying on the sofa watching television and Tippy was on the sofa with me. She got my attention because she was sneezing; at the time, the thought came to me that she was getting a cold. A short time later, my daughter came into the family room to play with her and I looked at her and said, "She won't be with us much longer." Looking back, I realize now I even shocked myself by such a comment. I do not know where that thought came from or even why I had said it. However, there it was; the comment was made.

Later that same night, I woke from my sleep at exactly 3 A.M. and sat up in bed; and much to my amazement, my husband did exactly the same thing and at the exact same time! Someone or something woke us. We both got out of bed and found our Tippy in the hall, very sick. Immediately, my husband telephoned the vet to take her to the emergency department and while he was getting dressed, she stopped breathing. I screamed to my husband and knew that she was gone. Through my sobs, I watched my husband take her to the car. I tried to compose myself to go upstairs to wake my children and tell them the devastating news. A short time later, my husband returned with our baby, telling us that the doctor had confirmed that she was dead. The next day, we had the unbearable task of taking her to her resting place in my hometown of Spaniard's Bay, cuddled in her doggie bed and blanket, with all her favorite toys. After burying my baby, Tippy appeared to me while we were in the car returning home. Was this all in my imagination because I was so distraught and grief stricken? I do not have an answer.

That same evening, I fell to my knees in prayer to God, if there is a God, and begged Him to take care of my baby and, if possible, could He please give me a sign that she is safe and okay. It was at this exact moment that I instantly heard her all-too-familiar bark! Could this be real? Am I just imagining it? The next morning, I woke because there seemed something heavy around my feet. I sprung up in bed and, there was my beautiful, fluffy, white toy poodle, Tippy! I let out a squeal and the tears started to flow. All she did was look at me with those gorgeous eyes and then she disappeared. I slumped back down into bed and silently thanked God for my special visit.

Later during the same week, I was in my car driving to work and suddenly Tippy appeared to me once more. She was sitting on the passenger seat and looking straight ahead, as she would always do, and then turned and looked at me. It was not just for a few seconds; she stayed there for the complete drive to the college where I worked. I pulled my car into the parking lot, turned off the ignition and, with tears in my eyes, I reached down and kissed her on the head and told her I loved her. My lips seem to go right through the top of her head but that did not matter. I told her I was so happy that she had visited with me and that I needed to go to work. I recall walking away from my car, knowing that this would be the last time that I would see her, and sure enough, when I returned later in the afternoon, she was gone.

Now it is two months later, Christmas time, the evening of December 28. This evening seems no different from any other evening, or so I think. My husband and I decide to go to bed early and I am relaxing and reflecting upon my day. All of a sudden, I can feel myself lifting out of the bed! As I am lifting upward, I realize I am going right through the sheet and comforter and the upper part of me is moving upward almost at a 45 degree angle! I glance backwards and to my complete astonishment, I see myself still lying in the bed with my husband lying next to me! It is at this instant that I realize that I am out of my body!

69

As I keep moving, I find I am in a vertical position. I look down at myself and realize that I am still wearing my long nightie that I had worn to bed. As I lift my head, I see that I am floating right through the upper part of the wall, opposite the bed! I am moving faster, travelling, and it is amazing! I do not know where I am going; however, I feel safe and feel very much at peace. I am flying in the air, outdoors! I am moving so fast that the tail of my nightie is flapping in the wind. I am high above the ground but not too high, because I can clearly see all the valleys and the mountains below me. At one point, I realize that I have travelled quite a distance, and know that I am no longer in Newfoundland because there is no snow on the ground. In fact, I realize that I cannot even be in Canada because there is no snow to be seen anywhere. I am moving at a speed that is very enjoyable and relaxing, and it feels so natural!

The next thing I know I am starting to slow down. I find myself moving toward a huge, white mass, and gently I land upon it. As I look around, all I can see is whiteness everywhere. I must be standing on a cloud. I do not know what else it could have been. It is white and fluffy and feels soft beneath my bare feet. There is nothing else around. As I stand there looking into the whiteness, I notice figures standing ahead of me. There are seven of them. I am standing at one end of the cloud and they are in front of me; six are standing in a formation. There are three on each side and they are about six feet apart from one another, facing each other on the opposite side. The seventh figure is standing at the end of this formation, in the distance, opposite to me. They are all dressed in long, white robes with long sleeves, hoods and white rope belt, tied around the waist, hanging down on the left side of each robe. I do not know whether these figures are male or female but I sense they are all male. No one speaks and no one is looking in my direction; however, for some unknown reason, I know I am supposed to walk down the aisle between them.

Without hesitation, I start to walk down the aisle toward the seventh figure that is standing at the end of the cloud. I can see he is taller than I am, and is also dressed in a long, glistening white robe with long sleeves, a hood, and a white rope belt tied at the waist, hanging down the left side. As I walk closer, the whiteness becomes brighter and brighter and the features of this male figure become more distinct. Even though it is extremely bright, I find it to be very soothing and refreshing. It is a magnificent glow! I keep walking and I see two beautiful, piercing eyes, which seem to sparkle with an exuberant brilliance, every color of the rainbow, with a radiance of love. This figure is now in full view of me, and I recognize the figure immediately! I start to cry uncontrollably! I run and fall to my knees at His feet! Bent down, to the right side of this figure, with my head bowed, I continue to cry and sob uncontrollable tears of joy! I am experiencing an overwhelming sense of love, a very deep massive love. I can feel His hand on my head, and through my tears of joy, I repeat, *"You are real! You are real! You are real!"* I keep saying it, *"You are real! You are real! You are real!"*

He does not speak but I am able to hear His thoughts, and He is saying, *"It is all okay, my child."*

This figure is *God!* This figure is *my Heavenly Father!* The presence of love and peace is enormous! I am experiencing an indescribable love. The love I feel coming from my Heavenly Father I am unable to explain in human terms, and I continue to sob and sob and sob, all the while repeating, *"You are real! You are real! You are real!"*

I can still hear His thoughts as He speaks to me. *"My child, you have great work to do. I have bestowed upon you much greatness. You are to teach…teach many, for you have been prepared. Keep learning. You are wise and therefore chosen for a great mission while on the Earth plane."*

I am astounded by the words my Heavenly Father is saying to me, and as the tears keep flowing, I am unable to respond.

My Heavenly Father continues. *"The veil of secrecy must be lifted. The time has come. This is the time for transformation of all things."*

I can still feel the weight of His hand on my head and I feel so much love transmitted to me. These feelings of love are extraordinary and so enormous!

He says to me, *"It is necessary for the people of the Earth plane to learn; for many have faltered. Go, my child, in peace and love; and always remember your greatness."*

My entire being is permeated with an all-encompassing sense of love and peace that is impossible for me to explain, and if I had not fully known the will of God before, it is clear at this moment. I have an all-knowing sense and know that the real treasures in life are love and peace, and that I can become the happiest, most ecstatic human being if I choose, because love heals all wounds, and we are all part of a divine plan!

The next thing I know I am back in my bed! I glance over at my husband who, I can tell, is still sleeping. I am lying there, wide-awake, and feeling so much love and peace! I am astounded at what I have just experienced! The tears are streaming down my face as I lay there, and with the tears are the feelings of an enormous, vast love! The love is so exorbitant, that it is impossible for me to begin to describe the extent of it except by comparing it to all the love I have in my life. I know the feeling of love because I have love from my husband, my darling two children, my relatives, friends, neighbors and some people in my workplace. However, if I could put all of this love together, and if I were to multiply it a thousand times, it still would not come close to the amount of love I experienced from my Heavenly Father!

It is at that moment I realize that I had been a "doubting Thomas" all my life, and now I do not have to doubt anymore. There is a God! There is a Heavenly Father! I have proof! My Father in Heaven knew how badly I needed to meet with Him face to face and allowed me this spectacular visit with Him. I am His child, and He loves me dearly and I love Him. I come to terms with the fact that I am here on Earth because He wants me here and I realize that I must have agreed to come here to serve a purpose. With these thoughts in my mind, I have an awakening of the truth, as I quickly recall the very same message given to me by my Aunt Mildred many years ago!

My thoughts swiftly take me back to the words expressed by my Heavenly Father during my fantastic visit. He said to me, *"It is all okay, my child."* I now understand that the very life I am living is exactly the life I am supposed to be living here on Earth, it is the life that God has chosen for me. No matter what goes wrong, nothing is truly wrong; for my Heavenly Father is watching and protecting me. He told me it is all okay.

As I lay in my bed, with the tears flowing like spring rain, I recall He also said, *"My child, you have great work to do."* I have great work to do! What great work do I have to do? Why did I not ask what this great work is that I have to do?

"I have bestowed upon you much greatness." What greatness do I possess? I am just an ordinary person who is a daughter, sister, wife, mother, friend and colleague; like most people on this Earth. What greatness do I have that others do not? Why me? Who is going to believe all of this when I am finding it difficult to believe it myself? However, I know what happened to me. I am wide-awake and I know what is real. I had the most extraordinary trip that one could ever imagine, and that I know to be true!

"You are to teach...teach many; for you have been prepared." If only I had stopped crying long enough to ask Him what it is, I am supposed to teach. He said that I have been prepared. How have I been prepared? The thought is no sooner in my mind when the answer comes to me as I go back to my childhood days. The school I attended was only a small, one room school and the students were from kindergarten to grade three, and there was only one teacher. I always caught on quickly. I remember completing kindergarten and grade one all in the same year. When I was in grade two, I completed my work much sooner than my friends, so consequently my teacher had me teach the younger students in kindergarten and grade one, while she taught grades two and three. I was also a Sunday school teacher for about four years. I continued with my education after graduating from nursing school, attending university and graduating with my Bachelor Degree in Education, and later with my Master Degree in Education Administration. Due to my interest in education, I chose to teach in the different health sciences programs, including nursing. I have been prepared to teach! I have the education and the teaching experience from a very young age!

"Keep learning." I must keep learning. I have always tried to learn something new each day because I felt if I did not do this, then I considered my time wasted. In my younger years, I believed that the word 'can't' was not in my vocabulary, and now I realize that I have always held this belief about myself. I have always had the attitude that the sky is the limit for me. My thoughts go to my dad, who I realize has had an enormous positive influence on my life in many ways, including the value of education. Yes, I am still learning and I realize that my Heavenly Father knows this and this is why He told me to keep learning.

"You are wise..." Am I really? But then, who am I to question my Heavenly Father? If my Heavenly Father says I am wise, then I must be. I do know that I have been reading spiritual books all my life; for my thirst for spiritual knowledge seems to be never ending, and so I do know I have obtained a lot of knowledge over the years. In addition, maybe I am far wiser than I give myself credit for; however, I know I must be patient for time will reveal all. This I know to be true.

My Heavenly Father also said to me, *"...and therefore chosen for a great mission while on the Earth plane."* What is this great mission? I guess only time will tell.

My thoughts seem to be racing a mile a minute. *"The veil of secrecy must be lifted."* What is this veil of secrecy? I no sooner have the question in my mind then an answer comes to me. The people living here on Earth do not know who they really are and where they came from, nor do they know where they are going. They think they are all-powerful, physical beings with knowledge of all things, but little do they know that they actually know very little. They have allowed the physical world to overpower their minds and many have lost their way. *"The time has come."* The time has come for the people living here on Earth to know the truth. *"This is the time for transformation of all things."* The Earth has regressed, rather than evolve as it should, and it is because of the people of the Earth. It is time for positive change.

My Heavenly Father said, *"It is necessary for the people of the Earth plane to learn; for many have faltered."* I understand this comment because many people living here on Earth are not living a respectful, honest and loving life. I know many people have fallen by the wayside for whatever reason. Many people need to change their ways for the better and they have to learn to live differently. Many times during my life, I have refused to listen to the news because the news each day revealed the horror and sufferings of this world, and therefore I found it extremely difficult to listen to or watch. The negative impact the media portrays each day is exposing my soul to the traumatic reality of the world I live in and I find it all too heart wrenching, even to this day. There is too much cruelty, pain and suffering.

As I wipe away my tears with the end of my bed sheet, my mind takes me back to the loving voice of my Heavenly Father. *"Go, my child, in peace and love; and always remember your greatness."* I will always cherish these words. He called me His child! I am a child of God, our One and only Creator, and He is my Father in Heaven who loves me dearly. As the tears trickle down my face, the thought comes to me that God does not reside in each one of us, as some people think, for God is our Heavenly Father who resides in the spiritual world. However, God is a part of us because we all came from Him and we are His children. We are a spark of our Heavenly Father's light of love and our lights shine brightly, according to how much we walk in God's path of righteousness and love. I know that if each one of us chooses to follow God in all His ways, our light will shine with a brilliant glow for all to see.

I have had a night like no other, and it is as though time has stood still. However, I glance over at the clock on my nightstand and it says otherwise, for now it is the wee hours in the morning and it will soon be daylight. Even though it is late, sleep will not come because I am wide-awake and full of energy.

I will tell my husband of my experience because we have no secrets; however, I know it will be in time. I do not know when but it will be soon. I need time to reflect and to grasp everything that has transpired. First of all, I didn't even know that I could leave my body the way that I did, and secondly, I didn't know that I could travel the way that I did. If that is not remarkable enough, then I met my loving Heavenly Father! Who is going to believe all of this? I can hardly believe it myself! Yet, I know it actually happened! I know my husband is going to have difficulty believing what I experienced, and of course, I truly understand. This is all so incredible! It is so powerful, so life changing! My visit was so amazing that I now know that God is real. I met Him. I touched Him. I spoke to Him, and He spoke to me through His thoughts. I have been a "doubting Thomas" all my life but now I do not have to doubt anymore. God is real!

Now I know that time will reveal all. In the meantime, I will graciously walk in my Heavenly Father's path of righteousness and love. I know that I am here on Earth to do His work, which I graciously accept, and I know in time all the closed doors in my life will swing wide open and my life's work I will know, for my Heavenly Father said so.

CHAPTER 6

Why Is The Devil Always Chasing You?

...for the devil is come down unto you,
having great wrath,
because he knoweth that he hath but a short time.

The Holy Bible: Revelation 12:12
King James Version

Because it is still Christmas time, we are all very busy visiting relatives and friends, and entertaining in our own house. It is another evening and both my husband and I decide it is time for bed. My husband fell to sleep very quickly, which is usual for him, while I am still awake and have just finished saying my prayers. I am once again relaxing and reflecting upon my day; however, I am reflecting upon the most amazing trip I had the night before also.

As I start to drift off to sleep, I start to experience a fear that leaves me paralyzed. I am snuggled in my bed when all of a sudden, I feel very hot as though I am burning up. I think I must be running a temperature and that I am coming down with a cold or the flu. I start to push off the comforter and open my eyes. Standing by my side of the bed is a large, dark figure! I am unable to pick out the distinct features of this figure because of the darkness it possesses; even the eyes are dark. I feel such a massive amount of hatred directed towards me from this being! I feel such terror! The fear I feel is indescribable! I want to scream but nothing comes. I quickly move closer to my husband and pull the comforter back over me. This figure is dressed in a long, black robe and it has a hood.

I feel it is a male presence and surprisingly enough, I know instantly it is the evil one, whom many refer to as Satan or the devil! His hatred for me is so intense and the anger directed towards me is enormous! I freeze with fear! I have never experienced such a feeling of hatred and fear in my life!

I am so scared I feel as though my body is paralyzed with terror. I want to scream to my husband so he can help me, but there is nothing! Then, almost instantaneously, I realize that there is another presence in the bedroom with me! I am unable to see this presence; however, I do sense it is very loving and concerned for my well-being. The loving presence speaks to me and I recognize the voice as a male, *"Recite the Lord's Prayer."* I start to say the Lord's Prayer to myself, *"Our Father which art in heaven."* To my astonishment, I can instantly feel the anger and hate slack off and I can see this hateful being move backwards. I continue. *"Hallowed be thy name. Thy kingdom come. Thy will be done in earth, as it is in heaven."* About a third of the way through the Lord's Prayer, I can see this evil, dark being continue to move backwards and the intensity of his anger and hate fading with him! *"Give us this day our daily bread. And forgive us our debts, as we forgive our debtors."* I am now half way through, and this hateful, dark figure is in the distance and the anger and hate is still going with him! *"And lead us not into temptation, but deliver us from the evil one."* This dark figure is in the distance and almost out of sight. *"For thine is the kingdom, and the power, and the glory, for ever. Amen."* I have completed the Lord's Prayer and much to my astonishment, this evil being is completely gone and the anger and hate with him!

I can still sense the presence of the loving soul with me and I feel completely safe. The feeling of fear has now completely disappeared. This is all so remarkable! In a soft and loving voice, the loving presence says to me, *"You have nothing to fear my child; for the evil one has vanished from you for all time. You have done extremely well. We are all so very proud of you. Get well rested; for a new day dawns."* The loving male voice addressed me as "my child!" Immediately, I recognize the loving voice as that of my Heavenly Father! There are absolutely no words to describe the feelings of love that are showered upon me. I now feel an unbelievable sense of peace, joy and love.

On different occasions over the years, my mother would say to me, "Why is the devil always chasing you?" and my answer would always be the same, "He can chase me all he wants, but he'll never catch me." As a child and a young adult, I did not even know myself why I gave such an answer, but now I do, for I know the truth. The evil one, the devil, realizes now he will never have me, because no matter how hard he tried with his temptations, I never faltered, and now he knows he has lost me forever.

I am all too aware of some people living here on Earth who are willing to sell their souls to the evil one to gain Earthly power in the form of money or control. Unfortunately for them, as they will find out later when their time has come to leave this home we call Earth, it will come back to haunt them. They will have to pay a very high price when they return to the Other Side, for the evil one only promises the treasures of darkness.

Just the night previously, I had visited my loving Heavenly Father and I realize the evil one knows about my special visit. He had come to let me know he hates me. It made me realize that he has finally given up because he knows there is no hope. His pursuits had all been in vain. He will never win me over. There are many times that I can recall being tempted to do wrong, and to give into the evil ways of the evil one and his followers; however, I always remained steadfast and never once even considered following him.

There were times when others tried to influence my life in a negative and hateful manner; however, their attempts failed also. One such time was when my husband accepted a new job in Vancouver, British Columbia, and had left Newfoundland in August. The following December, I took our two children and our toy poodle, Tippy, and boarded the plane for Vancouver. Because of the different lifestyle of the bigger city life and consequently the high crime rate, as a family we did not adjust very well at all. Consequently, as soon as our children finished their school exams in June, we had them on the first plane back to Newfoundland.

It was the next month, July, that I returned to Newfoundland. I was out shopping and had run into my friend Linda, and of course, we got chatting. During our conversation, I noticed she had this weird look on her face as I was telling her about how I had just returned home, and our children had returned back home the month prior, and that my husband would be coming home in September because he had been offered a new engineering position in Newfoundland. I remember being concerned because of the expression on her face, and I asked her if there was something wrong. Her reply was quite shocking! She said to me, "Olive, you're not going to believe this."

"Believe what?" I asked.

"Olive, I was told that you and Dave are divorced!"

"Are you kidding me?"

"No, Olive, I am not kidding you," she replied. "I was told that you are divorced and that you were still living in Vancouver and you kept the children with you, and that Dave had left you and was already back here in Newfoundland!"

We just stared at each other in disbelief and instantly broke into hysterical laughter. After composing ourselves, I finally blurted out, "Linda, this is unbelievable! There is no truth to any of this! Who would put out such a malicious and hateful rumor?"

She answered, "Olive, I really don't know who started this but obviously it is all hateful, malicious gossip!"

"It most certainly is hateful, malicious gossip. And you did say that Dave had left me, right?"

"Yes, I did because this is what I was told."

"Well, I can tell that this is wishful thinking for someone, and I do have an idea who would be so nasty to start such a rumor."

"You know someone who would actually start such a malicious rumor, knowing there is no truth to the rumor at all?" Linda asked with an expression of bewilderment.

"Yes Linda, I most certainly do, and what this person is trying to prove is beyond me, because she knows full well that in time she is going to look like a fool."

Now my friend and I are once again laughing hysterically, as Linda asked, "Is there any truth to the rumor at all? Were you and Dave maybe having marital problems and you considered staying in Vancouver to live?"

Again I laughed as I responded, "No, Linda, there is absolutely no truth to the rumor what-so-ever. Dave and I never experienced any marital problems at all, and it is just the opposite. We are very happy. This person who started this hateful rumor is definitely a fool."

Gossip with the intent to willfully and maliciously deceive others is definitely wrong. Whether a lie has a label as a fib, a white lie or a black lie makes no difference, for a lie is a lie. A fib, according to many, is a small lie so therefore it is not damaging, but there is no such thing as a small lie. Some people even try to convince themselves that there are such things as black lies and white lies. They consider that a black lie is false information, whereas a white lie is only partly false information and the complete truth is exaggerated, and therefore to tell a white lie is not as bad as telling a black lie. In reality, there is no such thing as a black lie or white lie, or a lie of any other color. A false statement made with the intent to deceive is a lie, whether complete or partial. A lie is inexcusable. Lies are destructive and hateful behaviour and to compound this hateful, evil behavior, the liar may try and justify the actions by resorting to telling more lies; for telling one lie leads to another and then another, and in time a web of deceit has been weaved. Those who choose to participate in malicious gossip and resort to telling lies become the true followers of the father of lies, the evil one, the devil, and becomes a slave to the power of lies. Any person walking this Earth who resorts to stooping so low and telling lies is following Satan, and therefore has become one of his followers. The one lesson that I have learned over the years is that if a person is inclined to be untruthful and resorts to lies, eventually the price of deception will have to be paid. If a person creates a negative, malicious and hateful thought, word or action of intent to harm another, little does he or she know that the person harmed the most by the distortions of evil is himself or herself, for in time they will be inflicted with soul sickness. Unresolved issues can also cause soul sickness. These unresolved issues over time fester, and lead to sickness within the soul, and sickness within the soul is eventually seen in the physical body.

The cause of soul sickness is rejecting God; this brings illness to the soul, which in turn, brings illness to the physical body. When the physical body experiences symptoms of discomfort, such as a headache, the soul is experiencing pain and agony and is crying tears from the soul. One of the most common ways of rejecting God is by telling lies. One such individual I have known for many years has resorted to telling lies for as long as I have known her, and my Guardian Soul tells me that in time, this person is going to develop some type of crippling disease of the feet because of all her sins. Soul sickness stems from the seeds of evil. This person will have sickness caused by self-infliction and needs to acknowledge that she is responsible for her own illness. If this person is willing to acknowledge that she is responsible for her own sickness and then asks for forgiveness, not only from God but also from all those whom she has done harm, forgiveness can be granted and the sickness will disappear. As God forgives her, He can also help her heal.

The souls who represent darkness will plant the seeds of evil. The seeds of evil are deep, profound hateful tactics such as manipulation, deceitfulness, lies, gossip, greed, anger, hostility, agitation, irritability, aggressiveness, frustration, envy, rudeness, selfishness, bitterness, jealousy, vengefulness, turmoil, resentment, impatience, unkindness, and harshness. These types of souls expect to live by their own rules of power; for in reality, they feel powerless and have low self-worth. Therefore to gain power, they need to be at the center of attention, and have the compulsion to control and the desire for external control, and therefore will try to control others.

"In addition, the seeds of evil can be recognized by the negative and hateful actions, such as shouting, screaming, arguing, bullying, threats, foul language, hitting, and assault, all forms of abuse, such as, physical, sexual, mental, emotional, verbal, and cruelty to animals, and thoughts of murder or murder. And murder includes killing any form of life, for example, killing birds and hunting down animals just for pleasure. The negative behavior of hate can destroy the soul, for if you allow your soul to experience hatred from others, you are being disrespectful to yourself and in turn, you are being disrespectful to God.

The real person, who is the soul, who follows our loving God is completely free of all negative, hateful, and evil desires. A soul who lives by the laws of God with love and has advanced higher, rejects people or other souls who reject God and who follow the evil one. Without love, these souls become their own worst enemy; for when a soul chooses to follow the evil one, the soul will eventually experience helplessness, hopelessness, and desperation, and will resort to trying to negatively influence the loving soul in different situations and circumstances. Those walking in the devil's path of hate and control will not understand the loving soul. The lower level soul will use every hateful tactic she can think of in order to try to bring the loving soul down to her low, dark level. This type of soul will scorn, ridicule, lie and gossip about the loving soul because of the anger and inability to control. It is of vital importance to know that no matter how much love you give a lower level, dark soul, this soul will not return love because of all her darkness. The loving soul must be prepared and on guard at all times, and consequently finds it extremely difficult to be in the company of such a lower level, dark soul.

The loving soul who follows God fears no one, feels beneath no one and doesn't feel inferior or superior to any one; for the loving soul has respect and love for all God's people and treats them as equal. The loving soul respects all differences of humankind and therefore considers all with respect and love regardless of the race, religion, color of the skin, educational background, social status, financial status, sexual orientation or any other difference; for genuine love demands respect. The only time a loving soul will reject another soul will be because she recognizes the evil that is present, and consequently the loving soul needs to keep away for her own protection.

Protection from evil is necessary. Protection can come by recognizing the spiritual power and spiritual strength that comes from the possession of spiritual or religious objects. For example, holding prayer beads, wearing a cross around the neck, having a religious book in one's possession like the Holy Quran or the Holy Bible, will aid in protection from evil. These spiritual or religious items hold great spiritual power, and represent protection and will therefore keep the soul safe and free from harm. In addition, prayer is of the utmost importance because a prayer to God for protection is also very powerful.

When you choose to walk in God's path of love, you will begin to experience a different kind of power, for it will not be the physical power but spiritual. There will be no more feelings of fear and low self-worth; no need to feel the need to be at the center of attention, no compulsion to control others, and no desire for external power; for the true power will come from within. In order to have true power, one must plant the seeds of love. The seeds of love are: compassion, kindness, forgiveness, tolerance, acceptance, generosity, peace, patience, truth, hope, faith, gentleness, mercy, grace, knowledge, joy, helpfulness, giving, longsuffering, goodness, understanding, friendship, contentment, vision, endurance, speaking gently, speaking kindly, speaking words of truth, honesty, doing charity, and being positive in all thoughts, words, and actions.

I know and understand the concept of saved, for I experienced it. One of the worse things a person living on this Earth can do is to think or believe there is no such one as the evil one, for this is a grave mistake. The evil one and his followers are alive and well and are out in full force. I know this because I have proof!

CHAPTER 7

Yes, But You Will Be Going Home.

For he shall give his angels charge over thee,
to keep thee in all thy ways.

The Holy Bible: Psalms 91:11
King James Version

My first encounter with my Guardian Angel takes place in my garden on a beautiful summer's day. It is July 18 to be exact, and I am in my garden admiring the beauty and growth of the trees, bushes and flowers, for my garden is in full bloom. I love to watch a new plant or tree grow and I love to watch flowers blossom. Almost every day I can see the growth spurting forth when I plant a tree or bush. I treasure the time I spend in my garden because I find it brings me much pleasure and I find it very relaxing. More importantly, watching nature take its course gives me much love, peace and serenity. So here I am again, walking in my garden admiring my beautiful trees, bushes and flowers and yet I am not fully at peace for I cannot help but think of my dad.

My father had been quite sick and spent some time in the Intensive Care Unit at the hospital. His doctor is amazed that he is still alive; for he said he should have been gone long ago. According to the test results, his heart is very weak and barely pumping and his doctor considers his survival a miracle. I know my prayers to God and my father's strong will to live and to never give up, are the reasons why he is still here with us. He is a fighter and we all know he is going to fight to the very end. He is not going to leave us very easily. He loves us all too much and he loves life. He will only go when God decides to take him and not one minute before.

The doctor decided to call a meeting with the family. After quick introductions, my father's doctor proceeds to address the idea of palliative care services. He is adamant that nothing else can be done for my father and in the best interests of all, he suggests that the best care at this time is for my father to be transferred to the Palliative Care Unit. I know this would be a quick death sentence for my father, and even though I know he does not have much time left, how he should live out his last days should be a matter of choice; and the very person that should make this decision is not even present. Without hesitation, I very quickly say what is on my mind. In no way do I agree with this suggestion. I also do not agree with such a meeting without my father being present. Even though my father's physical health has deteriorated, his mind is still quite sharp and clear and he is quite competent to make such a major life decision for himself. After I leave the meeting, I return to my father's hospital room where I find him sitting on the side of his bed, and so I sit in the chair opposite to him. With a look of concern on his face, he asks me what is wrong. I guess I cannot hide my hurt; however, I smile and just say, "You will soon be going home." With his tear filled baby blue eyes, he replies, "Okay, my doll, okay."

Now it is over a year later, and my father is still alive and is able to enjoy his beautiful garden. Yet, as I think about him, a sadness sweeps over me as I remember my dad's words just the previous day. My husband and I were visiting our parents because it was my father's birthday, July 17. We are all sitting in our lawn chairs in his garden, chatting away and just enjoying each other's company. Our glasses are empty and so my mother takes them to refill and my husband offers to help her, and so they both leave and go inside the house, leaving my father and me alone. We sit quietly enjoying the beautiful summer's day in my parents' mature garden, which is full of life with flowers, shrubs, and trees blossoming. As I look around, I realize how beautiful my father's garden really is in the summer months. "Dad, your garden is so beautiful this time of year. Everything is in full bloom and looks so amazing." His comment is one I shall never forget, because the words he spoke had a great impact on me. He agrees with my comment and with sadness in his voice, he answers, "Yes, but someday soon I have to leave this all behind." The truth of his words pierced my heart because I know what he has said is so true. This is my dad's home and his beautiful garden, but we both know all too well that someday soon he will be leaving it all behind. My father's words had such a devastating impact on my soul that the reality of living life here on Earth really sunk into my brain on that glorious sunny afternoon.

It is now the following day and here I am standing alone in my own garden, admiring my own flowers, shrubs and trees. I am enjoying my time immensely, although these feelings are soon going to tumble down around me because the words that my father had spoken the day before surface in my mind, and once again pierce through my heart. "Yes, but someday soon I have to leave this all behind." My father is so right, for the cold hard reality is that our time spent here on Earth is only short. I slump to the ground in despair, as I say to myself, "Oh my, it is so true. Someday I will have to leave this all behind also." I feel very sad and become emotional, and I can feel the tears filling my eyes. Then, to my astonishment, a male voice from behind me speaks with great conviction and love. "Yes, but you will be going Home."

I immediately turn around to see who is in the garden with me, and much to my bewilderment, there is no one there! I cannot believe my eyes! I look all around the area but no one is in sight. I know a male voice has spoken to me and I quickly say aloud, "Who are you?"

The loving, male voice answers, "Gabriel."

My reaction is of great shock. "Gabriel?"

"Yes, Gabriel."

"Are you the angel Gabriel that I have read about?"

The loving voice responds, "I am your Guardian Angel."

I blurt out, "I have a Guardian Angel?"

With a loving laugh, he replies, "You most certainly do."

Immediately I experience an overwhelming sense of peace and love and an all-knowing feeling. My sadness quickly disappears and I feel so much love and joy. It is astounding! I can feel the tears of joy streaming down my face as I crouch down to the ground for more support. This is all so incredible to me. As I compose myself, I quickly wipe away my tears of joy and ask, "Are you still with me?"

"Yes, my dear, I am here."

"Are you really a Guardian Angel?"

"Yes, I am a Guardian Angel. And I am not just any Guardian Angel; I am *your* Guardian Angel."

"Does everyone have a Guardian Angel?"

"Yes, everyone does have a Guardian Angel, and not only does everyone have a Guardian Angel to watch over them from a distance but each soul on the Earth plane also has Guardian Souls to guide and protect them. However, unfortunately most living here do not realize or understand that they have Guardian Angels and Guardian Souls. When they come over here, they become too grounded in the physical world and forget who they really are and where they come from."

"Is this true for me, Gabriel? Did I forget also?"

"Not really, my dear. It just seems like you did, but you didn't allow yourself to become too grounded over here." There is silence. "This is why you are here, enjoying God's beauty which He has created for you in this beautiful garden of yours. You still remain spiritual and therefore you embrace God's gifts of nature with its entire splendor."

"I really do enjoy being in my garden. I love to watch the growth spurt forth each day. It's like a miracle to me."

"Yes, I do understand. This means that you have not allowed yourself to become caught up in the physical side in which you live."

"Gabriel, why is it some, or as you say most, people who live here on Earth become too grounded?"

"It is because they allow themselves to dwell on all that is physical and forget about the spiritual. This is a grave mistake. In time, when they return to the Other Side, they have a lot of repentance to do."

"What do you mean by repentance?"

"They have to repent before all and they must try and understand how foolishly they dwindled away a lifetime."

"You mean a lifetime wasted?"

"Yes, my dear, this is exactly what I mean. Too many souls are caught up in the race of living the physical life. When this is so, many return with a lifetime of regrets."

"This seems so sad."

"Yes, it certainly is sad. Those of us in the spiritual world do not want this to happen but unfortunately, many live in stubbornness and greed. When these souls are on their deathbed, do you think they are going to think of all their material wealth and their material possessions?"

"I doubt that very much, Gabriel, and even if they did think of all of their material wealth and material possessions, it may be because they know their end is near and that everything they accumulated in their lifetime cannot be taken with them."

"Yes, you are absolutely right. These types of souls live their lives on the Earth plane with extravagance and overindulgence. They may think of the position or title they hold in a job, or the position or title of their spouse which they thought was so important, but what real meaning is there? Then it could be their social status in society, the money, the stocks and bonds, the big house or houses, the fancy car or cars, or all the man-made toys of the physical world, but in the end what purpose does it all serve? These are all manufactured possessions that have no real value or power. And when the end finally comes, which it will; for no one escapes the death of the physical body, eventually there is an extremely high price to pay."

There is silence for I am trying to understand everything. I break the silence and ask, "Why are some people so greedy and want so much for themselves, when others have so little?"

"It is because of love."

"How can this be? If they are truly loving, they would not squander so lavishly on themselves and give to others who are so much in need."

"My dear, the love I am referring to is the love for themselves in a selfish and greedy way; for they have the love for money and power, and all that it brings with it in the physical world."

"Oh, I understand now."

"These people are lost souls living a fool's life; for as the old saying goes, a fool and his money are soon parted. These selfish and greedy souls living on the Earth plane, in time, will have to part with it all. They do not know the true meaning of love and power, for the power of love is not selfish and greedy but just the opposite. The true power of love is permanent and lasts for all eternity. This power comes from within the soul, directly from our Creator. People who truly know the meaning of love and who walk in the path of our loving God are incapable of such selfishness, greed, extravagance and overindulgence."

"You don't consider me one of these people, do you, Gabriel?"

His reply is instant. "No. You have learned to live your life in moderation. You are not extravagant and you never will be. Living in the physical world is about living in moderation; which means exactly that, living in moderation and not living with extravagance or overindulgence for there has to be a balance of all things. There has to be a balance also with work and play, and work must include helping others. It is important to live each day to the fullest. You have nothing to fear."

"Gabriel, what you are saying is true. I always considered wealth different from what many people I know consider wealth to be. When my son was small, he would ask me, 'Mommy, are we rich?' My answer was always the same. 'Yes, we are very rich because we have so much love.' Of course, my son would come back with the response, 'But Mommy, love doesn't make a person rich; money does.' My answer to my son would always be, 'No, you are mistaken; for only love can make a person truly rich. It has nothing to do with money.'"

"We are all so very proud of you. We know you are striving to do your best. We also know that you have encountered many setbacks but you continue to move forward. You will be rewarded greatly."

I feel the tears well once again in my eyes, as I remember all too well the grueling times I have embraced and the difficult people who have stepped in my path during my life journey.

Gabriel speaks again. "You have done extremely well. We are aware of all your problematic encounters and all the souls who have done you harm. The day will come when they will have to repay their spiritual debts; for no debt ever goes unpaid. They have to undo their wrongs which they have done to you and they have to ask you for forgiveness."

"They need my forgiveness?"

"Yes, my dear. What a soul has done to you, she also has done to herself; for when she passes over to the Other Side, she will experience the same pain and suffering she caused you. She will continue to experience this pain and suffering until she has undone her wrongs and asks forgiveness from you. If the soul who has committed the act of hatefulness, owns up to the act, and sincerely apologizes and vows to act lovingly forever more, our Creator forgives. However, the soul must be completely honest and sincere. And it is entirely up to you to offer forgiveness; and forgiveness has to be granted by you in order for her to be free from her spiritual debt."

"And what happens if the person doesn't own up to her hateful actions and sincerely apologizes, what happens then?"

"If a soul or person, as you like to say, chooses to not pay the spiritual debt, then the soul has to live with the torment of the negative and hateful actions she has caused, and consequently the soul does not advance but instead moves down to a lower level than before. And the soul will take the spiritual debts with her when she returns to the Earth plane for another lifetime."

My thoughts take me back to certain individuals who have tried to cause me harm and have been very hateful towards me.

"All these individuals will have to pay their debts of hatefulness towards you."

It is at this moment that I come to realize that my Guardian Angel can hear my thoughts. As I wipe away my tears, I state, "Gabriel, you can hear my thoughts!"

"Of course, my dear. You can also do this."

Instantly my mind takes me back many years ago, when my Aunt Mildred told me the same. "I remember now, Gabriel, I had an aunt who told me I could do this, but I guess I really didn't believe her."

With a chuckle, he answers, "Yes, I know."

Quite surprised by my Guardian Angel's comment, I ask, "Do you know my Aunt Mildred?"

I can hear another chuckle as he says, "Yes, I know your Aunt Mildred."

"I guess I should have listened to my Aunt Mildred."

I can hear another chuckle as he replies, "Know that you must remember who you really are. If you do this, you will not experience so much difficulty during your life because you will be more prepared for the evil doers."

I am completely in awe by this comment as I pick myself up from the ground and ask, "Are you sure I can do this? I can really hear other people's thoughts if I want to?"

"You most certainly can. And not only can you do it but everyone else can too."

"Everyone can?"

"Yes, everyone, because people living on the Earth plane are all souls, which means they are spiritual beings and not physical beings. This is where the term psychic comes from, for it means of the soul. Therefore, because we are all souls, we are all psychic. In addition, because we are all souls, we are intuitive, meaning that our feelings come from our souls. You too have intuition, meaning you are intuitive, which just means that you have feelings or emotions which come directly from the real you, your soul."

"Really?"

"Yes, really. Because we are all souls or spiritual beings, we possess spiritual abilities. The problem is that most don't realize that they have spiritual abilities."

"You say spiritual abilities. Do you mean there are other abilities that I have and don't realize I possess?"

"Yes, you most certainly do. You have been blessed with extraordinary gifts and you have many spiritual abilities, more than the average soul."

"Gabriel, what do you mean more than the average soul?"

"I mean that you are much further advanced spiritually than most walking this Earth plane. Many are ignorant of who they really are and where they come from, and consequently many live in ignorance."

"What are these spiritual abilities you are referring to?"

"The first spiritual ability, which we have discussed earlier, is the ability to hear the thoughts of another, and this special ability is referred to as clairaudient. A soul such as yourself, who in time will use this hearing ability will be able to hear other souls thoughts, and also when they speak, whether these souls are in a physical body or not."

My thoughts seem to be going a mile a minute as my brain tries to understand everything I am being told.

"You need to listen with love in your soul and be open to everything that I am telling you."

"I will, Gabriel."

"You are a soul medium or a psychic medium, as many on the Earth plane like to say, and this means you have the ability to communicate with Guardian Souls, Guardian Angels, and souls who have left this Earth plane and crossed over to the Other Side. You are a go-between, so to speak. But not only can you communicate with souls on the Other Side, you also have the ability to communicate with all souls, no matter where they are."

"Gabriel, if you are saying we are all souls, does this mean I am able to communicate with everyone here living on Earth?"

"Yes, this is exactly what it is I am saying. When we wish to communicate, we can communicate with all souls whether they live here on the Earth plane or whether they live on the Other Side."

I am dumbfounded. "You mean I am actually able to communicate with other people, regardless of where they are living?"

"Yes, this is correct."

"How do I do this?"

"You already know how to do this. The term used for this spiritual ability is called telepathy."

"What is telepathy?"

"It just means not having to speak out loud. Through telepathy, you can carry on a conversation, just the same as when you speak aloud. It is communication through thoughts. When souls communicate with you, do not interpret the information; in other words, do not add your own interpretations or suggestions for there can be misunderstanding of information. This misinterpretation can very easily become convoluted into inaccurate facts."

"This is mind-boggling! I will actually be able to do this?"

I can hear a chuckle as the loving voice responds, "My dear, you can do this now if you wish. The choice is yours. However, I want you to understand that souls who live behind the veil on the Other Side can communicate either positive energy or negative energy. If the soul communicating is an evil soul, it will communicate negative, hateful energy; if the soul is a loving soul, it will communicate positive, loving energy. Souls who live here on the Earth plane are no different. There are some souls living here on the Earth plane who are evil souls and they communicate negative, hateful, evil energy. Then there are souls living on the Earth plane who are loving souls and these loving souls communicate positive and loving energy."

"I certainly know about the evil ones, Gabriel, because I have met them."

"Yes, this I know to be true."

"Of course, I have also met loving people."

"Another special ability you have is clairvoyance, which means "clear vision." This is the ability to see more than the physical eyes can see for you are seeing with the eyes of your soul."

"I have heard of this. Some people call it second sight or being able to see with the mind's eye or the third eye."

"Yes, my dear. However, it is not seeing with the mind's eye or a third eye because there is no such thing. What it really means is being able to see through the eyes of the soul, as I have already told you."

I am in deep thought and unable to respond.

"You have the ability to see a soul on the Other Side or, if the soul chooses to pierce through the veil that separates the Earth plane from the Spiritual plane, you will see the soul in the physical world, the same way you can see souls living on the Earth plane. Children possess this spiritual ability because they are souls who have recently come from the spiritual world. When children speak about seeing others that someone else is unable to see, this means that these children are actually seeing souls from the Other Side. Unfortunately, my dear, most adults dismiss this as their "imaginary friends," and therefore consider it to be just the child's imagination."

"I know this to be true for many parents."

"Another spiritual ability is that of clairsentience which means "clear feeling." The term clairsentience simply means that you will be able to sense or feel another soul's energy. You are already very capable of doing this, aren't you?"

"Yes, you are right. When I am around other people, I seem to be able to pick up their emotions without them telling me how they are feeling."

"In time, you will use all of the spiritual abilities that I have talked about with you. You also have the gift of clairessence, which means you have "clear smelling." This is the ability to smell odors beyond your physical sense."

"I can actually do this?"

"Yes, and you will also be able to help many who want to advance their spirituality by using the process of regression."

"I don't understand. What is the process of regression?"

"It means you have the ability to take people back in time to revisit their past lives which they have lived."

"I can really do this?"

"Yes, my dear. You have the ability to do a past-life regression with a soul, or with the person, as you Earth souls like to say. This is very important spiritual work because you will be able to help many."

"How will I be able to help many people?"

"You will help many because there are many souls living on the Earth plane at this time who have brought a lot of unresolved issues with them into their present lifetime, and these unresolved issues are causing them problems and preventing some from moving forward. You are one of these people."

"I am?"

"Yes, my dear. Do you not have a great fear of public speaking?"

"Yes, I do!"

"Well, this is because of a traumatic event which happened to you in a previous lifetime. And hasn't this great fear of yours, at times, prevented you from moving forward while living your life?"

"Yes, it has."

"You will go through the process of a past-life regression yourself, because you will have the opportunity to meet someone like yourself, who has this great ability, and you will learn from him. You will become an expert as a past-life regressionist, and as I said, you will be able to help many."

My thoughts are running wild because of all of this new information and I am not sure I fully understand everything I am being told.

"Do not despair. You have been given many gifts and they will all develop at the proper time for you."

"Gabriel, you are hearing my thoughts again."

"You know I can hear your thoughts, as you can hear mine, but only if you choose."

"I have heard it said that thoughts are real, and at the time, I couldn't understand why. Now I do."

"Yes, thoughts are real. And why is it you understand now that thoughts are real?"

"Because others can hear your thoughts and therefore this is why thoughts are real."

"Yes, my dear, you catch on quickly."

I chuckle and reply, "Yes, I guess I do."

"And the gift of psychometry has also been bestowed upon you."

"It has? What does this mean?"

"Psychometry means you have the spiritual ability to pick up energy from an object and to interpret the information coming from it. All information is embedded into objects when a soul uses or holds it."

"I'm not sure I understand. What type of information can possibly be in an object?"

"Objects such as rings, watches, clothing, or any item a soul uses will hold information about the soul and will provide information such as the soul's emotional state. All energy from a soul transfers into any object or item a soul uses or handles. Therefore, any other soul exposed to these objects or items can pick up information. This ability is very important when trying to locate missing souls who have lost their way on the Earth plane."

"Gabriel, do you mean people who have gone missing?"

"Yes, my dear, and in time you will use this special ability in order to help find missing children and missing adults on the Earth plane."

"Do you mean I will be involved in helping to find children and adults who have gone missing?"

"Yes, this is so. You have the capability of holding a piece of clothing or toy belonging to a child that has gone missing, and you will be able to read important information regarding the child. You will also be able to make direct contact with the child and therefore will be able to see the surroundings where the child is and you will be able to speak directly to the missing child. This is also true for any adult who has gone missing."

As I listen very intently, the loving voice continues to offer me information that is beyond my wildest dreams.

"This is what some call mediumship. It just means that you are a medium, which means you are the go-between. You are the soul who is able to communicate with other souls, whether they have crossed over after the death of the body and live on the Other Side, or whether they still live on the Earth plane. You will be able to see and hear the other soul, and you will also be able to pick up the emotions, as well as vital information about the soul, and in the case of a missing child or missing adult, this information will be extremely valuable. You have this ability."

"Gabriel, how will I be able to see another person if I am not there with him?"

"My dear, this is referred to remote viewing. You have this ability. It does not matter where the soul is, you will be able to see. For example, if it is a missing child you are helping to find, you have the ability to make contact with the child and therefore you will be able to see and speak to the missing child. And because you have the ability to see the child, you will therefore be able to ascertain as to whether the child has crossed over to the spiritual world or if the child is still in the physical body, and therefore still in the physical world."

"Are you sure I am able to do all of this?"

"Yes, I am sure. You will be able to work with the grieving parents of the missing child and to help find answers to their questions."

"This is all so incredible."

"You will also be able to pick up vital information from a soul who has gone missing by using your writing skills. Some call this ability automatic writing. You just need to take pen and paper or if you prefer, go to your keyboard on your computer, and ask questions to the person you wish to contact and wait for the answer. The answer will appear in your writing or on your computer screen."

"This is all so unbelievable to me, Gabriel."

"You have great work to do. The time has come for you to understand who you really are and why you have come to the Earth plane at this time. As I mentioned to you before, most become too grounded in the physical world and forget who they truly are and why they have come here, and this is very unfortunate and therefore most return having very high prices to pay."

"When you say return, do you mean return back to where they came from?"

"Yes, my dear. They have to return to the spiritual world, where they belong."

"So we are all just visitors here?"

"This is correct. Each of you is only here for a short time. Each soul's cause of death and his or her age at death is predetermined before the soul came to the Earth plane to live, but this can be changed at any time."

It is at this moment that I experience an epiphany. "Gabriel, this means that people here on Earth don't really die."

"Yes, this is correct. There is no such thing as death, as many souls living here on the Earth plane believe. There is no such thing as dead spirits or dead souls; for the soul does not die, the soul is eternal. All souls are alive; the only difference is where they live. Souls who live here on the Earth plane at this time are living souls, and the souls who live on the Other Side at this time are living souls. Death just means a sloughing away of the old and returning Home."

"What do you mean by this?"

"I mean sloughing away of the physical body. The physical body is like an outer garment for the soul. The physical body is only temporary and is just a vehicle for the soul to use while living in the physical world."

With urgency in my voice, I quickly ask, "Does this mean that my father will not really die?"

"It most certainly does mean this, my dear. Your father's travels on the Earth plane are ending; for his time is drawing near. This simply means that the time has come in which his lessons on the Earth plane are finished."

I quickly respond, again with urgency in my voice. "Gabriel, even though my father's body will die, my dad will still be alive?"

"Yes, this is so. Death means a transformation. The real you, your soul, lives inside a physical body while living here on the Earth plane during this lifetime. When your soul is ready to return Home, the soul leaves your physical body. The physical body remains on the Earth plane but the soul does not. Once death occurs, it is the physical body that dies, and only the physical body; for your soul lives on. The physical body is like a social costume, which a soul wears during his journey on the Earth plane, and when his physical body is no longer needed, his soul departs and returns Home."

"Death really is a transformation."

"Yes, you are correct. Another way to look at this is to compare the physical body to a vehicle. The vehicle in which you drive, such as a car, cannot be driven without the driver, which is you. The car remains parked and will not move unless you get inside and drive the car. The same is true of the physical body, for if the soul is not inside the physical body, the physical body will not move, it will lay dormant. The car in time will deteriorate and break down and will no longer be of any use, and so this is the same for the physical body. As you know, the physical body ages and all its functions gradually break down. The physical body dies and when the physical body dies, the soul leaves the physical body at that time and returns Home."

"I remember my Aunt Mildred saying the same thing, many years ago."

"Yes, my dear, I remember also."

"When you say returning Home, where do you mean?"

"I mean to the Other Side, my dear, to the spiritual world where we all belong; for that is our true Home. Death should be looked upon as good and therefore you should be happy and at peace about the passing of your father. Your father will be returning to his true Home; for his mission in this lifetime which he has spent on the Earth plane as your father will be completed."

I slump to the ground once again as I cup both my hands over my face and sob, for the words which this voice has spoken have pierced my most inner being. Through my sobs, I remember all too well my feelings of never belonging here on Earth. All my life I recall having these feelings, especially when I was a small child growing up. I also recall the wonderful visit I had so long ago in my room when I was a student nurse, the visitor who said she was my Guardian Soul, and who then told me that I didn't belong here. I ask my Guardian Angel, "Why didn't someone tell me this when I was a small child? I always felt so lost and alone because I never felt I belonged here."

"My dear, the truth was never revealed to you when you were a child because it would have been too much of a burden for you to bear. As a child, you would not have wanted to stay on the Earth plane if you knew Earth was not your real home."

"Oh my, it all makes so much sense to me now."

"When each soul comes to the Earth plane for another lifetime, a veil of forgetfulness is in place, and the newly born soul needs to forget in order to function on the physical plane."

"And so, this is what happened to me. The veil of forgetfulness was in place?"

"Yes. We know this caused you great concern and anguish as a child because in the beginning, you knew you didn't belong on the Earth plane; yet if the veil of forgetfulness had not been in place, you would have found it too unbearable to stay on the Earth plane."

"I understand this now, Gabriel."

The loving voice speaks with such intense love and compassion. "My dear, you now have great insight. Use your knowledge and gifts very wisely; for if you do, you will help many."

I am unable to respond.

"Because of who you are, you have the capability to heal; for you are a spiritual healer. This gift was bestowed upon you a very long time ago."

Astonished by this remark, I quickly ask, "I am a healer?"

"Yes, my dear, you most certainly are. In past-lifetimes, you have been a healer, such as a shaman."

"I have heard the term 'shaman' before. I don't fully understand the full meaning."

"The term 'shaman' refers to an individual who practices religious rituals in order to access the spirit world for the benefit of others, in order to heal them. The person referred to as a shaman is a messenger between the physical world and the spiritual world, and heals the physical body by first healing the soul, for all illness and sickness originates from the soul. Therefore, if the soul is restored in balance and harmony, the physical body will also be restored in balance and harmony. When the soul heals, the physical body then heals. And so, my dear, in simple terms, a shaman is a healer."

"I do know, Gabriel, that I have a tremendous desire to help people, and I have always felt this way."

"Yes, and this is because this is the true essence of who you are and the spiritual work you have always chosen to do. Healing has been your one desire, for through healing, you help many in many ways, for you are also a spiritual counselor. It is through your spiritual readings that you are able to provide spiritual counseling and consequently give spiritual healings. For you have recognized from long ago that the soul needs to be healed before the physical body can be healed. You are very wise and thus many gifts have been bestowed upon you."

I find myself in deep thought; for amazingly enough, I understand what my Guardian Angel is saying to me to be true, at least the part about me wanting to be a healer. I am a Registered Nurse and have always had the deep longing to help people in any way that I can; and not just in the physical sense, for I specialized in Mental Health Psychiatric Nursing. However, I have always felt that I was capable of much more. Now this loving voice is giving me all this information, which I find remarkable!

"My dear, you are capable of much more."

"You said, it is through my spiritual readings that I am able to provide spiritual counseling and consequently give spiritual healings. What do you mean by spiritual readings?"

My dear you will help many by doing spiritual readings or soul readings, and it means just that. You have the ability to access the soul and thus, obtain vital information about the soul, or the person as you like to say, and by doing this, you will have great insight and therefore will give spiritual counseling. This will aid the individual soul immensely and consequently will provide spiritual healing."

"How do I do spiritual readings?"

"This will come natural to you, my dear. There is no need for concern."

"Okay."

"You are also an energy healer."

"I am?" I question in a surprise tone of voice.

"Yes, my dear, you most certainly are."

"What does this mean?"

"You heal by transmitting your energy of love, along with your powerful prayers, to the one needing to be healed. However, the one needing healing must first believe in you and your divine gift to heal, for if the one who needs the healing does not believe in you, the healing will not take place. There must be complete and absolute trust and acceptance that you are capable of healing."

"Gabriel, what you are saying makes so much sense to me because it reminds me of some years ago when my boyfriend, now my husband, and I had warts on our hands. A friend of mine, Betty, told me about this old woman who lived in our small town, who had special abilities to heal. One of the healings she was able to do was to make warts disappear. Betty told me she had warts on her hands and she had decided to go to this woman for help, and to see if she could make the warts go away, and sure enough she showed me her hands and the warts were gone! Well, I am sure you can imagine how thrilled I was to know this. Dave and I had tried the traditional treatments from the pharmacy but it did not help. Dave even resorted to going to his doctor who had prescribed a type of treatment, which was supposed to kill the virus. The warts did decrease in size but never did completely disappear. Therefore, I decided to tell Dave about this special person in Spaniard's Bay who is gifted. Well, back then, Dave was a non-believer of almost everything and for sure, he did not believe that some woman could actually make his warts go away, when even his doctor was not successful. Therefore, he did not intend to visit such a person.

"Well, I took it upon myself to go alone. When I knocked on her door, the door opened and the most beautiful, older woman stood in the doorway. I told her why I had come to see her and asked for her help. She simply wanted to know my name, and wanted to know how many warts I had and I told her. I also asked another favor of her and that was to see if she could help my boyfriend. I was honest with her and told her that he refused to come with me to meet her because he did not believe that she could actually make warts disappear. However, this kind woman smiled at me, asked me his name, and asked how many warts he had on both his hands. I said good-bye to this special, gracious woman and walked away.

"Amazingly enough, within the first week, I could see the warts on my hand shrinking, and not only did I see the warts on my hand shrinking, but I also noticed that the warts on Dave's hands were also shrinking! I was excited as I told him of my findings; however, much to my surprise, he simply attributed the fact that his warts were shrinking because of the treatments from his doctor. He did not accept the fact that this older woman had this special ability and gift. He insisted that the warts started to disappear because he had visited his doctor weeks prior, and not because of some elderly woman that he had not even met. I was quick to point out that after the medical treatments, his warts did decrease in size but did not disappear and were growing back even larger than before. I also pointed out the fact that I had not visited a doctor for any treatment, and yet, all my warts were shrinking. Again, he dismissed all the facts and refused to discuss it any more. After two weeks, all my warts on my right hand were completely gone, and all the warts on Dave's hands had completely disappeared.

"I had given it much thought afterwards as to why my husband's warts had disappeared, even though he was so skeptical, and such a non-believer of such things. In conclusion, I knew in my heart and soul that it was because I was such a strong believer and not only did I believe this special lady could heal me but because my beliefs were so strong, she was also able to heal Dave as well."

"This is exactly what happened. The person wanting healing must first acknowledge the sickness, have belief and then ask for healing. The healing may happen immediately or it may take days, weeks, months or even years, for it all depends on the person's belief in God, as well as the person's belief in you. All healings are from God. Our Heavenly Father has provided you with this gift of healing to be of service to Him, and his people on the Earth plane."

"Well, I truly believe that my husband's warts would never have disappeared but for me, because I was the believer and had the faith that it could be done."

"Yes, my dear, you are absolutely right in saying that. Your belief in the power of healing allowed not only you to heal, but also your husband. And so you not only can heal others, like the older lady you referred to in your story, but you must also teach others that they are capable of healing themselves."

"I have to teach others how to heal themselves?"

"Yes, negative experiences of past-lifetimes can be healed. And you can help heal many."

"How do I do this?"

"You already know; it will all come to you when the time is right. And you will also heal many during this present life-time; for many have brought soul sickness upon themselves."

If I am hearing correctly, did Gabriel not use the term, 'in this life-time'? What does this mean? My thoughts are going wild. I blurt out, "What do you mean by this lifetime?"

"You know very well what I mean." With this comment, I can hear the loving voice laugh. "Please do not forget what we talked about earlier. You have been here on the Earth plane before, as well as all the other souls living here now. As I said earlier, in one lifetime you were known as a shaman, and you helped many."

"So, reincarnation is real?"

"Yes, reincarnation is most certainly real."

"I have always believed this to be true. A poem by John Masefield says it all.

> *Arrayed in some new flesh-disguise,*
> *Another mother gives him birth.*
> *With sturdier limbs and brighter brain*
> *The old soul takes the road again."*

"Yes, my dear, the old soul does take the road again. And as I said, you have spent other lifetimes on the Earth plane and so have all the others living here, and after this lifetime, you have to return one more time."

"This is incredible!"

With a chuckle, he answers, "If you think so, my dear. Souls have to learn their lessons and until they do this, they have to return to the Earth plane for other lifetimes. However, you only have to return one more time."

"So, are you saying I have had a previous life?"

"You most certainly have. You have been reborn a number of times."

"Meaning I have been reborn as a baby?"

"Yes, my dear. I am aware that some souls on the Earth plane refer to being reborn as something different. Their interpretation of the word reborn is not what it should be. Some consider being reborn to mean being reborn into a particular Earthly religion. This is not what the word really means. The true meaning of the word means just what the word implies, born again into another lifetime."

"This is so true, Gabriel! I know of people who say they have been reborn, meaning that they now profess to be of a certain religion; for example, some say they are born again Christians."

"Yes, they have lost the true meaning. Over time, the true meaning of the word reborn has lost its real meaning."

"This reminds me of a quote from the Holy Bible in John 3, Verse 7, Jesus said: *Ye must be born again.* So is this what this quote really means?"

"Yes, it most certainly does."

"This is all so interesting."

"And when you were reborn in other lifetimes, you have changed many conditions; for the main purpose of returning to the Earth plane from the Other Side is to benefit from life's lessons, and to learn and move forward spiritually, and therefore advance your soul."

"I'm not sure what you mean."

"I mean that you have changed your sex. For example, in this lifetime you are a female; however, in your previous life you were born a male. And you have experienced death as a woman, a man and a child."

"Well, if I was born a male, does that mean that I was homosexual?"

"Yes, my dear, you most certainly were. All souls living on the Earth plane will experience being homosexual."

"Why is this, Gabriel?"

"Because being homosexual is a gift from God."

"I doubt many people believe this! There are many walking on Earth who are very prejudiced and think that if a person is homosexual, they are not worthy, and many times their hatred has led to violence, where lives have been shattered and lives taken."

"Yes, I am fully aware of these souls, and so is our Heavenly Father. Souls with such prejudiced thoughts of hatred towards others will have a very high price to pay upon their return; for nothing goes unnoticed."

"Gabriel, when you say being homosexual is a gift from God, what exactly do you mean?"

"Souls living on the Earth plane just don't happen to become homosexual, or choose to be homosexual, as many tend to believe. Being homosexual is a divine and holy right, as well as being heterosexual."

"So what you are saying is that one doesn't choose to be homosexual while living here on Earth; one is born either homosexual or heterosexual, is this correct?"

"Yes, this is absolutely correct. If a soul living on the Earth plane is homosexual in this lifetime, this is a divine right because God has bestowed this gift upon the soul. One cannot become homosexual, no more than one can become heterosexual, for only God has this power over the soul. Sexuality is a gift bestowed upon souls of the Earth plane. Whether the soul is homosexual, heterosexual, or bi-sexual, it does not matter, as long as it is between two consenting adults."

"This makes so much sense to me."

"This is because you are very wise, my dear, and one with great understanding."

"And so in my previous life, I was a male and therefore I was homosexual, and I would think that I suffered a lot at the hands of such hateful, prejudiced people. Is this true?"

"No, this is not true, simply because you died as a young child."

"Wow!"

"In other lifetimes, you have been born into royalty, with financial wealth, and you have been born into poverty too. So, you see, you know what it is like to be financially rich and you also know what it is like to be financially poor, as it is for other conditions."

"This is all so astounding."

"If you think so, but you have also been born into different races, in different living conditions, and also different religions."

"I have been different races in different lifetimes?"

"You most certainly have, my dear, and the same is true for all people living on the Earth plane. But also remember that on the Other Side, we are not members of a particular race, and if a soul is of a particular race, it is of his choosing."

"I doubt very much that most people realize this!"

"Most souls, or people as you like to call them, don't realize this, even though if they search deep within their soul memories, they will remember. Each soul knows and understands the life experiences he had to incur in each lifetime. And he also knows that if he keeps repeating the same mistakes, he will have to keep repeating the same negative conditions until he learns the lessons."

"If there really are no different races on the Other Side, Gabriel, why are there different races of people here on Earth?"

"The differences in people on the Earth plane, including the different races, are for others to learn tolerance and to learn love. So you see, the soul who is referred to as a bigot should not treat others with such hatefulness and cruelty; for in time, he will most likely find himself living and experiencing that same lifestyle."

"And is this what you mean when you said I have experienced different living conditions?"

"Yes, my dear. However, you will never live a life as a bigot because you are too far advanced."

"I respect all people, Gabriel, and I truly know that I don't even begin to understand hate."

"That's because you do not possess hate or evil in your soul; your soul is so far removed from such darkness because you are on such a high spiritual level. You are a soul that represents our Heavenly Father's light and love. All souls were created from God; however, the dark souls choose to become dark by separating themselves from God and following the evil one of darkness."

"When children grow up in a home where hate is taught rather than love, is this how hatred is learned?"

"Not really, my dear, because if a newly born soul is brought into the Earth plane for another lifetime and is already a loving soul, no matter the hatred environment that child is exposed to, this will not change the soul if he or she doesn't want to be changed. For example, if either the mother or father teaches prejudice and hatred for another in the home where the small child is growing up, the parents expose the young child to a negative and hateful environment, however, if the child is a soul that is highly advanced spiritually, the child will not become prejudiced or use hate towards another. Most likely in that type of situation, you will find the child leaving the home at a very young age because he cannot tolerate such hatred."

"And what if the newly born baby comes from a much lower spiritual level? Does this mean that the child will grow up already prejudiced and showing hatred towards another?"

"Yes, this is correct. However, if the child is growing up in a home where there is no prejudice and hatred and there is much love, the young child has the opportunity to change, and to grow and advance spiritually. It is natural for any soul to resist change; however, if the change is to help the soul learn spiritually, then the soul should accept the change graciously; for the soul will be following his chosen path of his life journey."

"And you also said that I have been different religions in other lifetimes?"

"Yes, my dear, you have practised other religions in other lifetimes such as Buddhism, Christian, Jewish, Hindu, Muslim, and other religions; as is the case for all the other souls living on the Earth plane. Therefore, you see, it is so foolish for souls to hate another because of his particular religion, for in a previous lifetime that same soul could have been of that very same religion. So in essence the soul hates himself."

"I find everything you are telling me to be so remarkable."

"All the great religions of the Earth plane teach love. Love represents God. Regardless which religion a soul practices while living on the Earth plane, all religions are paths leading to God."

"Are you saying that there is only one God, regardless of all the different religions?"

"I am saying exactly that. All paths of love lead to God."

"I always believed this to be true, Gabriel. I remember a quote from the great scientist, Albert Einstein. *All religions, arts and sciences are branches of the same tree.* Therefore, it certainly makes sense to me that all religions are branches of the same tree because the tree represents God."

"It is also during these different lifetimes that a soul can remember traumatic events from his past-lifetime which can cause profound fear in his present lifetime. These are called soul memories."

"Can you tell me more about soul memories?"

"Soul memories, my dear, are when a soul can recall a memory of some type of emotional situation. The soul memory can be either positive or negative. A negative soul memory may be a frightening or hurtful experience which may have had a very serious impact on the soul, and consequently the soul may experience a high level of pain or fear."

In deep thought, I suddenly realize that this has happened to me. "I remember one year I went to church on Good Friday, and during the service, I became very emotional. I felt the pain and suffering as though I was actually witnessing our Lord Jesus die on the cross. I found it so devastating I have not been able to go to church on a Good Friday since. Do you think this is because of a soul memory?"

"Yes, it is a soul memory. You are remembering the death of our Lord Jesus because you were there at the time."

I can hardly believe what it is I am hearing. "I was there at the time?"

"Yes, you were one of the people in the crowd mourning such an injustice."

"This makes a whole lot of sense to me because I always wondered why I found it extremely difficult to attend the service on Good Friday of the crucifixion of Jesus."

"Your soul memory brought back the emotional turmoil and despair that you had encountered on that day."

"I know I have many fears and I honestly don't know where they came from. Does this mean I have gone through other terrorizing events in my past-lifetimes?"

"Yes, this is the reason."

"I have a fear of snakes, which I know I didn't get from living in Newfoundland."

With a chuckle, my Guardian Angel replies, "This is true, my dear."

"And I have a fear of deep water, and heights."

"I also know that you have a great fear of speaking in public, as we already discussed."

"Yes, I do. My father was always big on education and wanted me to attend university after completing high school, but I refused to go because I knew I had to present papers in class. The fear of public speaking prevented me from pursuing my nursing degree at the university. However, I did apply to go to the Grace General Hospital School of Nursing and did complete the program, but within my first few of months I was going to quit because one of the instructors told me I had to present a paper in class."

"But you didn't quit, did you?"

"No, I didn't. I telephoned my parents and told them I was packing because I had to come home. I explained that I could not get up in front of my class and present my paper. They told me to go see an instructor that I found to be kind and understanding and that I liked, and explain my dilemma. Therefore, this is what I did. I went to see Miss Joan Collingwood. She was very understanding, and she informed me that if I chose not to present a paper in class, then this was my decision, and that no one could force me to do otherwise. In addition, for the remainder three years of nursing school, I refused all requests to present. Each time I would lose marks, but that was okay with me. Therefore, in the end I graduated. I have always wondered where this great fear came from."

"All of these fears of yours have come from previous lifetimes."

"I remember another time when I must have had a soul memory because I found myself in the most bizarre situation. After I had graduated from nursing school, I visited a doctor who specialized in phobias, and consequently, I was able to overcome my fear, at least to some degree. I was able to continue my studies and consequently attended university. However, during one of my classes, the professor had all the students participate in a drama situation. He had us move our chairs in position, as though we were on a train, and he instructed us to pretend we were actually taking a train ride. During this train ride, the train had come to a stop, and when it did, other students acting as soldiers, ordered us off the train, one at a time. As each person walks off the train, we can hear the sound of a shot, and we know that each passenger taken off is murdered. As I sit waiting for my turn to come, I become very anxious, so much so, I feel as though it is actually happening to me. I look around at the other students and they do not seem to have the same reaction to this event as me. However, it becomes quite evident to me that the others, including the professor, recognize my unusual behavior. When it comes my turn to face my accusers, I protested very loudly, and refused to leave the make-believe train. I have never forgotten how terrified I felt during that class even though I knew it was all make-believe."

"This was definitely a soul memory. You were recalling another time when you were falsely accused, and you were reacting."

"This is incredible. Soul memories are very powerful."

"Yes, they most certainly are very powerful."

"In my opinion, there is far too much hatred in this world. And as my father used to say, it's not the world that is the problem, it's the people living in it."

"Your father is also a wise soul; for this is one of the reasons he was given to you as your Earthly father."

I am unable to respond to such a comment because I feel myself again becoming emotional as I think about my dad, and how much I have learned from him over the years, and I am still learning. I always considered my father to be my greatest teacher in life, and now I have the insight as to why I feel this way.

"Your father loves you very much, my dear; as you also love him very much."

"Yes, I do, Gabriel. He is a wonderful father to me. He has always been so kind and loving. He believes in fairness and equality and is a huge advocate for education and hard work."

"Yes, I know. He is also one who understands true power."

"What do you mean?"

"I mean that your father in this lifetime understands and knows that real power does not come from the material world. However, this is not true for others. Many living on the Earth plane have acted and are still acting very foolishly. They believe that money brings prestige and power. In essence, it brings just the opposite, for all their material wealth means nothing in the end."

"Gabriel, I know what you are saying is so true. My friend, Edgar, made a whole lot of sense to me one day when he said, 'For all my years living on this Earth, I have yet to see a hearse towing a U-Haul on the way to the gravesite.'"

"Your friend is very wise, my dear. There are too many on the Earth plane that have too much abundance and have become very greedy and selfish, and live their lives very extravagantly when many are in so much need."

"As my grandmother used to say much craves more. It seems to me that the more some people have, the more they want, for no matter what they have, it never seems to be enough. They never seem satisfied. It seems they become obsessed with material wealth and that's how they live their lives."

"Yes, you are correct. These types of individuals feel insecure and inferior because they fear they will lose all of their material possessions and they feel and know that someone else will always have more. And so they always try to strive to always get bigger and better."

"Well, I have heard the phrase that bigger is not necessarily better."

"What you have heard is correct; for bigger is not necessarily better."

"I find it very difficult to understand how these people can live their lives in such a way."

"It is because they are greedy, my dear. In addition, because of their greed, they allow children to suffer and perish every day. They have many lessons to learn, with many spiritual debts to pay for their actions or lack thereof. These souls are given countless opportunities to change for the better; for the more they acquire, the more they think it to be another great achievement. However, this is not the real reason why the material wealthy souls of the physical world are given more; it's to help them to understand that they don't need more, they need to give."

"So the more financially rich people become, is not for the purpose to become richer financially, as they think, the purpose is for them to learn and to understand that it is another chance to share their abundance and to change. Is this correct, Gabriel?"

"Yes, it is most certainly correct. I will give you an example. Say a woman goes into a store to purchase some goods, and at the checkout, the clerk gives her too much money back. If she chooses to keep the money, she has placed herself into spiritual debt. She thinks she has come into an unexpected gain of money, and she has, but she has lost tremendously spiritually. And this type of individual will keep seeing these types of situations occur in her life, and she may consider herself lucky but luck has nothing to do with it; for spiritually it means she has been given another chance to make things right, not to choose to go into spiritual debt, and in the long run, redeem her soul."

"Many have so much and yet many have so little. There just doesn't seem to be any justice."

"Believe me, my dear, there is justice. These souls living on the Earth plane possessing such material wealth and choose to not share will, in time, have many regrets and many spiritual debts to pay. In essence, they will most likely find themselves to be in spiritual bankruptcy and most likely in spiritual poverty once they return to the Other Side, and have to face all the consequences of their actions of greed."

"I do know that greed is one of the main reasons for such turmoil here on Earth."

"Yes, my dear, you are correct. You understand and this is one of the reasons you have been chosen to teach. We are very troubled because there are many broken souls."

"How can I teach others?"

"The plan is in place."

Astounded by such a comment, I quickly reply, "Plan? What plan? What do you mean by the plan is in place? What do I have to do?"

"All you have to do, my dear, is to follow."

"Follow what?"

I can hear my Guardian Angel chuckle. "Follow what is presented to you. You have great work to do and you have a lot to accomplish."

"What is this great work?"

"You will teach others in many ways but one of the most important ways will be through your writing. You will write."

Again, I am amazed at what I hear. "Write? What does this mean, I will write?"

"You will write a book."

I am almost in a state of shock as I reply, "I will write a book!"

Again, I can hear the familiar laugh as my Guardian Angel answers, "Yes, you will write a book to share your life experiences with the world and in doing so you will help millions of souls in all walks of the physical life, regardless of age, race, gender, or religion."

I am speechless! My head feels like it is spinning and I feel dizzy. Some time ago, my beautiful daughter gave me the book, *The Simple Abundance Journal of Gratitude* by Sarah Ban Breathnach, as a Christmas gift. I loved my gift but it took no time at all for me to realize that what I thought all along was true; I do not possess any writing skills. Thinking back at what I wrote in my journal, how can I possibly write a book! This seems like an impossible task!

"No need to be concerned. Just because you didn't do much writing in your journal doesn't mean you don't have the ability to write; for everything is in place for you, all you have to do is follow."

As I try to compose myself, I am finally able to respond and ask, "You know about my journal?"

With a chuckle, Gabriel replies, "Yes, of course I do. And there are different ways to put words on paper than just with a pen."

"What do you mean?"

"I mean, do you not use your computer?"

"Yes I do," I quickly respond. When I was a small child, I would marvel at the typewriter on the desk in the upstairs hall of my friend Karen's house. For some unknown reason to me at the time, I recall being absolutely fascinated with this typewriter. I remember making a promise to myself that someday I would learn how to type; why I made this promise, I had no idea. Years later, I applied to go to nursing school but was told I was too young and had to wait a year. Therefore, I attended college and was enrolled in the Secretarial Science Program, where I learned how to type. Now, many years later, my typing skills have paid off. Even though I did not pursue a career as an administrative assistant, I use the keyboard almost daily while using my computer. Nevertheless, my thoughts go back to my writing abilities. "I don't know anything about writing. I am not an author. I don't know how to write a book!"

Again, another laugh as my Guardian Angel comments, "You are very wise. You possess many abilities, more than you realize. All you have to do is to sit in front of your computer, and place your fingers on the keyboard and see what happens. As I said, you have much to accomplish. One of the main purposes of your life on the Earth plane is to help as many lost souls as possible."

"I don't know if I can do this."

"My dear, never underestimate your abilities. Our Heavenly Father has bestowed upon you many blessings."

"What am I supposed to write about?"

"It will all come in time, as I said. Do not be concerned. Everything will fall into place like pieces of a jigsaw puzzle. Your husband will help you with the title of the book, and suggest you call it House of Angels."

"Oh, I love that name!" I quickly exclaim.

"However this will not be the title. You will call your book *Secrets of My Soul*. You will first want to use the title Secrets of the Soul, but later you will change it to *Secrets of My Soul*. You will meet a kindred soul during your travels, and this kindred soul will impress upon you the need to change the wording in the title."

"What is a kindred soul?"

"A kindred soul is someone you have met before and who has a strong spiritual bond with you and is considered a friend."

"Who is this kindred soul and where will I meet her?"

"In time you will know everything, and the kindred soul you will meet will not be a female but a male. In the meantime, you have great work to do and much to accomplish, for your book will cover the world with God's grace and love. It will be a catalyst for change, for there are many fallen souls. This book will appeal to people from all lifestyles and all walks of life who are searching for the real meaning of living life here on the Earth plane. The time has come for souls to discover the truthful answers about their life's journey. In addition, remember when you are writing your book, do not use eloquent words. You need to use simple, honest, and everyday language. This way, all people regardless of intellectual or educational abilities can read and understand, for God's gift of opportunity has to reach as many souls as possible. Also, maintain truthfulness at all times; for you must be conscious of the people you are writing about when sharing your stories. I leave you with these thoughts. In addition, always remember that you are never alone and we are all very proud of you. You have great work to do."

I feel the presence leave, and yet I truly feel as though I am not alone. As I wipe away my tears and pull myself up, I smile and look upward, knowing I have had the most wonderful experience! I stay a long time and continue to enjoy myself in my garden, all the while allowing all the messages given to me to sink into my brain.

I have come to realize that this is my first encounter with my Guardian Angel Gabriel, and I do indeed have a Guardian Angel watching over me, loving and protecting me at all times. I now know I have nothing to fear in this lifetime. With this realization, I now have a completely new perspective about living life here on this Earth.

PART 3

MY LATER YEARS

CHAPTER 8

My Guardian Souls

Are they not all ministering spirits,
sent forth to minister for them who shall be heirs of salvation?

The Holy Bible: Hebrews 1:14
King James Version

It is August 2000 and I am experiencing a soul memory! I remember just a few years earlier meeting my Guardian Angel for the first time in my beautiful garden on a hot summer's day. It was during this meeting that he explained to me the meaning of soul memories and now it is happening to me! This is my first trip to the Middle East and I am in Abu Dhabi, the United Arab Emirates. I endeavored to broaden my professional life by accepting a nursing position, teaching in a college, and later becoming the Director of Nursing Education for the same college.

Upon my arrival, I check into the beautiful Beach Hotel, located directly on the beach, with all expenses paid by the company as part of my employment contract. My new employer has arranged for me to live in a new condominium complex, which is in the final stages of completion and will not be ready for at least another two weeks.

As soon as I boarded British Airways at Heathrow Airport in London, I felt very comfortable. I was excited but not nervous, as I thought I would be, considering such an adventure. As the aircraft touched down on the runway in Abu Dhabi, I know instinctively I have lived in this culture before! The Western culture is so much different from the Middle Eastern culture and I know I have never visited any part of the Middle East, but it is all so familiar to me! This is incredible! From the souk shopping for traditional Arab style 18, 22 or 24 carat gold jewellery, to wearing the traditional female Arabic abaya and hijab, to the popular, traditional Arab food dishes such as hummus, tabouleh, falafel, baklava, mamoul, harisseh, sharma, and Arabic coffee. From the daily call for prayer in the mosques and the traditional Arabic communication and greeting etiquette to the traditional Islamic holidays, such as Eid and Ramadan where fasting takes place for a month; it all seems quite normal to me, as though I have lived in Abu Dhabi my whole life. I settle into my gorgeous hotel room and my new lifestyle with ease and grace, while anxiously waiting to move into my new home.

Inside my new condo in Abu Dhabi

The day finally arrives for my big move and my new condominium, with all its new furnishings, is breathtaking! Everything is wonderful. I am very busy unpacking in my new home and settling in, and most days after work, I usually go to Al Falfa Plaza to shop, because this plaza is directly across the streets from my condominium building. I say streets because I have to walk over four-lanes of streets, with an island of grass and shrubs in the center. Once I cross these streets, I then have to walk over another street, which is running parallel to the previous streets. The only area that is grass is on the island in the middle of the four-lane streets. All the other surrounding areas where I have to walk are sand except for the concrete sidewalk leading into the plaza.

This day is no different. I have just returned from work and once again, I am on my way to Al Falfa Plaza. I make sure I have my handbag, cell phone and my keys before I leave my condominium. All my keys are on one large key chain, with the key to my condominium attached by a smaller, plastic ring. I do my shopping at the plaza and return to my beautiful apartment, taking the elevator up to the third floor. When I arrive at my doors, I lay my two shopping bags down in order to retrieve my keys from my handbag so I can unlock my door. I stare in disbelief! The key to my condominium door is missing! The plastic ring has broken and my key is gone. Immediately, I decide I will leave my bags by my door and back track to the plaza. While at the plaza, I speak with the manager of the supermarket and I check with security to see if anyone has found my key and handed it in. There is no key to be found, anywhere. I start to walk back to my condominium, looking very carefully on the ground.

I reach the entrance of my building, speak to the superintendent telling him of my predicament, and ask, "Do you have a master key?"

He quickly explains, "There is no such thing as a master key for each individual apartment, because of security reasons."

As I take a big sigh, I ask, "Do you have any suggestions to help me?"

He answers, "The only thing you can do is to call the fire station and request for someone to come and cut the lock. This also means you will not be able to lock your door during the night and will have to wait until morning for the replacement of a new lock. It also means this process will be very costly. I think you should think about this."

I take the superintendent's advice and decide to walk once again to Al Falfa Plaza and to keep searching on the ground for my key. I head out towards the plaza, looking very intensely over the sand as I walk. The streets and the grass and inside the plaza are not very difficult areas to search, but the sand is. I also know that the sand is very fine and this makes it extremely difficult for me. There are also silver pop tin covers everywhere. In my mind, I am expecting to find my key laying on the ground; all I need to do is to find it. Now on my way back to the condominium building and still searching frantically for my key, I walk very slowly.

My thoughts are running wild, trying to find some solution to my problem. I am thinking I will get a taxi and go to the Beach Hotel for the night. I have my credit card on me and I have money for the taxi. I figure it is best for me to go to the hotel, go to the restaurant and have my dinner, relax in my hotel room, have a good night's sleep, and when I am feeling refreshed in the morning, take on this dilemma. As these thoughts are swirling around in my head, I realize that I would not have a change of clothes in the morning, in order for me to go to work. Inconvenient because not only do I not have a change of clean clothes, but I do not have any make-up, shoes, or my attaché case for work. As these thoughts are going through my mind, I am still slowly walking on the sand searching for my key. I suddenly stop because the thought comes to me that my Aunt Mildred should be with me. Up to this point in time, I know I have a Guardian Soul watching over me all the time and my Guardian Soul is my Aunt Mildred. Therefore, it occurs to me to ask for help. In my mind, I say, "I know you are with me and I need your help. I do not need to explain my circumstances because you know everything already. You know where my key is. Please, guide me to my key."

I keep walking slowly over the sand and am almost at my condominium building. I suddenly stop without knowing why. My head bends towards the ground. I find myself staring directly at a tiny amount of silver shining through the sand. I automatically think it is the pull-off tab of a can of pop. Even though this thought is in my mind, my body bends over and my hand reaches and pulls the small silver piece of metal out of the sand. I can hardly believe what it is I am seeing! It is my key! As tears fill my eyes, I smile and thank my loving Guardian Soul, my Aunt Mildred. I am so grateful. I happily return to my condominium building to tell the super my wonderful news.

My thoughts take me back to the day I visited with the psychic person Beth, and during my visit she informed me that I have a Guardian Soul watching over me at all times, and not just any Guardian Soul; my Guardian Soul is my aunt who had died many years ago before I was born. Even though I am in such a far-away county in the Middle East, so far away from my family, friends, and all that is familiar to me in the Western culture, I do not feel scared or alone. I know I am never alone because I have my loving Guardian Soul with me, who guards and protects me every minute of every day.

Since arriving in the Middle East, I have become ill. I need surgery and my husband and I feel it is better for us to return to Canada. My husband decided to join me in Abu Dhabi and had arrived about a month earlier. Without hesitation, we board the Boeing 777 British Airways, which heads for London, England, and from there we board an Air Canada flight for Toronto, and then a connecting flight to Newfoundland. I am happy to be home, and especially to see my children and our dog, Katie.

As I look at the calendar hanging on the wall in my kitchen, I cannot help but notice the date, February 28. Here is my spiritual number and I am going to meet with Beth again. I met with Beth after my Uncle Abel died and now some years later, I want answers to more questions.

I have no trouble finding Beth's house because I remember being here before. The door opens and the same petite woman is standing in the doorway, greeting me with a big smile. She says, "You don't look familiar. Have you done something different to your hair?"

I chuckle and answer, "Yes, I have."

"Well," Beth exclaims, "This is why I don't recognize you. I know it has been a long time."

"Yes, it's been a long time and I have to say there's been a lot of water which has passed under my bridge in that length of time."

Beth laughs as she asks, "And is some of the water muddy?"

"Yes, definitely, some of the water is indeed muddy!"

Beth offers to take my coat and then she offers me a tea or coffee. I graciously accept the offer for tea. Once the tea is ready, Beth guides me downstairs to the same small room I visited the last time. Nothing has changed. It is the same as I remember.

Beth starts by asking, "Who is it you would like to contact?"

I reply, "I would like to contact my Uncle Stan and my Guardian Angel, Gabriel."

"And what makes you think you have a Guardian Angel?"

"Because I know I have someone around me, someone who guides me and helps me in times of need."

"Yes, but that could be your Guardian Soul," Beth quickly points out.

"Yes, this is true because I also know I have a Guardian Soul, my Aunt Mildred; however, I also know I have a Guardian Angel."

"And how do you know this?" Beth questions with a chuckle.

"I know I have a Guardian Angel because he spoke to me one summer's day while I was in my garden, and he told me he is my Guardian Angel and his name is Gabriel."

"Well then, let's see if we can make contact with your Guardian Angel."

I sit comfortably back in my chair and sip my tea as I watch Beth concentrate. "If you are able to only get Uncle Stan to visit at this time, this is fine with me."

In no time, Beth starts to speak. "I can see a female here in the room with us."

"Would it be Aunt Mildred?"

"She just answered yes. Who is Aunt Mildred?" Beth asks.

"She is my aunt who died a very young woman. She died on October 14, 1930 before I was born."

"So, you didn't know this aunt?"

"This is correct. She was only thirty years old when she died. She was married to my Uncle Abel and they had three children. She had a child die the year before her death; he was only five years old. He died on February 12, 1929. Beth, the last time I was here you made contact with Aunt Mildred for me."

"I make contact with so many who passed over, I don't remember everyone."

"Yes, of course, this is understandable considering it's been so long since I saw you last."

"Do you have any questions for your Aunt Mildred?"

"Yes I do. I want to know why I was so upset when Uncle Abel died."

"She says you asked this question before and your Uncle Abel told you the time wasn't right. Is this what happened, Olive?"

"Yes, you made contact with Uncle Abel for me and I asked him that question some years ago."

"And what did he say?"

"He told me that the time wasn't right, but that's a long time ago."

"And so you want to know if your aunt will tell you the answer?"

"Yes."

"Well, I don't think she's going to tell you either because she is shaking her head no."

"I do not understand the big secret. And when is the time going to be right?"

"She is not answering. She is speaking again. You have to be mindful of your health."

"I have to be mindful of my health? What does she mean by this?"

"She says sometimes you take the troubles of the world on your shoulders, and this causes you much stress and worry. Olive, do you really do this?"

"Yes Beth, I'm afraid I do."

"Well, that's not good. You need to stop that. Oh my, we have another visitor; it's a male."

"What does he look like?"

"He's not necessarily tall and he is a slim man. He has light reddish hair that's in the brush cut style." With a chuckle, Beth utters, "I don't know who I got here now."

We are both laughing as I answer, "It really sounds like Uncle Stan."

"He is laughing also and he is nodding his head yes. Who is Uncle Stan?"

"His name is Stanley Earle. He is my uncle who died on July 26, 1999."

"You must have been close to this uncle."

"I was close to Uncle Stan but then I was close to all of my uncles. Nevertheless, it is only since his death that I realize how close I really am to him. I was even present at the very moment he took his last breath."

"You were there when he died?"

"Yes. He had become quite sick, and my mother, sister and I went to the hospital to see him. It was during the last moments of his life and we stayed outside in the corridor of his hospital room, because we felt it was a time just for immediate family. However, a short time later, one of my cousins came out and asked if we would like to be inside. He left this world very peacefully."

"And so now he's here to talk with you. Why do you think he has come after so long?"

"Well Beth, it really hasn't been that long."

"I don't understand, you said he died about a couple of years ago."

"Yes, but shortly after his death, he started to visit me in my house."

"You're kidding me?" Beth exclaims.

"No, I'm not kidding. When I said it has only been after his death that I realize how close I am to him, that's what I mean."

"How do you know when he comes around you?"

"He blinks a light and then I know he is with me."

With a chuckle, Beth asks, "And how does your husband feel about your dead uncle visiting you in your house?"

I am now laughing. "Beth, the first time I told my husband about Uncle Stan visiting, you should have seen his face!"

As I start to continue with my story, Beth interrupts me. "Your Uncle Stanley and your Aunt Mildred are now laughing with us." As Beth retrieves a tissue from the box on her desk and wipes her eyes from the tears of laughter, she blurts out, "Olive go on; I can't wait to hear this."

"Well, it was one afternoon and my husband and I go down to our basement because my husband wants to show me how tidy he has organized everything. There are four lights in the basement, with only three light bulbs turned on. We are looking at our lawn furniture, which we have stored in our basement for the winter, when all of a sudden, the light above us which is not turned on, starts to blink! We both look up and there, directly above our heads, is the light bulb blinking! In complete amazement, my husband shouts, 'What the hell!' Now I have to retrieve a tissue from the tissue box to wipe away my tears of laughter, while I watch Beth double over in laughter. I continue my story. And we are both standing there looking at this light bulb blinking at different intervals. I tell him that this light has blinked like this before when I have been down here. He looks at me with this weird look on his face and exclaims, 'Really!' I tell him, yes really, I have been down here in the basement before and have found that this particular light bulb blinks. My husband quickly responds, 'That bulb must be faulty.' I answer, 'Really?' He looks at me and states, 'Yes. It must be a faulty light bulb; what else could it be?' I tell him, I have been down here in the basement and have found the other light bulbs to blink also and it is not just down here, because it has happened in other parts of the house. He just stares at me with such a shocked look on his face. 'What do you mean; you have found the other bulbs to blink also?' I tell him I believe that there isn't anything wrong with the bulbs but that it means we have a visitor. Of course, he looks at me with such a bewildered look on his face, and questions, 'And who is this visitor?' I tell him, Uncle Stan. He shouts, 'Uncle Stan! You mean your Uncle Stan who died?'

By this time, Beth is roaring with laughter and she has me roaring with laughter also, and I am now finding it difficult to finish my story. After using more tissues, we finally are able to calm down for me to continue. I explain that Uncle Stan visits me often and his way of letting me know he is around is by manipulating the lights. He just keeps staring at me. I tell him to keep looking at the bulb and see if it will stop. With this, sure enough the bulb stops blinking. He then goes over to turn off that light; however, as he approaches the switch on the wall, he realizes the switch is not on! I don't think his nerves could take any more, and as we leave the basement, my husband turns off the three lights that are on."

"Oh, Olive, that is so funny."

"Beth, can you ask Uncle Stan why I was so upset about Uncle Abel's death and his funeral?"

"He heard your question, Olive, so I don't have to ask him. It's because you are his child."

"I am his child!" I exclaim. "What does this mean? Is he telling me that my own father is not really my father?"

"He is nodding his head no. This is not what he means at all."

"Then what does he mean?"

"You were the small child that died years ago."

"I am the small child that died years ago? What is he talking about?"

"He answers remember that Uncle Abel and Aunt Mildred had a child die at the age of five?"

"Yes."

"Well, you're that child!"

"I am that child?" I ask in astonishment.

"Yes, he says you are that child."

"What does he mean, I am that child?"

"You were that small child that died in your previous life."

"Oh my, it all makes perfect sense! When Uncle Abel died, I was so upset because I was not only crying for the death of my uncle, I was also crying for the death of my father!"

"Oh, Olive, this is absolutely amazing!"

"Yes, and now I know why Uncle Abel wouldn't give me any information when I asked him before. He told me the time wasn't right."

"Your Aunt Mildred wouldn't tell you either, so she must think the time is not right either, but obviously your Uncle Stanley feels differently."

As I stare at Beth with shock, she is looking at me with the same type of expression on her face. "This is incredible, Beth. This means that Uncle Abel and Aunt Mildred were my father and mother in my previous life. I was that small child that died at the age of five! And then I reincarnated into a new life, with new parents, and my parents in my former life, are now my uncle and aunt in this lifetime."

"Olive, it all makes so much sense. Your uncle and aunt did not want you to know this because they felt the time was not right. But I think the time is right because it will help you understand why you grieved so much over the death of an uncle."

"Yes, Beth, it certainly helps me to understand why I reacted so strongly to Uncle Abel's death. At least I know I'm not crazy!"

Beth roars with laughter. "Oh my, I have another gentleman here now!"

"Is he related to me?"

"He answers he's Uncle Edward."

Now I am laughing even harder, as I reply, "Beth, I don't have an Uncle Edward."

"Well, now you have him laughing. He seems to be a man with a great sense of humor, and a man with a lot of power around him. He likes to keep things in perspective. He runs a tight ship, so to speak."

"Beth, I really don't know who this is."

"Well, you have him laughing again. He seems to find it funny that you are saying you don't know him. Maybe he's an uncle from your past and you don't remember him."

"I know there's nothing wrong with my memory and I know I don't have an Uncle Edward. What does he look like?"

"He has a round face, but not totally round, and he has dark hair which is graying. He is stocky in stature and he looks about 5'6" tall, not tall, tall. He is a fine looking man and he is dressed casually. He seems to be somewhat old fashioned in his ways. This man dresses fairly well and he likes nice things. He liked nice cars."

"I really don't recognize this person."

"I'm sure if you went back you would probably find him among your ancestors."

"Can you tell me more about him?"

"He is one of your Guardian Souls."

"He is one of my Guardian Souls?" I question with great surprise.

"He is nodding his head yes and smiling."

"Beth, please ask him how many Guardian Souls I have."

"He heard your question, Olive, and he said just two."

"Two? So does this mean that my two Guardians Souls are him and my Aunt Mildred?"

"He answers yes."

"I remember years ago when I spoke to Aunt Mildred for the very first time and she told me she was my Guardian Soul. I asked her what it meant, and she said she was assigned to watch over me and to protect and keep me safe on my journey of life. Is this also what this person Uncle Edward says a Guardian Soul means?"

Beth replies, "He is nodding his head yes and he says you are never alone, because your Aunt Mildred and him take turns to be by your side. They watch over you, guide and protect you from harm."

I sit in complete wonder, trying to allow my brain to absorb this information. It all seems so surreal to me; for not only do I have one Guardian Soul to watch over me, now I have two.

"He states you worry too much. You take the weight of the world on your shoulders."

"Well, I do agree with that statement. He certainly sounds as though he knows me."

"It seems that way because you have him laughing again. You allow yourself to become too worried at times and this is not good for you."

"I know that I tend to worry too much, but how do I stop worrying?"

"He answers worry is a negative concept and it does no good. Worrying can only lead to issues with your health."

"Yes, Beth, I do understand this, but how do I stop worrying?"

"Your Uncle Edward says to worry means that you think you have control over a situation, when in reality this is far from the truth. Well, this certainly makes sense to me."

"Yes, Beth, it does. I will take his advice."

"This is good advice, Olive. This uncle seems to know you quite well."

"I'll have to check with my mother and father to see if they know of an Uncle Edward."

"Yes, this is a good idea. This gentleman who calls himself Uncle Edward must be a distant relative of yours, and you don't remember him."

"Yes, Beth, you must be right."

"The female is speaking. She is one of ours. Both males are nodding their heads yes. It seems you are one of them."

"I am? What does this mean?"

"I really don't know what this means, I will have to ask."

"I guess you don't really have to ask, Beth, because they already can hear you, right?"

Beth grins. "Yes, you are absolutely right. They already know what it is we are saying to each other." Beth continues. "The gentleman who says he is your Uncle Edward states you are on the same level as them."

"I am? What does this mean?"

"I have no idea, Olive."

"Your Uncle Stanley is now speaking. You will get your answers in time by infused knowledge."

"Infused knowledge? I know I have heard this term before. What does this mean?"

"I really don't know; I haven't heard of it."

"I will have to look up that term in the dictionary when I go home."

"Your Uncle Stanley says a child gives you messages, the messages come from a phone call, from a card, a note or a letter. He tells you things because he is told to tell you. This is infused knowledge. You know who this child is."

"Wow, Beth, all of this makes so much sense!"

"So you do have a child that does these things that he is talking about?"

"Yes, I most certainly do. I do know now what he means by infused knowledge. I know this really happens."

"This child must be someone close to you?"

"Yes, he is."

"This is all very interesting, indeed."

"Beth, can you ask if I will be returning to Abu Dhabi?"

"Where is Abu Dhabi? I have never heard of such a place."

"It is in the United Arab Emirates, in the Middle East. My husband and I just came home so I could have surgery on my right leg and once I am fully recuperated, we have our airline tickets to return."

"Your Uncle Edward says you will not be going back to Abu Dhabi."

"We're not?" I exclaim.

"That's what he says and he seems so positive about this."

"This is quite surprising news!"

"He states you are going to be changing roads, and in time you will be making changes that will be for the better."

"I am going to be changing roads! What does this mean?"

"Well, my interpretation of changing roads means that you will be taking a new direction in your life. In other words, the things you are doing now, you will not be doing later on."

"Okay, but changing roads how?"

"Well, you have already been told that you will not be returning to the Middle East, that's certainly changing roads, don't you think?"

"Oh my, yes most definitely, now I get it. Well, what roads will I be going down, if I am going to be changing roads?"

"Uncle Edward answers within the next three months, you're going to be hurt again. It is going to be an upsetting time and there is much confusion. You will have to deal with your emotions. There are going to be tears shed; however, you are going to survive it, and to consider this time you have now, as the calm before the storm."

"Calm before the storm! What does he mean by this?"

"Your Aunt Mildred states you are going to go through a rough time and you are going to cross swords with a female. This female is very immature for her age and she is a gossiper, a talker. Do you know who this is, Olive?"

"I have some idea."

"She says you're going to want to clear up some issues around you and once you do, things are going to start turning for you. The dark clouds will pass over. By the summer, there will be happiness around your home again. Things will start to settle."

"Beth, I'm really taken back by all of this because I thought that once I recuperated from my surgery, I would be returning to the Middle East. My husband just accepted a new engineering position before we left for Canada. His employment offer included many benefits, such as a new fully furnished condominium, and a company car. I have also been working over there and my job offer has excellent benefits. Therefore, you can see why I am finding it difficult to believe all of this. I just can't see what would be so drastic that would make us change our minds about not returning. Also if we stay here, we are both unemployed so none of this makes any sense to me."

"I can certainly see why you have concerns and why you are having trouble believing what you are being told."

"Beth, can you ask them to give me more details?"

"Your Uncle Edward is speaking. You will have a well-deserved break. Doors are going to be opening with new opportunities. Everything will pan out beautifully. You will see."

I am sitting here with Beth and I am lost for words. All of this seems to be such drastic changes, and why this would be happening to me at this time in my life, I do not know.

"Your Uncle Edward says you are coming to the end of your seven-year cycle, and you are starting a new seven years. Everyone has a seven-year cycle, but we all get it at different times. Some people can go all their lifetime and get nowhere. A seven-year cycle means people create a chain link; they are happy bitching and complaining about their life and they do not have the will to change it, or they do not bitch and complain and are willing to change. It is up to every person to either change or not change. After your seven-year cycle, it means you are seven years older, and you are beginning a new seven-year cycle, and for you it means you are building a new foundation. You have proven you are willing to work hard to make the changes that are necessary in your life."

"I have heard this said before; we all have seven-year cycles during our lifetime."

"And your Aunt Mildred is speaking again. Always remember that you have a Guardian Angel watching over you at all times. They're now fading in the distance, Olive."

"They are leaving?" I exclaim.

"Yes, all three of them, and they are all smiling and waving good-bye. And your Uncle Stanley says that they love you and they're watching out for you all the time."

"How can they be watching out for me, if they are all leaving?"

"Oh, Olive, even though they are walking away in the distance, they can very easily come over here to our side."

"Do you see either one of them here with us now in the room?"

"No, I don't but that doesn't mean that one of them won't come over to be with you. And also I know that they are able to watch you from a distance."

"I know this to be true because this is what my Guardian Angel told me when he visited with me. He said he would be watching from the distance."

"I have to say, Olive, you are very lucky to have such loving souls in your life."

"Yes Beth, I am, aren't I?"

"You most certainly are."

Beth and I say our good-byes and part, knowing our paths will cross again another time.

CHAPTER 9

An Untimely Death

Death is simply a shedding of the physical body
like the butterfly shedding its cocoon.
It is a transition to a higher state of consciousness
where you continue to perceive, to understand,
to laugh, and to be able to grow.

Elizabeth Kubler-Ross, M.D.
On Life After Death

The results of the medical tests show the small tumor is benign, and I am so happy to hear this news. I have been walking with the aid of crutches for the past two weeks, since having surgery on my leg, and today I am finally able to put the crutches aside.

It is Good Friday, April 13, 2001 and my husband and I are in our house making plans for dinner, when the ringing of our telephone interrupts us. I answer and the caller wishes to speak to my husband. I call my husband to the phone and I recognize immediately my husband's voice changing; he is speaking in a very sad tone of voice. He finally hangs up the receiver and looks at me with such sorrow on his face. I instantly know he is about to tell me sad news.

He states, "Billy was found dead this morning."

My immediate reaction is one of great shock and sorrow. I pull a chair towards me and sit down. I feel weakened by this news. Billy is our nephew and only twenty-eight years old and now, he is dead! I find myself just staring at my husband Dave, as I blurt out, "What could have happened?"

"I asked that same question but the answer I was given was that no one seems to really know."

"Oh my, this is all so strange."

"Well, as we know Billy has diabetes and so maybe it's got to do with the diabetes."

"Yes, you could very well be right," I answer.

The day of the funeral arrives and we get through the day as best we can, because we are unable to attend the funeral. I find comfort knowing I have my Heavenly Father to turn to in prayer. I pray for Billy's safety and well-being and I personally ask God to receive Billy with His love on the Other Side.

Nighttime has arrived and both my husband and I feel exhausted. We decide we will go to bed early. I am having trouble falling to sleep but when I do, I have the most beautiful dream. This is not just an ordinary dream; it is a very vivid experience and so real, I am able to remember every detail. The next morning, I am sitting having breakfast with my husband and I tell him about my magnificent dream. As I revisit every detail, I have an epiphany and excitedly exclaim to my husband, "Oh my, this was not really a dream at all, this was an actual visit that I had with Billy!"

My husband looks at me with tears in his eyes. "You were actually with Billy?"

My reply is instantaneous. "Yes, I definitely was with Billy last night! He came and visited with me. He had a huge smile on his face and I knew he was so happy to see me, as I was to see him. There was a deep connection of love between us, which I had not realized had existed while he lived on Earth. We shared a very, special bond of love for one another. He talked about how terribly sad he was that we were not able to attend his funeral. He could see and hear everything that had transpired since his death."

"How could he possibly see and hear everything?" my husband questions.

"All I know is that this is the information which he gave me. And he also wants you to know that he understands."

"He does?"

"Yes, he most certainly does." I have to retrieve a tissue for I can feel the tears coming as I continue my conversation. "The remainder of the time we spent together we talked and laughed and enjoyed being with each other. We had a lot of fun together. I remember asking him if he still had diabetes and he said no. He was no longer sick but very healthy."

As I dry my eyes and my husband does the same, he asks, "Billy is really healthy now?"

"Yes, Dave, this is what he told me."

"Billy is really at peace?"

"Yes, Billy is really at peace. And he knows we love him very much."

I can tell my husband is somewhat relieved by my news, however, as the days go by, I can see he is still finding it difficult, knowing we did not attend Billy's funeral. I know an overwhelming sense of grief consumes him. He is struggling with the recent turn of events and I know that he needs to find closure. I think that once he returns to work he should be able to put everything behind him and start to live his life in the carefree and loving manner that he is accustomed to.

It has been almost a week since Billy's funeral and we both feel it is time to go back to work; however, we will not be working in the Middle East. Strangely enough, we have decided not to return to Abu Dhabi, the United Arab Emirates. Since the death of Billy, both my husband and I have come to terms with the fact that life is very fragile. We talk it over and we both agree that we have to get our priorities straight; to live so far away in the Middle East from our children is not the right decision to make. Yes, we have jobs with very high salaries, which would have been tax-free money, and fantastic benefits; but living life to the fullest does not necessarily mean it is about sacrificing for the sake of money. Money cannot buy love, nor can it bring happiness and peace, and it certainly cannot bring back a loved one who has died. Life here on Earth is too short and precious to squander away over the almighty dollar and material possessions. We have made our decision and we both know it is the right choice for us.

I am now in my bedroom recalling the last time I had a meeting with Beth and she told me that Uncle Edward said that Dave and I would not go back to Abu Dhabi to work. At the time, I thought this to be a very strange comment. It did not make any sense to me that we would not return, yet, here I am realizing that it makes perfect sense to me now. I chuckle as I think about that day of my meeting, knowing I did not truly believe Uncle Edward's comment; that is if I have an Uncle Edward. I have to remember to ask my mother or father if I have an Uncle Edward. Another life lesson for me; our Guardian Souls know our life plan!

All of a sudden, I can hear my husband calling my name in a frantic tone of voice from downstairs. As I approach him, I can see he is crying and laughing at the same time. I know I am looking at him with a look of bewilderment on my face. "Dave, what is it?"

He grabs me and gives me a big hug, and at the same time, lets out a big sigh of relief. He exclaims, "Ol, you're not going to believe this!"

"Believe what?" I question.

He now gets himself a tissue and starts to wipe away his tears. He turns to me and answers, "Ol, I just had a visitor."

"You just had a visitor?"

"Yes, a visitor. And you're not going to believe who visited."

I know I am still looking at him with confusion because I know I did not hear the doorbell ring and I certainly did not hear anyone enter our house. Then again, I was upstairs. As he just stares at me, I ask, "Are you going to tell me who visited you?"

With another big sigh of relief, he starts to cry again as he says the word, "Billy."

"Billy!" I exclaim.

"Yes, Billy. I was standing here in the kitchen, here by the sink, and my head was down because I was getting dishes ready for the dishwasher, and when I looked up, Billy was here in the kitchen."

I am now going to the tissue box because I need a tissue to dry my tears also. "What did he look like?"

"He looked very healthy and very happy."

"What did he say?"

"He looked at me with a big smile and said, 'Good-bye, Uncle Dave.' That's all he said."

"Oh Dave, this is so fantastic. This is truly a gift from God. We have both been so blessed."

"Yes, and I consider this to be a miracle."

"Did you say anything?"

"Yes, I said, 'Good-bye Billy,' and then he slowly faded away with a huge smile on his face. I felt a lot of love from him. It was then I called out to you."

"I am so happy for you, darling, you needed this."

"Yes, you are definitely right. I feel so much relief and I feel normal again."

As I give my husband a hug and a kiss, I look at him and say, "Billy knew you were hurting and he knew you needed to say good-bye to him in order to find closure."

With a smile and tears in his eyes, he nods his head yes. Billy's visit with his uncle gave my husband the opportunity for closure, which I know he needed so badly and now I realize that Billy knew this also, and this is why he visited.

CHAPTER 10

A Meeting with My Guardian Souls

For there is nothing covered,
that shall not be revealed;
neither hid, that shall not be known.

The Holy Bible: Luke 12:2
King James Version

Beth has been a long-time friend and I feel I need some guidance from her because I am so distraught by the turn of events, up to and after Billy's death. I contact Beth and ask to meet with her. Once again, I find myself sitting in the small room with Beth, telling her that I would like to make contact with my Aunt Mildred; for I need answers to many questions that I have.

It takes no time at all. "Your Aunt Mildred is now with us. She is sad about the trouble in your relationship. Is there trouble in your relationship?"

"Yes, Beth, I'm afraid there is." I sigh and can feel the tears filling my eyes, so I have to reach into my handbag to retrieve a tissue.

Beth continues. "She says time has changed many things."

I confirm to Beth by nodding my head yes.

"She states talk to Dave and see what changes can be made. I take it, Dave is your husband?"

"Yes, Beth, Dave is my husband."

"Your Aunt Mildred expresses that you have to make changes around the situation by talking to him and telling him how you feel. You need to be honest and tell him your true feelings."

I am hanging on to every word that Beth is telling me. "Beth, I feel Dave already knows how I feel. It is him that has to deal with the issues in our relationship."

"Oh, Olive, there's a gentleman who just stood next to your Aunt Mildred. I do not know who this man is, but he is not a tall man, short to medium height, and he has red hair with a brush cut style."

"That is my Uncle Stan."

"Oh yes, I remember, I recognize him from the last time that we met."

"Yes, that's right, Beth. Uncle Stan came to visit with me the last time I was here to see you."

"Your Uncle Stanley expresses that Dave is not showing his emotions, and as far as he is concerned, it's a waiting game."

"A waiting game and just what would he be waiting for? I don't understand; what is he waiting for, for things to get worse?" I quickly reply.

"Your Aunt Mildred answers that you have to make changes around the situation, and one of the changes is to write the letter."

"Write the letter?"

Beth responds with a surprised look on her face, "I don't know what letter she is talking about. None of this makes any sense to me; however, if she is telling you to write a letter, it means you need to write a letter. I can see your Aunt Mildred sitting at a large, beautiful, wooden desk, holding an eloquent pen, writing a letter, and this signifies to me that you must write your letter."

"Send it to whom?"

"She says that you will know who to send it to in time."

"And just what am I supposed to say in this letter?"

"She is smiling. You will know what to say."

I question in astonishment, "I do?"

"One thing I do know is that Guardian Souls will not lead you astray. They love you and they are here to guide and support you in any way that they can."

"I only really know Uncle Stan because my Aunt Mildred died before I was born."

"Olive, you just think you don't know your Aunt Mildred; believe me, if your Aunt Mildred is one of your Guardian Souls, you know her really well and she knows you really well."

"Beth, I'm not sure what it is you are really saying."

"I am saying that you know your Aunt Mildred before you were born this time on Earth. You know her from the Other Side."

"Oh, yes of course, and also she was my mother in my previous life. Now I understand."

"Your Aunt Mildred is upset and is crying because she says your husband would be a lonely soul. You are supposed to be together and you will not stay apart. You can rebuild and be happy but you have to make changes. There has been too much negativity and the negativity has turned into hatefulness, and you have endured it far too long. The time has come to make positive changes."

As I sit with Beth, I can see by the expression on her face that she is just as puzzled by all of this as I am. "I am trying to make sense of all of this."

"Your Uncle Stanley says, write the letter and pass it on."

"Who do I write this letter to?"

"Your Uncle Stanley answers, time will tell you."

"Time will tell me?" I question.

"Yes, your Uncle Stanley is nodding his head yes. And he states sometimes you have to walk away."

"Beth, surely goodness Uncle Stan is not saying for me to walk away from Dave?"

"Your Uncle Stanley replies no. Dave is not the one causing upset in your relationship."

"Okay, this is true. So who am I supposed to walk away from?"

"Your Uncle Stanley answers anyone who causes problems for you and Dave. In other words, don't have anything else to do with these people."

"Okay, this makes perfect sense to me."

"Your Aunt Mildred is speaking. Some people are not willing to change. I know this to be true, Olive, some people can go their whole lifetime and stay in the same nasty and hateful rut."

"Well, I certainly have to agree with this."

"Oh, Olive, there's another gentleman here and he says he is your Uncle Edward."

"Well, apparently, Beth, I have an Uncle Edward but I don't know who this uncle is."

"Your Uncle Edward states both you and Dave need to think it through because the time has come for you both to walk away, and if the time is not now, it is coming."

"Beth, I do know that I have battled ignorance and hatred for many years and consequently I find it extremely difficult to be around certain people."

"Your Uncle Edward declares the time is coming."

"The time is coming?"

"Your Uncle Edward is nodding his head yes. He says it is impossible for two things to occupy the same space at the same time; for where there is hate, there cannot be love."

"That makes a whole lot of sense to me, Beth."

"He continues to speak. During your lifetime here on Earth, you will make contact with many souls. Each and every one of these people that you come in contact with is there for you for a particular reason, even the negative and hateful ones."

"Actually, my philosophy in life is that it is all meant to be. As strange as that may sound, I truly do believe that. I truly believe that there are times in our lives when we are supposed to encounter negative people and negative circumstances. The only problem I have is trying to understand why God wants me to experience so many negative and hateful people and circumstances, and it seems He thinks I can handle more than the average person can. I do not know why He thinks this, but He must have His reasons! I have been dealing with negative, hateful people all my life. I can honestly say I am not getting used to it, but I seem to handle these stressful times differently. I know I am a fighter, and I know the main thing is to ensure that these negative, hateful people will not bring me down to their level, no matter how hard they try. I always do what is right and make sure I come out on top. I do believe in the end, I pave the way for those coming behind me to have life a little easier. I just wish I could understand a little more why God chooses to put me into certain situations, the way that He does. However, I do know that life is not supposed to be easy; for living life here on Earth is a challenge and we are here to learn and to grow from our experiences."

"Your Uncle Edward says that the main reason for any relationship is for you to have a spiritual experience, which in human terms would be called a human experience, and it is to help you to learn and advance. No matter the situation or the circumstances, it is of the utmost importance for you to understand that it is a spiritual experience for you. So, Olive, what you believe to be true, is exactly what your Uncle Edward is saying."

"Yes, he is agreeing with me, isn't he?"

"Yes, Olive, he is."

"I remember the words of Teilhard de Chardin: *We are not human beings having a spiritual experience. We are spiritual beings having a human experience.* I have never forgotten that quote because it has such powerful meaning."

"That's a very interesting quote, Olive. Oh, your Uncle Edward is speaking again. When you begin to live your life as the loving expression of God all the time; then you will know the true meaning of success while living here on Earth. And he says remember the things we have told you earlier."

"Yes, Beth, I can see where both Dave and I need to talk things out. Maybe the time has come for real change."

"Change is not necessarily always a bad thing. Change can bring about much happiness and peace."

"Yes, I know this is true."

"Olive, I feel you are truly blessed to have such loving, devoted and wise souls, as your relatives, who are guiding and protecting you. Not all people I do readings for are as blessed as you."

"I know I am truly blessed and I know my husband Dave is truly blessed also because of the loving relatives I have in my life."

"They are all smiling and they are now starting to fade into the distance. They are waving and they all say good-bye."

With tears in my eyes, I say, "Good-bye Aunt Mildred, good-bye Uncle Stan, good-bye Uncle Edward."

I thank Beth for her valuable time and for giving so much of herself, and tell her that I am sure I will be back again.

As I drive away from her house, I recall all the comments. I think about Aunt Mildred, I think about Uncle Stan and I think about Uncle Edward; and just who is Uncle Edward?

Later that evening, I telephone my parents who are living in Florida. My mother and father have been going to St. Petersburg, Florida for over twenty years. They purchased a house there, spend the winters in Florida, and return to Canada in the springtime each year.

My father answers the phone on the first ring. "Hello."

"Hello, Dad, how are you today?"

As always, my dad's voice sounds so cheerful as soon as he recognizes my voice. "Very good, very good. How are you, my doll?"

Dad and I chat for a while and then he calls out to my mother to take the phone. We say our good-byes and then my mother and I start chatting. I begin by asking Mom how she is doing and how Dad is doing. After so long into our conversation, I ask, "Mom, do I have an Uncle Edward?"

Her reply is an immediate, "Yes."

"Yes!" I exclaim.

"Yes, you have an Uncle Edward; he's your great uncle. He is your father's uncle. But we didn't call him Edward, we called him Ned."

"Oh my, you mean Uncle Ned from Spaniard's Bay?"

"Yes, Uncle Ned who lives in the two-storey house, next to Bob and Rita; his wife was Aunt Mary. They've both been dead a long time, but you must remember Aunt Mary and Uncle Ned don't you?"

"Yes, Mom, I most certainly do. Their son is Ralph Neil."

"Yes, Ralph was called after your father."

"Oh yes, I remember."

"Ralph is the one you and Dave bought your house from, isn't he?"

"Yes, Mom, you are absolutely right."

After talking to my mother, I hang up the receiver of the phone and laugh to myself, thinking how living life here on Earth can be so intriguing.

CHAPTER 11

At Death's Door

Yea, though I walk through the valley
of the shadow of death,
I will fear no evil:
for thou *art* with me;
thy rod and thy staff they comfort me.

The Holy Bible: Psalms 23:4
King James Version

Awakened from a deep sleep, I see my son standing in the doorway of my bedroom. He is speaking to me in a concerned voice. "Mom, where is our black car? Our car is not in the driveway!" My son had gone out earlier in the evening with his friends for a coffee at their favorite coffee shop, Tim Horton's, and has now returned home.

Trying to open my eyes, I ask, "What are you saying?"

In a frantic tone of voice once again he states, "Mom, our black car is not in the driveway. Someone must have stolen our car!"

Before I can answer him, he says to me in the same frantic tone of voice, "Mom, where is Dad?"

With this comment, I turn my head to the left, and realize that my husband is not in bed next to me. I remember that my husband and I were watching television in our family room earlier in the evening, and I had gone to bed without him. We always like to watch the national news at 10:30 in the evening; however, this particular evening I decided I would go to bed early. I remember feeling sleepy, and so I told my husband that I was feeling too tired to stay and watch the news with him. As I got up from the sofa, I recall my husband telling me that he was going to stay and watch the news. As I walked away from the sofa, I heard Dave say, 'I have to go out and get gas.' I remember asking, 'Can't you do that in the morning?' He answered me but because I was too far from him, I did not understand the words of his reply. Now, here I am lying in bed realizing my husband must still be in the family room. I look at my son and say, "Check the family room. Dad was watching television when I came to bed."

The only reply my son gives me, as he walks away from my bedroom doorway is, "But Mom, it is two o'clock in the morning!"

By this time I am fully awake and realizing the serious impact of my son's words.

A short time later my son returns. "Mom, Dad is not in the family room, and I checked the other rooms. He is nowhere to be found!"

I quickly remember what my husband said to me earlier and I reply, "Oh yes, your father said he had to go out and get gas."

Once again, in the same frantic tone of voice, my son replies, "But Mom, it's two o'clock in the morning!"

It is now starting to sink into my brain what my son is really implying. He knows it is quite out of character for his father to be out getting gas at two in the morning. I try to comfort him by saying, "Dad will soon be home. He is just gone to get gas. Go to bed."

My son leaves and goes to his bedroom and I can hear him in his room, getting ready for bed. I am thinking to myself that my husband will be home any minute. I am listening intently to hear his car pull up in our driveway, and to hear him in the foyer of our house. The next thing I know, I hear the telephone ringing. I can hear my son pick up after the first ring. "Hello." My son is back standing in my bedroom doorway, speaking in the same frantic tone of voice. "Mom, you are wanted on the phone!"

I anxiously reply, "Who could want me at this hour in the morning?"

"I don't know, Mom. It's a man."

I jump out of bed, grab my dressing gown and go to the phone. "Hello."

The male voice on the other end of the telephone line introduces himself. "I am Constable St. Croix and I am with the Royal Newfoundland Constabulary. Are you the wife of David Noseworthy?"

I quickly reply, "Yes I am. Is there a problem?"

Constable St. Croix answers, "I am calling to let me know that your husband has been in a serious car accident, and that you should come to the Emergency Department of the Health Sciences Centre."

I start to feel weak and immediately I lean my body on the wall. "Is my husband okay?"

The police officer does not answer my question, but states, "Mrs. Noseworthy, you need to come to the Emergency Department of the Health Sciences Centre."

"Has anyone else been injured in the accident?"

The answer is, "No, just your husband."

I can hear my son speaking to me in a panicky and raised voice. "Mom, come on, we have to go!"

I tell the police officer we are on our way, and hang up the phone. With that, I return to my bedroom and get dressed.

I can hear my son saying to me once again, "Mom, come on, we have to go!" By this time, my son is now shouting at me. "Mom, come on we have to go!"

I know I am rushing as fast as I can, so I do not understand why my son is getting upset with me.

My son drives and it takes no time at all. We enter the Emergency Department of the hospital, and waiting for us are two police officers. One asks if I am Olive Noseworthy, and I answer, "Yes." I then introduce my son to them. They proceed to tell me that my husband has been in a serious car accident and that he is inside with the doctor. I tell them I need to go in and see my husband. I follow the police officers, who take me to one of the nurses.

The nurse introduces herself as Tina and then takes us to one of the cubicles. As she draws the curtain back, I start to feel faint as I see my husband lying flat on the stretcher, wearing a neck brace, and hooked up to intravenous therapy. As I approach my husband, it is only then that it finally hits me! The tears start to fill my eyes, as I bend down and kiss my husband on his forehead. I try to speak but the words just will not come; it is as though there is something caught in my throat. I start to take pieces of glass out of his hair; there are shattered pieces of glass everywhere. The doctor enters the cubicle and introduces himself as Dr. Guy Hogan, the orthopedic surgeon. He proceeds to tell me the time my husband arrived at the Emergency Department and his condition. He states, "Your husband has his left ankle broken, and his lungs and liver are bruised." However, it is the next sentence that really startles me. "Your husband has some bleeding on his brain and he also has a severe injury to his spine; his back is broken and he should be paralyzed, but he's not. He needs emergency surgery."

My legs start to crumble and the next thing I know I find myself almost sloughed down on the floor, and I realize that I am collapsing. My son's arms are around me and he tries to get me to sit down in a chair, but I refuse. I manage to pull myself up with my son's help. I follow the doctor out to the nurses' station and confront him. "What do you mean he has bleeding on his brain and his back is broken, and he should be paralyzed?"

He then proceeds to tell my son and me the full extent of the injuries. "Your husband has some bleeding on his brain but it is not extensive and I expect the bleeding to subside in time; however, he does have a spinal injury and his spine is crushed."

"Crushed?" I exclaim. "What do you mean crushed?"

He answers, "I am unable to explain any better than what I have already told you. He is a very lucky man. He is alive and not paralyzed. His condition is nothing short of a miracle. I have to excuse myself because I have to prepare for the OR. He needs emergency surgery."

My head is spinning. I feel faint, weak and nauseated. I can feel my son's arm around me as he guides me to a chair and helps me to sit down. Tears are streaming down my face and my son is hugging me. He is crying also.

One of the nurses comes over to comfort us and offers us tissues, as she says to me, "Take some deep breaths." She then asks, "Are there any other family members that you should notify?"

My thoughts quickly go to my daughter who is so far away. She had graduated from university and is now on vacation with her friends in Europe. I look at my son. The tears keep pouring down my face like heavy rain and I cannot seem to compose myself.

I now have the daunting task of trying to track down my daughter. The last time she called, she told me she was going to Paris. I thought my best option was to call her friend's mother, and to see if she can find her for me.

The nurse then asks, "Is there anyone else you would like to call?"

"Yes, I need to call my sister, but I will do it later in the morning, considering it is so early. I will wait until around 6."

She responds with a smile. "I understand. Please come to me when you want to use the phone."

My only response is a nod. I eventually compose myself and my son and I return to the cubicle. I continue to take the glass out of my husband's hair and as I do, I say to him, "Everything will be okay." I do not know how convincing I sound because the reality is that I honestly do not know if what I am saying is true.

He cannot speak because of the neck brace that he is wearing but I know he understands because of his facial expression and the look in his eyes. I continue talking to him, explaining what the doctor has told me. I explain as best I can about the spinal injury, that there is no paralysis, and he needs emergency surgery to repair the damage. I also explain to him that he has a fracture of his left foot but this is minor surgery. It is then one of the nurses comes in and tells me that the police officers want to speak to me again.

I do not want to leave my husband, but I know I need to speak to the police officers, regarding the car accident. I find my way to a small, private room where the two police officers are waiting for me. They greet me, and motion for me to take a seat opposite to them and they then proceed to give me the details of the car accident. They are giving me a lot of information but most of it is not sinking into my brain, but what does sink in are the following words. "The car is completely demolished and it appears that your husband rolled his car about six times." My brain is trying to comprehend how the car could have rolled six times! The same officer proceeds, "When we came upon the scene of the accident, my first thought was that there aren't any survivors, because of the condition of the car."

My response is a groan as I put both my hands over my face and take a deep breath to take what is coming next.

He says, "The car is completely flattened and the Jaws of Life had to be used in order to free your husband from the wreckage. And to be honest with you, once I realized the driver of the vehicle was alive, I considered it to be a miracle, because I truly don't have an answer as to how your husband survived such a severe impact."

I am now in tears once again and having to wipe my eyes. As I try to compose myself, the second officer asks me if I am feeling up to continuing. I manage to nod my head yes.

The first police officer continues. "Do you know why your husband was out that hour of the night driving?"

I relay the story of earlier in the evening when my husband said he had to get gas, and the only gas station open late at night is in the area where the accident had occurred.

One of the police officers states, "Your husband's car was the only vehicle involved and he must have been speeding in order to have done the damage that has been done."

Surprised by this remark, I respond, "I find it difficult to believe that my husband was not going the speed limit. This does not seem at all like him. My husband is a very cautious driver and I do not even remember him ever getting a speeding ticket for all the years I have known him. This behavior would be really out of character for him."

The other police officer declares, "Your husband is very lucky to have been found. The area of the accident is on a straight stretch of highway, but the highway curves, and rather than Mr. Noseworthy making the curve in the highway, his car went straight and therefore went into a rock wall. But before hitting the rock wall, it looks as though his car flipped head on for approximately three times, hit the rock wall, and flipped again another three times sideways."

I feel as though someone has pulled my lungs out of my body because I am finding it difficult to breathe. I find it unbearable to hear what the police officers are telling me. I am speechless as I wipe my eyes from the tears flowing down my face.

The same police officer asks, "Are you okay for us to continue?"

I manage to nod my head yes, as he questions, "Was your husband the type of person who usually wore his seat belt?"

My answer is immediate. "Yes. He always wore his seat belt and made sure that we all did when we were in the car with him. Why do you ask?"

"Because when we came upon the scene of the accident, your husband was not wearing his seat belt."

I am dumbfounded. "My husband always wore his seat belt."

"It could very well be that the seat belt snapped upon impact."

I nod my head in agreement because this is what makes sense to me.

"The impact smashed the car's ceiling and it appears your husband was pushed across to the passenger's side; when we found him, he was pinned between the driver's seat and the door, crushing his left leg."

I am unable to utter a word.

The other officer then says, "It seems the only explanation for your husband's car accident is that he must have seen something as he was driving, such as a rabbit, and then swerved to try and avoid hitting it. It is then he must have lost control of his car and rather than make the turn, he swerved and went into the rocks, flipped his car on the impact and then hit the rock wall."

The area of my husband's car accident

Constable St. Croix agrees with this conclusion. "Yes, that makes sense to me. I do know there are rabbits in that location because it's a wooded area, even though it is in the city."

Constable St. Croix proceeds to tell me that the Emergency Response Team had received the 911 call around one in the morning. The call came in from a man named John Doyle who lives in the Shea Heights area. He said, "Mr. Doyle's son, Curt Doyle, was visiting his parents earlier in the evening because he was leaving Newfoundland the next day to go to Fort McMurray, Alberta to work. Curt had left his parents' house in Shea Heights around one in the morning and instead of walking the street to his Hamilton Avenue apartment, he chose to take a short cut through the wooded area and down the steep hill. When he was at the top of the hill, he could see the lights of a vehicle below, and he knew it must have been in an accident because the lights were shining in an area off the highway and in a rocky ravine. He quickly turned and ran back to his parents' house and told his father the news, and his father immediately called 911. Both Curt and his father then headed out the door and down the embankment to the wrecked car. It was Curt Doyle and his father John Doyle who stayed with your husband until the Emergency Response Team arrived on the scene."

The other police officer says, "Your husband is a very lucky man to be alive. Not only because of the condition of the car but also because of the location of the car accident."

All I am able to do is nod my head yes, as I wipe away the tears from my eyes.

He continues. "I don't know if you really know the area where your husband had his car accident, but it's an area which is not visible from the highway. Cars driving by the same area on the highway would not have been able to see the demolished vehicle. It was only by the grace of God that Curt Doyle was visiting his parents that evening, and had decided to take the short cut through the wooded area and to go down the rocky embankment. It is my belief that it could have taken days and maybe even weeks before your husband was located. Thinking about the whole situation, I would have to say, I consider it to be a miracle for your husband to have been found, at that particular time."

They both thanked me for my time and stated that they would be filing a report. I then returned to be with my husband and my son.

Upon my return, the nurse comes and informs me that a delay is necessary for the emergency surgery. "The blood work results have come back and it shows that your husband's plasma levels are far below normal. We are going to have to start giving him units of plasma. When his levels return to normal, the surgery will go ahead."

My question to her is, "Why would his levels of plasma be so low?"

The only answer she can give is, "I really don't know."

My son and I remain in the cubicle, where I sit next to the stretcher, holding my husband's hand, and keep reassuring him that everything will be okay. As we sit, my son looks at his watch. "Mom, it is now 6 o'clock. Do you want to call anyone?"

I return to the nurses' station and ask to use the phone so I can call my sister. Later in the morning, my sister and her husband arrive. I am so happy to see them because I really need a break. They stay with Dave while my son and I return home.

The first thing I do is call my friend, Lynda, and tell her my sad news. Lynda is more than happy to help find my daughter in Europe.

My son goes to bed to try to get some sleep, while I fall on my knees by the side of my bed and pray to God, through my tears, thanking Him for the miracles. Even though I am exhausted, I feel an enormous sense of peace and love, and feel a renewed burst of energy to take on the remainder of my day. I slowly get off my knees and go to my dresser to retrieve some clothes. My head bent down, I am looking in the top drawer of my dresser as I quickly decide on the clothes I will wear. As I lift my head, I look up and into the mirror above my dresser.

I stare at myself in complete astonishment! On my neck is my gold chain and on both my ears are my gold earrings! In addition, I am wearing lipstick! It all comes rushing back to me. I realize that when I received the phone call from the police earlier that morning, I must have gone into a state of shock. I cannot remember putting on my jewelry or lipstick, nor can I remember getting dressed! However, what I do remember is my son's voice, when he kept saying to me, "Mom, come on, we have to go!" I slump down on my bed and hold my face in my hands. The tears once again are streaming down, as the hours earlier rush back in my mind. I do eventually pull myself together and am able to get a shower and get dressed. I know I should eat something but my stomach feels as though it is doing somersaults and just the thought of food makes me nauseous.

As I stand in my kitchen, the phone rings and the voice I recognize instantly. It is my daughter. She tells me that her friends are helping her to get the first flight out as soon as possible. I am so relieved that my daughter is on her way home.

I return to the hospital and feel much better. I know it is a waiting game until my husband can have his surgery. The hours go by slowly and my son returns to the hospital to be with me. He tells me the phone did not stop ringing while he was at home. The word has gotten out about my husband being in a serious car accident. The news media has already reported about the accident. It is only now that I am able to start to put the pieces of the puzzle together.

The hours are going by very slowly while we wait for Dave's plasma levels to reach normal. It takes six units of plasma before the nurse announces she has informed Dr. Hogan and he is preparing for the operating room.

It is finally time for my husband to go to the OR. I tell him I love him and that I feel he will be safe and that the surgery will go according to plan. My mind knows of the complications of such intense surgery but my soul is telling me that he will return to me, with the surgery being a success.

My sisters and their husbands are now with my son and me as we wait patiently. We are no longer in the Emergency Department but are in a small room on the fifth floor of the hospital. It is a long and weary wait. Finally, after almost five hours, Dr. Hogan arrives. He calls me out and talks to me just outside the waiting area. He looks exhausted but I can see a twinkle in his eyes. His words I shall never forget, for they are embedded on my brain forever. "The spinal fusion of discs in his lower back went as planned. I consider the surgery a success."

I try to hold back the tears, but to no avail. I reach deep into my soul to ask, "Is he going to be paralyzed?"

He smiles and answers a simple, "No."

I am also smiling but now I am also sobbing. I say the words, but the words do not seem enough for all this man has done to help my family in such a time of need and sorrow. "Thank you."

He is still smiling as he replies, "You are welcome."

As I wipe away my tears, I ask, "Am I able to see my husband?"

As he starts to walk away from me, he says, "Yes, of course."

My son now has his arms around me and we are both crying tears of joy. As I look through the doorway of the waiting room, I can see my family crying also. The nurse comes to me and tells me I am able to go into the recovery room and see my husband.

Dave is very groggy from the anesthesia, which is to be expected; however, he is awake and I am able to speak with him. As I bend over and kiss him, my tears fall on his face. "It's over. Dr. Hogan says your surgery went as planned and that he considers it a success." I take a deep breath of relief and continue, "You are not paralyzed."

A few days later, Dr. Hogan and I meet and he explains to me the serious impact the car accident had on my husband's lower spinal area. He tells me that Dave's lower spine was crushed and that he should have been paralyzed because of the massive amount of damage. However, my husband was not paralyzed because apparently upon impact, all the nerves in the spinal area separated and moved before the impact. Dr. Hogan proceeds to demonstrate to me by holding up his left hand as a fist, and then takes his right hand and makes a fist, and proceeds to slam his right fist into his left fist, and as he does, before his right fist reaches his left fist, he opens his left hand and spreads his fingers out, and then slams his right fist into his left hand. Dr. Hogan says that he doesn't have a medical explanation as to why the nerves in my husband's lower spine spread out before the impact, crushing his spine. The only conclusion he can come to is that it is nothing short of a miracle.

My husband had survived a traumatic car accident, which could have taken his life, and if it had not taken his life, could have very easily left him paralyzed. Both the police officers and the doctors considered my husband's survival and medical condition a miracle.

Days later, my husband tells me he has no recollection of the impact or anything that happened during the crash, nor does he remember the pain. His memory of the actual crash is "wiped out." However, he does remember driving on the highway to get gas, listening to the music on his car radio and enjoying the drive. Everything else is a blank until he realizes he is alone in the car, pinned down and unable to move, with the car roof smashed on top of him. He does not remember not wearing his seat belt. He remembers it being a long time before he knew someone was with him and he says it is a voice he shall never forget for as long as he lives because the voice was so reassuring and calm; it made him feel that he was not alone and that he would be okay. The loving voice said to him, 'Hang in there. Help is on the way. Hang in there.'

As my husband retells his account of that May 8 night, I feel the most incredible peace and a knowing that what we are experiencing as a family is necessary. My husband survived for a reason, and in time, I will come to realize it is all about learning life lessons. The traumatic event of the car accident was required in order for my husband to move forward spiritually, and I now understand that the special experience really was for all of us as a family.

CHAPTER 12

Tragedy Turns Into Triumph

When things go wrong, as they sometimes will,
When the road you're trudging seems all uphill,
….So stick to the fight when you're hardest hit—
It's when things seem worst that you must not quit.

Edgar A. Guest
Footprints

Family members, friends and neighbors are truly amazing because of their love and kindness. There are gifts of food delivered to our house; there are phone calls, cards, flowers and emails sent to us in our time of sorrow and struggle. One of the emails I received is from my dear and wonderful friend, Anne, living in Dubai, United Arab Emirates. She writes:

Dear Olive,

I am so very sorry to hear the bad news about Dave. I only hope that this is not as bad as it sounds and I just do not want to accept it for Dave. Oh, God….I only hope and pray that he will recover soon without any problem to his spine and the rest of his body. Oh…I just can't imagine, it seems when trouble comes, it all comes together, and I don't know why for the both of you….you are the nicest people I've ever met. How did it happen? Well, it is a miracle. He is out of danger but we need to pray that he gets well, and you need to give him the moral support. I wish you both were here and then nothing would have happened….anyway, sometimes you just cannot avoid fate. God....I know He is with him and he will be all right soon. Please give him our wholehearted love and tell him that God loves him very much and that both Roger and I will pray for him. So, do not give up the battle. I know this is a real test of life. Know you are not alone.

Your so very worried friend, Anne

The days that follow are very stressful. My husband is experiencing "episodes" which the doctors are not able to diagnose. I use the word "episodes" because it is as though he is experiencing seizures, but they are not seizures; he is going in and out of consciousness. Consults go to medical specialists, and many medical tests are ordered; including an electroencephalogram, more commonly known as an EEG.

It is early in the morning and our son is at home sleeping because he had stayed with his father all night. He had come home exhausted and in tears, telling me that his dad was very sick throughout the night, and consequently they both had a terrible night. My daughter and I head straight for the hospital, to find that my husband is still not feeling very well. We are sitting quietly in my husband's hospital room, when the nurse comes in and tells me that it is time for Dave to go for the EEG test. I know he is very weak and not feeling very well, and because of my husband's unstable medical condition, the nurses decide it is best to keep him in his hospital bed and wheel the bed to the EEG testing room.

A registered nurse and the technician, who is performing the test, are in the room with us. Once inside the EEG testing room, the technician prepares my husband. He has to wear a cap that connects to the EEG monitor, which gives the reading of the test to a computer. He has to lie flat on his back while the technician runs the test, and because he is wearing a body brace, I know he is feeling very uncomfortable. It is during this time that Dave starts to regurgitate mucus from his mouth and slips in and out of consciousness. I am by his side and I keep turning his head as best I can, while wiping his mouth. I am starting to become very concerned because I know he could aspirate while lying on his back. This means that the mucus coming from his mouth can very easily go back into his lungs. Then my worst fear happens. He starts to gasp for breath and immediately I turn him on his side. Relieved, I glance over at the nurse who is standing off to the side of me, just watching and without even thinking, I shout, "Are you a registered nurse? Don't you realize he could aspirate?" She does not answer; she just stares at me. I am so distraught by the whole event.

It is at this moment my husband calls my name and in a very low and weak tone voice, he says, "Ol."

I put my head down next to his so I can hear him speak clearly. "What?"

"I love you. Good-bye." He then closes his eyes and drifts off. I know I am losing him! I feel frantic! Any moment I am expecting him to go into respiratory arrest and I will have to call for a 999 code!

I fear that Dave will leave us without our children being by his side. It is then I start to pray. I close my eyes and speak to God. "Dear God, if this is Dave's time to go, I will accept this, but please do not take him from me in this condition. Please let me take him back to his room and get him cleaned up and comfortable in his bed, and time so I can get our children to come to be with him." As soon as I finish praying, I open my eyes. My husband is still lying in his bed with his eyes closed, and not responding.

All of a sudden, he opens both eyes, looks at me, smiles and calls my name. "Ol." He is becoming fully alert and responding well. I bend down and give him a hug.

Realizing that God has answered my prayer, I speak privately to my Heavenly Father. "Thank you dear God for your love." I dry my eyes and look at the technician, giving him an affirmative nod of my head to let him know it is okay to continue. The technician continues his work and is finally able to complete the EEG testing. With the help of the nurse, we are able to get my husband back to his hospital room safely.

I wait outside his room while nursing care is given, and the nurses wash him and change his clothes.

The nurses come out of the room and I enter. Dave looks very comfortable, is fully alert and is doing exceptionally well.

Alone in the hospital room with my husband, I pull up a chair close to the side of his bed and take his hand in mine, as I sit quietly with him. My husband is lying on his back with the head of the bed raised approximately to a 45-degree angle, looking straight ahead, and looking very peaceful.

He then turns his head towards me, moves his head upward to the right, and rolls his eyes in the same direction. "They wanted me to go with them but I told them no, because I couldn't leave you."

I am in complete awe and am unable to utter a word!

"Ol, they wanted me to leave you, did you know that?"

"You said good-bye to me, so I knew you could be leaving me."

"I only said good-bye to you because I thought I had to go."

"And you didn't have to go?"

"No, because I told them I didn't want to go with them because I wasn't leaving you."

As I dry my tears, my husband continues.

"They were dressed in all black, Ol."

"How many were there?"

"Two." He then smiles at me with tears in his eyes, squeezes my hand, and says in a very soft and loving voice, "Ol, I love you."

"I love you too, darling." I know all too well, what his words imply. I know at that moment that Dave's love for me is so powerful that he will never allow others to come for him and take him against his will. His love for me gave him the will to stay on the Earth much longer. His determination to remain by my side is much stronger than his will to go with the souls from the Other Side.

As I wipe away my tears, I thank God for allowing him to stay by my side. I pray in silence, "Heavenly Father, I love you so much and I truly know that You love me. Thank you for not allowing Dave to be taken against his will." God recognizes my husband's devoted and endless love for me and He has answered my prayers. My Heavenly Father loves us dearly. I know deep down in my soul that my husband and I are truly blessed.

My husband's life as he had known it is shattered, and although I know he is truly grateful to be alive, he is struggling with the road he is going down, which could very easily lead to depression. As the days move by slowly, my husband's condition is still not improving for he is still experiencing "episodes." After being given numerous medical tests and after several medical consultants have examined my husband, there is still no diagnosis. We are all perplexed and especially the medical team.

It is during this time that our minister, Reverend Bob Rowland, visits and speaks with Dave, to help him unravel the mystery regarding his condition. It is no time at all before my husband has the most incredible insight regarding his health. Reverend Rowland prays with my husband and recites to him a quote. The quote taken from the Holy Bible: Matthew 19: 4-6: *And he answered and said unto them, Have ye not read, that he which made them at the beginning made them male and female, And said, For this cause shall a man leave father and mother, and shall cleave to his wife: and they twain shall be one flesh? Wherefore they are no more twain, but one flesh. What therefore God hath joined together, let not man put asunder.*

The recital of the prayer releases a flood of tears, which sent my husband the message that he needs to make changes in his life. The minister continues speaking to him and asks him to remember his wedding vows, taken from the *Book of Common Prayer: ...according to God's ordinance in the holy estate of Matrimony? Wilt thou love her, comfort her, honour, and keep her, in sickness and in health; and, forsaking all other, keep thee only unto her, so long as you both shall live?*

Reverend Rowland then recites another quote from Mark 6:11, in the Holy Bible: *And whosoever shall not receive you, nor hear you, when ye depart thence, shake off the dust under your feet for a testimony against them.* It is at this moment my husband is able to look at his problems from a spiritual point of view, which gives him tremendous insight and clarity. He completely understands the problems and issues that had persisted for years. And amazingly, a remarkable change comes over him. He is at peace, and not only is he at peace, but the episodes completely stop!

My husband's tragic car accident was a blessing in disguise; and the month of hospitalization provided him with an excellent opportunity for reflection and revaluation of his life. He now felt empowered and achieved exceptional clarity, which enabled him to express himself as he could never before. He now has a completely different outlook on life. He became a changed person; however, he knows that some people will never choose to change for the better, no matter what the circumstances.

The days that follow prove to be quite amazing. Some days later, I walk into his hospital room to find my husband quite elated and anxious to see me. He starts by saying, "Ol, I need to talk to you."

"Okay," I reply.

"Ol, are you ready for this?"

"I don't know, ready for what?"

"Ol, the most exciting thing has happened to me."

I can see he has become even more anxious, to the point of becoming excited. "What has happened to you that is so fantastic? Is it that you now enjoy the hospital food?"

He laughs. "No, that's not it, and it's far more extraordinary than that."

"What could possibly be more extraordinary than that?" I jokingly ask.

He looks at me with such an expression of excitement on his face. "Ol, I floated high above my body, so high that I was able to look down and see myself lying in the hospital bed!"

I am speechless and dumbfounded, as I stare at my husband.

"Ol, I know all of this sounds really crazy but this really happened to me."

"No, it doesn't sound really crazy. Are you forgetting my experience of travelling out of my body that cold December night?"

"Yes, actually, I had forgotten but I do remember it now."

"And it is not crazy because I know about out-of-body experiences happening to people who have been declared dead."

"Well, I'm not dead."

Now both of us are laughing as I listen intently because he really has my attention.

"Ol, I floated out of my body and out of the bed and floated to the ceiling of the room!"

"When did this happen?"

"A short while ago before you came."

"You actually floated out of your body?"

"Yes, I actually floated out of my body! I could see everything and I could hear everything!"

"What could you see?"

"At different times, I could see the nurse coming in my room to check on me, while my body was lying in the bed."

"Did she say anything?"

"Not to me, but as she was leaving, I could hear her talking to someone outside my room."

I retrieve a tissue from the box on the nightstand and wipe a tear that has trickled down his face as he continues. "I have drawings I want to show you. I want you to understand what has been happening to me. I drew these sketches to help me explain to you how I would suddenly have a sensation of leaving my body, and find myself at the top of the ceiling, looking down into my hospital room. I could see my body in the hospital bed, even though I knew I was watching from above!"

In utter amazement, I stare at the hand drawn sketch. It is remarkable! I have no doubt in my mind what my husband is telling me is true.

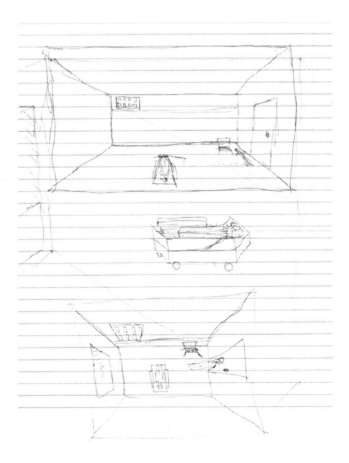

"That's not all."

"It's not?" I question with an excitement I am unable to control.

"No, it's not. I understand now that I am in an Automobile Trauma Recovery Program and I fully understand why."

"When did you realize this?"

"I realized this last evening, shortly after you left. I wrote everything down, so I could show you." He then passes me a paper, which has the following outline:

Automobile Trauma Recovery Program ~ Mon. May 7—
Thurs. May 17
Mon. May 7/2001 1st day of Program
Tues. May 8/2001 2nd day of Program
Tues. May 15/2001 Measured for Body Brace
Wed. May 16/2001 at about 9:30pm! (Understood the meaning of Program)
Thurs. May 17/2001 waiting to be fitted with Body Brace

The meaning of the Program is as follows:

- Reinstating to the basics of life

- Living with the everyday pleasures of life

- Learning to appreciate the helpfulness of others

- Learning to be there for others at their special time of need

- Learning how to deal with family issues & concerns

- Doing God's Will

- Do unto others, as you would like them to do unto you

My husband's car accident did not occur until after midnight on May 7, which would make it May 8, however, from the note that he has written to me, it clearly states that the first day of the Program started on May 7.

Floating out of his body and being able to view his body as well as his hospital room has had profound consequences for him. He now views life from a completely different perspective. I know deep inside he struggles with the meaning of everything that has transpired, yet I also know that he is at peace and he is learning valuable life lessons. He understands that everything that has happened to him was meant to be; and that he is supposed to learn many lessons; but more importantly, he has the gift of spiritual awareness.

On June 6, after a long month of waiting, my husband's doctor discharged him from the hospital, allowing him to travel to our house by ambulance because he cannot sit. On doctor's orders, he is allowed to sit for twenty minutes out of a twenty-four hour period, while wearing his body brace. He also has to wear a foot brace on his left foot. Months later, he was able to walk using a walker while still wearing his body brace, and then able to use crutches, and finally walk on his own, but still wearing his body brace.

My husband relaxing in his chair with Katie

Just a week later, after my husband arrived home from the hospital, he celebrated his birthday with all our close family and friends in attendance. It was a time for celebrating and we all celebrated with love and joy in our hearts, and thankful to our Creator for all His blessings bestowed upon us.

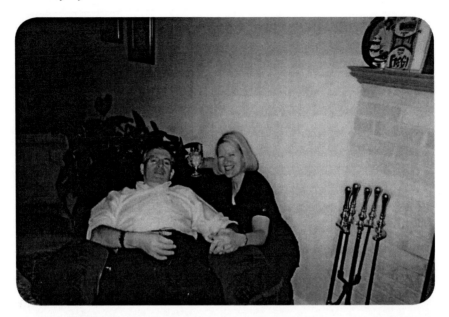

My husband and I celebrating his birthday, after his car accident

My husband has not been home from the hospital for two months, when a letter arrives in the mail. Just a couple of months prior, I had visited my friend Beth and during that visit, she told me to write a letter. I recall the conversation that I had with Beth at the time. "Your Aunt Mildred says that you have to make changes around the situation, and one of the changes is to write the letter." Now I know what letter it is I have to write. It is all crystal clear. It is my Guardian Soul, my Aunt Mildred, who has guided me through this ordeal and with a loving and a grateful heart, I sincerely thank her.

As the days go by and my husband is recuperating at home, he continues to improve in every manner. Not only is he improving physically, but he is also becoming more spiritual. It is during his time at home, he requests to read my manuscript, which I have been working on for quite some time, and the profound impact that my writing has on him is overwhelming. He feels a deep sense of shame for not taking the time and interest to read it while I was actually writing it. He can now relate to the spiritual world and knows the rewards of being a loving, caring, and compassionate person, and for some miraculous reason he has the ability to communicate on a different kind of level, a much higher level, a spiritual level. He is able to rise up to the level that I have been on for so long. He tells me that this is the first time that he can ever remember that he feels comfortable talking about topics that I enjoy, things he had always tried to avoid, change the topic, or just plain sit there and say nothing. Now he truly feels that there has been a definite change within him for this to happen, and it makes him feel much, much happier and at peace.

He knows he has a lot to be thankful for and is truly grateful. He knows now what I mean when I say that the hands of God are guiding me. He now believes that the hands of God, whom he dearly loves as well, are also guiding him. He says he remembers me saying so often, God is guiding the path I am travelling, and he firmly believes this to be the same for him. Because of everything that has transpired, he has a completely new outlook on living life.

After the tragic car accident, my husband has greater insight. The car accident changed his life for the better. He knows he has learned many valuable life lessons. I also learned many life lessons; one lesson being that my husband is not a complainer. Not once during the month of his hospital stay, and not once during his full year of recovery, did I ever hear him complain or make a negative comment of any kind. He took everything in his stride. I knew deep down he did not want to cause any extra burden on me or our children. I witnessed his perseverance, even when he was lying in bed and needed to go to the bathroom during the middle of the night. He never called out to me for help, but instead tried to put on his body brace himself in order for him to get out of bed. I heard him and got out of bed to check on him, and found him determined to do it himself because he did not want to disturb me from my sleep.

Still perplexed regarding the cause of my husband's accident, I wanted more answers and so I made an appointment with my friend Jack. Jack, who uses his gift of psychic abilities, confirmed that he could see Dave driving along the highway, listening to the music, and enjoying the drive, but it ended in disaster. He could see the accident happening and that at the time of impact, my husband thought of me. He said he did not fall asleep, and even though it was late at night, he was not sleepy, but he experienced a sharp pain in his head, and he lost control of his car because he pressed on the gas pedal, thinking it was the brake. It was then he experienced a blackout and lost control of his car, and his car flipped repeatedly, and crashed. Jack said he could see the demolished car, and he was surprised my husband lived. He said he could see it being such a terrible accident and that he could have died. He told me they had to saw the door off in order to get him out and that he could see that he had injuries, and that his back and one of his legs were broken. Jack said he could see the horseshoe in my reading and the horseshoe is upside down. I asked what this means and he told me that the horseshoe means good luck, but because it is upside down, I still have good luck; however, I have to go through difficult times.

My husband allowed his tragic car accident to foster positive changes in his life and consequently, it has been a positive experience for him and for us as a family. I truly believe that the car accident my husband encountered was all part of his life plan, and was really a blessing in disguise. It was something he had to go through in order to move forward, and he seized the opportunity to enhance his life in a more positive and loving way.

Looking back, I can clearly see that I responded in shock; however, I never did cry out in anger, to ask why. It seemed to me that this was all part of what we had to go through as a family and that we would deal with it all to the best of our ability. It was a long and arduous journey and not only did we overcome, but as a family, the traumatic experience of my husband's car accident and all the events leading up to his accident, and all the events following his accident, made us stronger than ever.

I have truly come to realize that living life here on Earth is about learning life lessons, and as I reflect on everything that has transpired since my husband's car accident, I know I have learned many. After encountering such an ordeal as a tragic car accident, I have learned that life is full of surprises and not always, what one would expect. An unexpected tragedy allows a person either to rise above the tragedy or to smother in it. Tragedies have destroyed marriages and families. I feel that with any tragic event in life, a family can move farther away from one another or move closer together. We moved closer together. The accident has made us all even stronger as a family, and especially my husband, for he is now stronger spiritually. The life-shattering experience gave us a completely different outlook on life, and we have risen above it all. We were close as a family before the car accident, but now I realize we are even closer. The deep, strong bond of love we have for one another, will never be severed, and will remain for all eternity.

CHAPTER 13

Soul Visitors

Be not forgetful to entertain strangers:
for thereby some have entertained angels unawares.

The Holy Bible: Hebrews 13:2
King James Version

The true gift of laughter comes from mutual respect and love and with the sharing of respect and love, comes joy. One such time in my life was when my friend Julie and I took a trip together. Julie wanted to take a vacation and asked me if I wanted to go with her. It did not take me long to decide because I really felt I needed a break. When she told me the date we would be leaving, the 28, I just chuckled to myself. I had realized for quite some time that anything of importance in my life occurs with my special numbers. I feel it is right to take this trip and now the date has confirmed it for me. I chuckle once again when I receive my airline ticket. The flight number is Air Canada 8826! Here are my numbers again!

We meet at the airport, check in and board the plane. Our flight is enjoyable as we chat and laugh all the way. We enjoy ourselves so much we lose track of the time, and it seems like no time before the flight attendant is preparing us for the landing. We get our luggage and Julie rents a car. Off we head to our hotel. It is an older hotel, very posh and elegant. We have both stayed here before many times and we both love it.

Our room is a suite and upon entering the room from the hallway, you enter the sitting area. The sitting area has a sofa, desk and chair, television, round coffee table in the middle of the room, and a mini-bar. There are two

windows, one on each wall overlooking the side and front of the grounds of
the hotel. Off the sitting area is a door, which opens directly through a short
hallway, which contains a clothes closet. Off the short hallway is another
door, which opens and leads into the bedroom. The bedroom contains two
queen size beds, a television, and a large dresser. There is one window in
the bedroom, which also overlooks the front grounds. Off the bedroom is
a door, which takes you into the bathroom. It is a typical bathroom, also
with a window overlooking the front grounds of the hotel.

Julie and I unpack and then go down to the dining room to have
our dinner. We find it very relaxing because the décor is very elegant
while the atmosphere is very warm. We find the service excellent and
the food delicious. We return to our room and decide we will spend the
remainder of the evening relaxing.

Around midnight we decide it is time for bed. Julie usually finds it
difficult falling to sleep and so she decides to get a blanket and pillow,
lie on the sofa and watch television, and hopefully fall off to sleep. She
says she will sleep there all night if she feels comfortable, and that she is
going to set the television timer to turn off the TV automatically around
2 A.M. I close both doors; the one off the sitting area and the one off
the bedroom because I know the sound from the television could keep
me awake. I get into bed and quickly fall off to sleep. Julie likes to get
up early in the mornings, but I like to sleep in and so we made plans to
meet in the dining room for lunch.

We meet in the dining room as planned and order lunch. We start
chatting, with Julie starting with the comment, "Olive, what were you
doing last night? You were making so much noise!"

"What do you mean?"

"You were up, going around the room. You were making so much
noise, you woke me."

"What are you talking about?"

"You woke me with all the noise you were making, it was so loud. I
got up and went in the bedroom to see what you were doing. I then got
in bed."

With this comment, I start to laugh. "Julie, I'll tell you right now, I
was not up going around the bedroom last night at all. As a matter of
fact, I didn't get out of bed not once, not even to go to the bathroom."

By this time Julie is laughing. "Olive, you had to have been up because I could hear you in the bedroom moving around!"

"If there was anyone up going around our bedroom, making a noise, it definitely was not me! By the way, when you came into the bedroom, where did you find me?"

"I found you in bed."

"Was I awake?"

"You had your eyes closed; you looked like you were asleep." I could tell by the expression on Julie's face that she understood the intent of my questions, and instantly broke into a fit of laughter, with me following right behind.

That evening after dinner, we decide to go to a movie. There is a movie playing based on a true story, *The Widow of St. Pierre*. It is playing at the old Majestic Theatre and we are both delighted to go because we love this theatre; it brings back such wonderful memories of when we were children, while visiting Corner Brook. We love the movie. We then return to the hotel and relax in the sitting room. It is almost midnight, we are tired, and so we decide it is time for bed. Julie decides she will sleep in the bedroom this night. We both prepare for bed and snuggle in, she has her bed and I have mine. Our plan for the next day would be the same. We would meet in the dining room for lunch.

The waiter takes our order and we start chatting. I begin by saying, "Julie, you're not going to believe this, but last night I woke up because I thought you were up, going around the room. You were making a lot of noise and you woke me." By this time, I am laughing and I have Julie laughing.

"What do you mean, you thought I was up?"

"I heard someone in the room making a noise. The noise woke me. I thought it was you. I looked around the room for you but I could not see you. I then looked over in your bed, and there you were asleep!" By this time, we are both laughing hysterically, and Julie has to compose herself, by having to leave the table and go to the washroom. Upon her return, we both desperately try to compose ourselves, knowing that we are making a spectacle of ourselves because others in the dining room are staring at us.

"Julie, I couldn't believe it! What or who woke me up, I do not know. I know it wasn't you because you were asleep, I could tell by your breathing. I felt there was someone in the room with us." By this time, I have to retrieve a tissue from my handbag to wipe my eyes because I am laughing so much that the tears are flowing down my cheeks. Julie is also hysterical with laughter.

That evening, we had reservations made at the Wine Cellar. We dressed early and went to the lounge to have drinks, before going to the restaurant. I wanted to treat Julie to dinner but she insisted on treating me. We both love the Wine Cellar and this night is no exception; we are having a wonderful time. Our table, situated on the far wall with a window just above it, is perfect. It is October and we are excited about Christmas coming. We talk about going shopping the next day. We were just starting dinner when I looked out the window and I could see it was snowing. I was so excited! It is the first snowfall for the year and we are definitely now in the Christmas shopping spirit. When I tell Julie it is snowing, she looks out the window and as she does, she declares, "Oh my, I just had a déjà vu."

"What do you mean you just had a déjà vu?" I know Julie has experienced déjà vu other times over the years, and now she is experiencing it once again.

She answers, "A sense of déjà vu just came over me and that all of this is very familiar to me, in every aspect. It is as though we have done this before, right down to the very detail."

Because she is experiencing déjà vu, I know we are in the right place at the right time. We are doing exactly what we are supposed to be doing. We are on the proper course of our chosen paths, and this makes our evening that much more special.

It is again around midnight and we are both very tired. We prepare for bed and snuggle in once again. Julie decides she is going to try to go to sleep in the bed rather than go out onto the sofa. We both go off to sleep very quickly. I am asleep for some time; however, I wake up because Julie is snoring, and she is snoring so very loudly. I call her name and she answers. I tell her she is snoring and to turn on her side. She says she is not snoring and that she is already on her side. I try to go back to sleep again, but it is no time when I can hear Julie snoring again. This time I think it best not to disturb her. I do not want her to be tired, by not having a good night's sleep. Our plan once again is to meet each other in the dining room for lunch the next day.

We decide what we are going to have to eat and order.

Julie starts the conversation. "Olive, I must have been doing a lot of snoring last night. I didn't know that I snore when I am sleeping."

"No, you didn't snore that much. First, I woke you and I told you to get on your side. Shortly after I heard you snoring again, but it wasn't for very long."

"Well, even if it wasn't for very long, it must have been really loud because I kept you awake," Julie replies.

"No, you didn't keep me awake."

"Sure you even came over to my bed and dug your finger into my shoulder and whispered to me to stop snoring!"

Well, by now we are both hilariously laughing.

"Julie! I didn't get out of bed and go over to you and dig my finger into your shoulder, and tell you to stop snoring!"

"Olive, you did! You dug your finger into my shoulder. You used this finger," and she proceeds to demonstrate.

We are both laughing so much we can hardly get the words out, and we are both finding it difficult to breathe.

"I'm telling you, I definitely did not get out of bed and go over and dig my finger into your shoulder! As a matter of fact, I slept right through the night."

"I'm telling you, Olive, you did," Julie insists.

"I'm telling you right now, if someone took her finger and dug it into your shoulder, it definitely was not me. I don't know who it was, but it was not me!" Once again, we are laughing so much we find it difficult to eat our lunch, and once again, we have the staff and other guests in the dining room staring at us in complete awe.

After I give it some thought, I wonder why I would be whispering to Julie to stop snoring, if she already had me awake!

CHAPTER 14

Living On Borrowed Time

Who can say where the road goes,
Where the day flows, only time.
Who knows? Only time.
Who knows? Only time.

Enya
Only Time

While vacationing in Corner Brook in October, I indulged in one of my favorite past times, shopping; and in particular, shopping at bookstores. I purchased books of interest and when I returned home, I placed my newly purchased books on one of the shelves in my personal library in our study. I love to read and therefore always like to have a supply of reading material waiting for me. I usually read more than one book at a time and I usually have other books sitting, waiting for me. I am always buying books. I need the comfort of knowing that there is another book waiting for me to read. To put it into perspective, it is the same as most people making sure they never run out of milk or bread. For many people, milk and bread are staple foods for the body, which most people eat every day; to me, books are staple foods for the soul, which I have to read every day.

It is now January and many of my newly purchased books are still in my personal library on the shelf, waiting for me. The Christmas season has kept me quite busy and I did not have time to do as much reading as I normally do. However, it is evening time and for no apparent reason, I go to the study and finger through the books on my shelf, and strangely enough, I am drawn to one particular book: *Over-Coming the Over-Whelming: How To Turn Adversity Into Success* by Charles King. I pull the book off the shelf and turn to the "Foreword." The first sentence starts with the words: *On March 6, 1988, the doctors told Charles King he only had six months to live...* Amazingly, here are my numbers 6 and 8, once again in my life! As I stare at my spiritual numbers, I know right away that this book holds some important message for me.

I finger through to the contents page and I stare at Chapter 8, which seems to stand out from all the other chapters. Again, I am looking at one of my spiritual numbers, the number 8! I return to the family room, sit on the sofa, and immediately finger through to Chapter 8, entitled: *Epilogue: Yea Though I Walk...* My eyes can hardly believe what it is I am reading! I am all too aware of this particular quote coming from Psalms 23:4, in the Holy Bible: *Yea, though I walk through the valley of the shadow of death, I will fear no evil: for thou art with me; thy rod and thy staff they comfort me.* I continue reading. *In light of the dismal prognosis, it was very apparent that my hope was clearly in the hands of God.*

Before I had started to read this book, my thoughts were focused on my husband's health, and how I felt he was seriously ill, but the tests ordered by the different doctors did not reveal anything. It has now been eight months since his tragic car accident, and by all accounts, he seems to be doing quite well. He has been seeing Dr. Guy Hogan on a regular basis since his discharge from the hospital, and he has been cooperating, especially when it comes to his routine care, including following the doctors' orders. Yet, I feel overwhelmed by the contents of this chapter in the book, and I am becoming emotional. It occurs to me that someone is trying to tell me something important.

I need to speak with my Guardian Soul. I have come to realize that I have two Guardian Souls watching over me at all times, one being my Uncle Edward and the other being my Aunt Mildred. I have also come to realize that they never come together, but they each come alone and always when the other one leaves, the other comes. They switch places every three days, so after Uncle Edward has been with me for three days, he leaves and Aunt Mildred returns. The switch always takes place during the night while I am sleeping. It took me a while to figure out that this was happening every three days. So here I am feeling I need to speak with either Uncle Edward or Aunt Mildred, knowing that one of them is with me, and if I have calculated right, Uncle Edward should be with me now. Therefore, I begin the conversation by asking, "Uncle Edward, are you here?"

I get an immediate reply. "Yes, I am here."

"Uncle Edward, do you know that I have been drawn to read this book by Charles King, entitled, *Over-Coming the Over-Whelming: How To Turn Adversity Into Success*?"

"Yes, my dear."

"Is it you who wants me to read this book?"

"Yes."

"Is it because the information contained in this book will allow me to understand Dave's medical problem?"

"Yes."

"Thank you, Uncle Edward. I will read this book and see if I am able to understand Dave's medical condition."

Uncle Edward replies, "Yes, please go ahead and read this book."

I have come to realize that I could very easily ask Uncle Edward to give me the message that I am supposed to learn, however, I know in the past, my Guardian Souls have made it quite clear to me that I need to figure out things on my own. And so, I sit comfortably in my chair in the family room and read. As I read, I understand that I need to pursue further medical consultation and request further testing, in particular an MRI for my husband. I also know that if further testing reveals that my husband does have a serious medical condition; it is indeed in God's hands. I know that if it is finally Dave's time to return Home, then I cannot stand in the way. I also know that if God believes that it would be in the best interests for all for Dave to remain here on Earth, He will cure him, even if the doctors feel they cannot do anything. I know it is in my power, through my Heavenly Father, to have Dave healed. Time will tell all.

I am hoping that the CAT scan will provide me with the answers I desperately need. It is now Wednesday, January 16, and I have to take my husband to St. Clare's Mercy Hospital for his appointment for the CAT scan. I have my doubts whether or not we are able to keep his appointment because it is snowing heavily and the winds are high.

However, with the guidance from my Guardian Soul, we arrive safely and my husband has his CAT scan procedure completed. As we leave the hospital, we realize it is still very stormy outside, but knowing I have Uncle Edward with me, I feel safe driving the car and eventually we arrive back home safely.

A week has passed and I am eagerly waiting for the long awaited answers to my questions regarding my husband's medical condition. I have to take my husband for his return check-up visit with his orthopedic surgeon, Dr. Guy Hogan. It is always a pleasure to see Dr. Hogan, and every time I see this man, I think about how much he has done to help us restore our lives back to normal.

Dr. Hogan is so pleased to give us some good news. With a big smile on his face, he tells us that the CAT scan results are normal and that Dave is now well enough to return to work on an "ease back program." My husband is holding my hand and I can feel him squeezing it. His instruction is for Dave to start at a maximum of four hours a day or at a shorter period, according to his level of tolerance. We think about it, and with Dr. Hogan's approval, we decide for Dave to return to work on "ease back" for a period of two to four hours a day, according to his tolerance level, for three days per week. The other terrific news that Dr. Hogan shares with us is that Dave can now drive the car! My husband's driving license had been revoked following the car accident, and now Dr. Hogan is pleased to inform us that his driving license has been reinstated and he can start driving the car whenever he feels up to it.

Later in the evening, I sit and anxiously wait for a telephone call from my parents in Florida. The thought is no sooner in my mind when the telephone rings. As my son picks up the receiver, I know without a doubt it is the call I have been waiting for. Sure enough, by the conversation my son is having, I know it is my father speaking to him. After my son is finished, he passes the receiver to me, and I gladly take it. "Hello, Dad."

I am so happy to hear the loving voice of my father. "Hello, my doll, how are you doing?"

Without giving it much thought, I quickly reply, "I am doing okay."

We continue our conversation by answering questions on how we are all doing, and in particular Dave. I also question how he is doing because I know his medical condition is getting worse. So I ask, "How are you doing, Dad?"

If there is one thing that I have learned about my father over the years, it is that he is an honest person and not a complainer. No matter how difficult things may get for him, he is not the type to complain or to make a fuss. In addition, I know that the last thing he wants to do is to cause me worry. He is by no means a selfish or self-centered person, and only wants what is best. He is always so friendly with people, and has a way of making other people feel special by greeting them with such a warm welcome. I admire my dad and I love him very much.

Unfortunately, during the last five years of my father's life, he has suffered a lot from arthritis in his hip and he finds it extremely difficult to walk and get around. Whenever I would be in his company, I could tell he was suffering with great pain; however, his only comment would be, 'Oh my, oh my, oh my.' Diagnosed also with congestive heart failure, at times, his life seems unbearable due to the pain and the difficulty he has breathing. Nevertheless, he always tries his best to be positive and upbeat. I can recall many times when he would say, 'No matter how hard I have it, there's always someone else who has it harder.' I know my father still does not feel very well but as always, he tries to sound upbeat and honest in his answer. "Fair, I'm doing fair."

I can feel the tears fill my eyes, as I pause. My heart feels so heavy. Two of the three main men in my life, whom I love with all my heart, are very sick and I feel so helpless. Without letting my father know, I am feeling so down, I quickly change the topic by telling him about the good news that Dr. Hogan has given us during our recent visit. "Dave is now allowed to drive the car again and he has been given permission by Dr. Hogan to start back to work on an "ease back program," starting this week."

I can sense the relief by the tone of my father's voice and that he is becoming emotional upon hearing our good news. "I am so happy to know that Dave is finally allowed to drive the car, and that he is able to start back to work. My doll, Dad is some glad to hear this."

"This is great news, isn't it, Dad?"

"Yes, it certainly is great news. I am happy to hear this news."

"I know you are, Dad."

"Where is Dave? I'd like to talk to him."

"Dave is lying on top of his bed, asleep."

My father comments with a sad tone in his voice, "Okay, my doll, I'll talk to him another time." He then says, "Your mother wants to speak with you."

I recognize my mother's voice. "Hello there."

"Hello, how are you doing, Mom?"

"I'm doing the best I can."

"I have some good news." I continue to tell my mother the same news I had told my father.

My mother is very elated to hear this news. "This is really good news, but are you sure Dave is really up to all of this? It won't be too much for him, will it?"

"I don't really know. I do trust Dr. Hogan, but as you know, he is an orthopedic surgeon and not a medical specialist. I have been bringing Dave to see Dr. Raman who, as you know, is a medical specialist and one of the best."

"Yes, I know Dr. Raman is one of the best because Dr. Raman is also one of your father's doctors."

We continue talking but now our focus of conversation is about my father. "How is Dad doing?"

"He is not improving."

There is silence as I am not able to speak. The silence breaks by my mother telling me that my father is experiencing the same signs and symptoms as he did a week ago. "He is still having difficulty breathing. He is short of breath most of the time."

My response is, "Dad doesn't sound very well."

She answers, "No, he's not."

My father has been quite sick, but he has always bounced back and the doctors are amazed at his recovery each time. Yet, the signs and symptoms my mother has just described to me are an indication that my father's medical condition is very serious and it appears to me he is experiencing heart failure. We all know there is nothing more that can be done medically; however, I know when the end comes, Dad would rather be back in Canada in the hometown where he was born and lived all his life than be in Florida.

She continues. "Dad wanted to call all the girls and he called you first."

I am somewhat stunned by this comment. "Why does Dad want to call all of us?"

"I asked your father the same question and his answer was that later on, he may not be able to phone all of you. He wanted to do it now."

Once again, I can feel the tears fill my eyes, as I understand all too well, what is being implied by my mother's words.

Before I end our phone call, I can hear my father in the background speaking to my mother. "Tell Olive to call us later in the week and to let us know how Dave made out driving the car and back to work."

Mom repeats what Dad said and I answer, "Yes I will." We say our good-byes.

I hang up the receiver and go to the bathroom to try to compose myself because I do not want my husband waking up and finding me so upset. Through sobs of despair, I come to the realization that there is really nothing in my control. It is like a light bulb going off in my head, as I understand that as a human, I have very little control over matters in my life! I realize that it is all in God's hands, and I have to follow to the best of my ability. The only thing that I know I can do is to pray. I have to pray to my Heavenly Father to make me strong and to be able to cope with what life is throwing at me. I know God will not forsake me and I know He will answer my prayers in the way that He sees what is best for me, at this time in my life.

Since that telephone call, I have been trying to understand everything my mother has been telling me. If there is one thing I have learned in recent years, is to listen to my feelings and the information presented to me. I feel I need to get the opinions of my sisters and we will decide whether we feel we should contact our parents and to make suggestions. This is a difficult situation because I do not want to cause undue worry and stress, especially for my mother and father; however, I also know that it would be extremely difficult for my mother if my father died in Florida. She would have to deal with all the necessary arrangements to get them both back to Canada, even though I know that some family members would go to Florida to help her. I am still getting the strong feeling that I need to prepare and to go where my thoughts and feelings are taking me. I feel I have to be strong because I do not know what else is in store for me.

At different times over the coming weeks, I would ask my husband if he was ready to drive the car once again, and his answer was always "no." However, today he tells me he is ready and today is May 8! It is not the ideal time considering the ice and snow conditions of the streets. In hindsight, I realize I was more nervous than my husband was. He did wonderful. We arrive back home safely and as he steers the car into our driveway, I quietly thank God for keeping us safe. It is a great milestone, not just because of his physical condition but also his mental state. Considering the tragic motor vehicle accident my husband experienced, I know it had to have had an emotional and mental impact on his health.

It is then he tells me he is going out again by himself because he needs to go somewhere. I become apprehensive and question his motives. He tells me he promised himself that he would do something for me to show his love and appreciation for all I have done for him. A short time later, he arrives back home with five sweetheart red roses arranged in baby's breath. He kisses me, hugs me, and tells me how much he loves me, and thanks me for everything. Tears fill his eyes and mine. The card with the roses reads: *I Love You Ol; I could never have recovered without you. I love you all the world. xxx ooo xxx Dave.* My husband also explains to me that each rose stands for each word: *Ol, I love you, Dave.*

Life seems good to us now, or so I think. It has only been a few days and I am upset and concerned because now for some unknown reason, my roses are not blooming! The roses are starting to droop, showing that they were once so gorgeous and so full of life but now they are dying a slow death. I do not want to throw them out because they were given with so much love, but I feel so sad when I look at them. In my mind, I am wondering if this is a sign from a loving soul from the Other Side. I have been concerned about my husband's complete recovery and now I am concerned that these roses are a sign to help me to prepare, but prepare for what?

I know my Aunt Mildred is supposed to be here with me and I have to speak with her because I am so concerned. I need her to help me understand what is happening. With a voice that is heavy laden with sorrow, I ask, "Aunt Mildred, are you here with me?"

"Yes, Olive, I am right here by you."

"Aunt Mildred, my roses are dying. Does this have any meaning?"

"Yes, it does."

"Are you trying to tell me something?"

"Yes, I am."

With this, I sense the feeling of sorrow to come. "Aunt Mildred, is it concerning Dave?"

"Yes, Olive, it is."

"I sense Dave is not as healthy and well as he appears, is this correct?"

"Yes, this is correct."

"Aunt Mildred, do I have to face impending bad news regarding Dave's health?"

"Yes, you do. You have to get prepared."

"Prepared for what?"

"Time will tell all, my dear."

"I feel I really need a break, Aunt Mildred."

There is only silence. After what seems like minutes, she questions, "What kind of a break?"

"I am thinking of staying a couple of days in Toronto with my daughter and from there I intend going to Florida."

She questions me by asking, "Do you think you should leave Dave?"

I quickly reply, "The CAT scan results came back normal and you know my son is at home with him and he has no problem with me leaving for a week. He says he knows I need a break."

Again, there is silence. Finally my Aunt Mildred speaks. "Yes, I am already aware of the CAT scan results and this is indeed good news."

"Yes it is, but I am still concerned even though the CAT scan came back normal. There still seems something that is just not right."

"You can only take one day at a time."

"Yes, I know you're right but I am concerned, so much so, I have asked Dr. Raman's secretary to make another appointment for Dave. I told her I would like an MRI done. She said she would wait and hear back from Dr. Raman and then would get Dave back in as soon as she can."

Aunt Mildred responds, "Yes, my dear, I know."

"Aunt Mildred, while I am waiting to hear back from Dr. Raman, I would really like to take a break."

The reply I get from my Guardian Soul is not one that I am expecting. "I am going to give you my advice."

"Yes, please, I truly appreciate you with me and guiding me to do what is right and loving."

"I feel that this is not a good time for you to leave Dave."

Surprised by this comment because I do not understand her motive, I reply, "Aunt Mildred, I really could do with a break."

"This is not a good time for you to leave home."

"I don't understand what it is you are really saying."

"I am saying you shouldn't leave Dave right now. I can see where Dave appears to be doing fairly well but I feel it is best to wait a couple of weeks and I will then know more."

"What do you mean, wait a couple of weeks?"

"You need to wait a couple of weeks, the time is not right."

"What do you mean, the time is not right?"

She quickly gives the same answer. "The time is not right. Leave everything alone. You should not request an MRI. It is not time."

Now I am somewhat shocked by her comment. "What do you mean, I shouldn't request an MRI?"

"It is too early for an MRI."

"How can it be too early for an MRI? This doesn't make any sense to me."

"You should not interfere with what is meant to be." After a short pause, my Guardian Soul continues. "You have to wait and take one day at a time. This is best."

As my brain is trying to wrap around the words my Aunt Mildred has spoken, my only response is silence.

My Guardian Soul says, "I can see Dave becoming depressed."

"Depressed?"

"Yes, I can see Dave getting depressed and the main reason why he is starting to get down is because at times he feels so tired and has very little energy, and the one thing that is bothering him is that he is concerned about you."

I can now feel the tears fill my eyes. "Aunt Mildred, this is now making sense to me because I know what you are saying about Dave is true. Most of the time he seems so tired."

"I can see this and he worries because he doesn't want to give you any added burden."

I wipe away my tears at the realization of what my Aunt Mildred is saying is true. I know my husband is not a complainer and I know that the last thing he would want to do is to give me more responsibility and worry. I listen intently to what my Guardian Soul is saying. "Okay, Aunt Mildred."

"In two more weeks, you will know one way or the other what you have to face."

"What does this mean?"

"My dear, it means exactly what I have said."

I feel so emotionally drained by the words my Guardian Soul has expressed to me, the only thing I can say is, "Aunt Mildred, I feel I have to go and rest."

"Yes, please rest. You need your strength."

It is days later and I have decided I need to go and see my family doctor, Dr. David Hart. As I get into the car and sit behind the steering wheel, I look up and directly in front of me, sitting right in the middle of the roof of our neighbor's house, is a "black crow." I am all too aware of the old saying regarding crows, one for sorrow and two for joy. Now here I am sitting in my car with one crow looking down at me! I just stare at it and it stares right back. The thought comes to me that Dr. Hart will give me information that will add pieces to the puzzle, but will also upset me.

Seated in Dr. Hart's office and crying because I am so concerned regarding my husband's health, I explain my husband's signs and symptoms, and my fear of abdominal complications. Even though the

CAT scan came back negative, I know that it is possible the results are not totally revealing the truth.

Dr. Hart confirms my suspicion and explains to me that it is possible there could be a medical problem regarding the pancreas. He proceeds to tell me that if a problem exists in the pancreas, it would be inoperable. This is exactly what I fear. My feelings are telling me that there is a serious medical problem, and unfortunately, the medical tests are not revealing everything. He confirms my concerns by telling me that an MRI is not necessarily going to give us more answers then what the CAT scan has revealed; however, he says he can put in a call to Dr. Raman and see if he recommends an MRI.

He then informs me that the next step he recommends would be a laparoscopy. A laparoscopy is the examination of the abdominal cavity by making a small incision in the abdominal wall, by using an instrument called a laparoscope. I know a laparoscopy should reveal a medical problem but then a laparotomy could be required. A laparotomy is a surgical incision into the peritoneal cavity, usually performed under anesthesia, and done as an exploratory procedure.

After much discussion, Dr. Hart recommends for me to wait and see if my husband's condition improves, and if it doesn't and his condition gets worse, then he will proceed accordingly. Even though I agree with Dr. Hart's recommendations, I fear the truth and any medical intervention may come too late. Still left with the unknown, and in a waiting game, I know I have to be patient. I will wait to see if my husband's condition deteriorates as it did on Christmas Eve and New Year's Eve, and then take the necessary steps. If his condition gets worse and he does not appear to be improving, I will seek medical care once again for him and visit Dr. Hart for further instructions.

Upon my return home, I try to go about my day in as normal a fashion as I can, considering my visit with our family doctor. My thoughts are running wild and I am not able to focus. After much resistance, I finally break down and sob. I feel so downtrodden. I honestly do not know how much more I can take. I know I have to become stronger than I am feeling, so I decide to splash some cold water on my face and reapply my makeup. I do not want my son or husband to know how upset I really am feeling. After calming down, I go down to my kitchen to make some tea.

Standing in front of my kitchen window while talking to my husband, I happen to glance out the window, and to my surprise, straight ahead, is a large, beautiful robin red breast! It is sitting on one of the branches on the tree directly opposite the kitchen window, and it is looking directly at me! It is very unusual to see a robin red breast this time of year because it is wintertime. It has been very cold and frosty with a lot of snow on the ground; and actually, the snow is so high it has reached the top of the fence in our back garden. I immediately tell my husband to look out the window, and as soon as he sees the beautiful bird, it flies away.

As I stare at my husband with great awe, and think that this occurrence is very unusual, I wonder what the date is and so I look at the calendar. It is February 8. As I think about the exquisite robin red breast that visited in my garden, I realize it is a sign of some sort. It has to be a soul sign given to me by a loved one. As I am thinking this thought, I instantly know that this is indeed so, and I know that there is a hidden message for me sent by someone to give me love in this form. With these thoughts, I immediately feel love and protection, and feel someone is sending me love to help me get prepared for something to come. I feel I have to be strong. I realize that Dave and I have an appointment tomorrow to see Dr. Raman in his office. Even though it is Saturday, he is willing to see us. I feel this is a meeting where we will have to make a decision of some sort regarding my husband's medical condition.

My thoughts now quickly go to my father who I know is very sick. I know I have to face the fact that someday soon my father will be leaving me, and I feel his time is ending here on Earth. With a deeply saddened heart, I know I must accept this news with grace and dignity. I cannot be selfish. I know all too well that my father is suffering now too much. Just the thought of my dad being in such an agonizing condition, my soul knows I have to take my troubles to my Father in Heaven in prayer.

CHAPTER 15

The Power of Prayer

And this is the confidence that we have in him,
that, if we ask any thing according to his will, he heareth us:
And if we know that he hear us, whatsoever we ask,
we know that we have the petitions that we desired of him.

The Holy Bible: 1 John 5:14-15
King James Version

Born into a Christian home, the seeds of prayer were planted early for me by my parents, and they have had a lifelong effect. As a small child, I learned that prayers are conversations with God, and to pray meant talking to God, asking Him for His blessings, help, and love, and that God listens to me from Heaven when I pray. I was taught to kneel down by the side of my bed each night; however, over time, I learned that my talks with my Heavenly Father did not necessarily have to be at night on my knees. I could talk to God at any time and in any place. I did not have to be in my house nor did I need to be in a church for I could be indoors or outdoors, in any place I chose. I also learned that I needed only me in order to talk directly to God, for my physical body is my gateway that lays the path of communication directly to God. In addition, I do not require a person such as a minister, rabbi, priest, or any other religious person in order for me to make contact with my Heavenly Father and to speak to Him. And so as a small child, I would say my prayers to God, which included The Lord's Prayer, my blessings for my loved ones to keep them safe, and my special child's prayer which goes like this:

In my little bed I lie,
Heavenly Father hear my cry,
Lord protect me through the night,
Keep me safe 'til morning light. Amen.

I have always believed in the power of prayer so as I grew older I continued to say my prayers. As an adult, however, my prayers changed. I continued to say the Lord's Prayer and the blessings for my loved ones, but now I included prayers to God for all the orphan children, as well as all the children who are suffering in this world.

During my early adult years, I made it a point not to ask God for anything for me. No matter what troubles I was facing, I never asked God for help. My reason for doing this is very simple. My rationale is that God has enough to do to offer blessings to those who are much more unfortunate than I am. Even though I did encounter problems throughout my early adult life, I know I have been very blessed with the life I am living, compared to the life of many other people. My belief is that many others deserve His time and attention more than I do and I feel it would be too selfish of me to ask anything from God. For many years, I prayed in this manner to my Heavenly Father, seeking only help and love from Him for others, never for myself. I also spoke to God in prayer each night before going to sleep, praying, "Dear God, please help me to shine your light of love on everyone that I meet tomorrow."

It was not until later in life that it finally occurred to me that God is all-powerful, that God's love and power is massive, and that He is able to care for all of His children, regardless of their need or circumstances. Therefore, I finally concluded that although it is good of me to be considerate of others and to put others first, it is also important to take care of myself, and so I finally started to pray for myself, as well as to continue to pray for others. As the years go by, I realize my prayers convey great strength and wisdom and that my prayers to my Heavenly Father are very powerful, and that God has always answered my prayers according to His will.

With a deeply saddened and heavy heart, I go to my Heavenly Father in prayer, for I have decided it is time to let my father go. With a strong conviction, I say my prayers and pray to God to take my dad when He knows the time is right. I have always prayed for God to keep my father here longer on Earth; however, I know that this request is being selfish on my part. I love my father too much and deep in my soul, I know I have to do what is best for him and not what is best for me. I fall to my knees and pray to my Heavenly Father to take my dad according to His will; for I feel my father is now suffering physically too much, and I ask God to make his passing quick and painless. I speak to my Heavenly Father, telling Him that I feel that my father has reached his full potential for learning and growing for this lifetime, and I do not want him to have to suffer any longer. I can feel the tears streaming down my face, knowing in my heart that I would gladly wish for God to keep my father here on Earth longer, but I know this would be wrong of me. I love my father too much and I am unable to stand by and watch him suffer any longer, and I have to give it over to my Heavenly Father who knows what is best, and who will do what is right according to His will. I also know that my Heavenly Father knows that my motive for my prayers to Him is an act of love and that my motive is pure and righteous.

I also pray to God to take my husband also, if it is His will. I do not want Dave to suffer either. I do not want him suffering physically but also I do not want him suffering emotionally and mentally. I know Dave would suffer greatly if he knows he has to leave me because I truly believe that my husband's greatest fear while living here on this Earth is leaving me. He loves me dearly and I love him dearly also, and for this reason, I do not want him suffering at all.

As I finish my prayers to my Heavenly Father, all of a sudden, a surge of warm energy rushes throughout my whole body, starting from my head and ending right down to both my feet. With tears gently rolling down my cheeks, I know God has heard my prayers. It is all truly in God's hands. I know I have to respect God's will. What is to be; will be. I will choose to walk in God's path of righteousness and love, knowing my Heavenly Father loves us dearly and that my Guardian Angel, my Guardian Souls, and my Uncle Stan from the Other Side are with me to guide, help and comfort me. Whatever the outcome, I know it to be right.

I also know that when my Heavenly Father does not answer my prayers right away, it is not that God does not hear me, it just means that I have to learn a lesson, or that the time is not right. For I know that everything is in God's time and not in mine, and that God's will shall be done on Earth as it is in Heaven.

CHAPTER 16

Spiritual Lessons

"I realized that the deepest spiritual lessons
are not learned by His letting us have our way in the end,
but by His making us wait,
bearing with us in love and patience
until we are able to honestly pray what He taught His disciples to pray:
Thy will be done."

Elisabeth Elliot
Passion and Purity

It is Valentine's Day, February 14, and my husband Dave arrives home with a box of chocolates for me; and my son comes home and gives me sixteen, large, silver, heart-shaped balloons. We are all in such a happy and loving mood and therefore I can sense a strong presence of loving energy in our house.

Even though my husband and my son are in such a good mood, I feel concerned because my husband is still not feeling well and most days he experiences fatigue and other symptoms, and I still fear he will never get completely well again. I know he is living on borrowed time, but just how much borrowed time I do not know. I do not know what God has planned for his future. It then occurs to me that these thoughts are coming to me because some loving soul is helping me to understand. I sense it is my uncle.

"Olive, I am here with you."

"Thank you, Uncle Edward. I know you are always there for me."

"Yes, my dear, and always remember that you are never alone."

"I know there are times when you are not with me but during those times, I have Aunt Mildred with me."

"Yes, this is correct; Aunt Mildred and I take turns to be with you."

"Thank you, this means so much to me."

"Always remember you have nothing to fear; you are guided and protected."

"I love you so much, Uncle Edward; and I know you love me."

"I most certainly do love you, my dear. You are a precious soul."

As I smile, I realize how fortunate I am to have this uncle in my life. "Uncle Edward, I need some answers."

"Yes, I already know. I can hear your thoughts."

My mind takes me back to the day in the hospital when my husband told me they wanted him to go with them, but he refused. "Uncle Edward, do you know what happened the day Dave had his EEG done?"

"Yes, I most certainly do."

"Then you know that Dave told me that there were two who wanted him to go with them, but he refused."

"Yes, I know."

"He said they were wearing black clothes and I am thinking this is because they thought they would be attending Dave's funeral. Am I right?"

"No, this is not the reason for them wearing black clothes."

"It's not?"

"They were wearing all black clothes because they don't have a choice."

"They don't have a choice?" I question with great curiosity.

"They don't have a choice about the color of clothing that they can wear."

"I don't understand."

"It is because this is the only color of clothing that they are permitted to wear."

"Uncle Edward, I still don't understand."

"My dear, one has to abide by the spiritual laws, and the spiritual laws dictate the color and type of clothing that a soul is permitted to wear, according to which level the soul resides on the Other Side."

"There are different levels on the Other Side?"

"Yes, there most certainly are. And how the person lives his or her life on Earth determines what level the soul will return to."

"Okay, this makes sense to me. However, I still don't understand why they were dressed in all black."

"Black clothing signifies that they belong to a lower level on the Other Side."

"So, because they are on a lower level, this means that the only color clothing that they can wear is black?"

"Yes, this is correct."

"So, if they want to wear any other color of clothes, they aren't allowed?"

"In order for them to be able to wear any other color of clothing, they have to be able to move up to a higher spiritual level."

"Oh my, it all makes sense to me now. And why the color black?"

"Black portrays darkness."

"And white portrays light?"

"Yes, my dear."

"And black portrays darkness, meaning hatred, and white portrays light, meaning love. Is this how it goes, Uncle Edward?"

"Yes, this is how it goes. Also, the level on which a soul resides determines the color of the black and to what extent."

"I'm not sure what it is you are saying."

"There are different shades of black. The blackest of black that a soul is wearing signifies that the soul is on a lower level than the soul who is wearing a lighter shade of black. In addition, it is not just the color of the clothing which a soul wears that signifies the level from which the soul resides, the color of the hair can also be black."

"So, a soul on a lower level also has black hair?"

"Yes, a soul on a lower level can also have eyes of black. The eye space is just hollow with darkness."

"So, the more wrong that a soul does while living on Earth, the darker and blacker the soul will experience when returning to the Other Side?"

"Yes, my dear. But it is very important to understand that the color of one's skin, or the color of one's hair, or the color of one's eyes, while living on the Earth plane, does not apply to the spiritual laws."

"People living on Earth with different color skin or different color hair, or eyes; this doesn't really have any great meaning. Is this what you are saying?"

"That's exactly what it is I am saying."

"We both know that there are some people on this Earth who look down on others who have a darker color skin or who have dark hair."

"The color of one's skin, for example, does not have to do with the advancement level of a soul while living on the Earth plane. People of the Earth plane who have different color skin, different color hair or different color eyes means only just that, it is just a difference in color. It has nothing at all to do with the spiritual level that a particular soul is from."

"Then Uncle Edward, why do people here on Earth have such a difference in the color of their skin?"

"It is solely for learning purposes. Some souls living here on the Earth plane need to learn love through tolerance. Just because one is of a lighter color skin than another, does not mean that the one with the lighter color skin is more advanced and therefore resides on a higher spiritual level on the Other Side. It may mean just the opposite. The soul with the black color skin could be a soul from a very high spiritual level from the Other Side. However, such a soul who chose to have black color skin is because the soul wants to help teach others about tolerance and respect, and therefore love. It is very foolish for one to think or believe that one is better than another just because of the color of the skin."

"Well, you must know that there are people who live here on Earth with such beliefs. We call them bigots."

"Yes, my dear, I most certainly do know this. These are souls operating from very low levels and have thoughts of ignorance. These souls need to learn tolerance, respect and love."

"I am trying to understand all of this, Uncle Edward. So are you telling me that some people here on Earth have dark skin just to help others learn tolerance, respect and love?"

"I am saying precisely this. Now, not all people who have dark skin have it for this reason. Some people have the dark skin because when they lived on the Earth plane in a previous lifetime, they had white skin, but as you say, they were bigots. They would not tolerate anyone who did not look like them. They looked down on these people and resorted to hatred, and consequently violence. Many loving souls suffered at the hands of these lower level souls and were tortured and murdered."

"I know, it is very sad that we have such a negative and hateful history of times gone by."

"It has much improved, my dear, but there are still souls living on the Earth plane who think they are better than others. However, deep down in their soul, their hatred comes from low self-esteem."

"I'm not sure I understand what it is you are saying."

"Any person or soul who thinks he or she is better than another is a fool. All souls in the beginning are equal. Therefore, for one to think that he or she is superior to another is completely wrong. One with such attitudes is telling the world that he or she is coming from a very low level on the Other Side. This is why some souls living here on the Earth plane dread death."

"Again, I'm not following what you mean, Uncle Edward. Why would those people fear death?"

"Some people living here on the Earth plane fear death because they know in their soul that once their time has come and they die, they have to return to the Other Side to a much lower level. They know in their soul that they won't have the same freedom and privileges as they do living here on Earth, during this time."

"Oh, now I understand. For example, people who have died and live on the Other Side, can no longer choose what color of clothes they can wear, even though they were able to wear different color of clothes while they lived here on Earth."

"Now you understand."

"It seems to me that a lot of people living here on Earth are going to be in for a rude awakening when it is their time to die and cross over."

"Yes, you are absolutely right. There are too many people living here now who are too selfish and self-centered and not very loving toward their kindred souls."

"I remember some time ago Aunt Mildred explained to me that a kindred soul is like a friend, am I remembering correctly?"

"We are all from the Creator and so we are all kindred, meaning we are all related. However, a true kindred soul is a soul friend, one that you can depend on and one you can trust."

"Well, for sure, my husband, son and daughter are my kindred souls because I know I can trust them."

"Yes, my dear, you are correct. You are also their kindred soul because they also trust you."

"There aren't a lot of people that I completely trust. Over the years, I have found that some people I thought I could trust have let me down."

"How do you think they have let you down?"

"They have let me down because I found out they are not to be trusted. They lied to me and so how could I ever trust that person again? If someone is willing to lie to me once, for sure she is willing to lie the second time."

"Yes, unfortunately you are right. Lies and deceit have ruined many relationships."

"I truly do not understand the logic in telling lies. Don't they understand that in time they are going to be caught telling lies, and then they lose all credibility and trust?"

"My dear, you are asking very important questions and in order to help you fully understand, your Guardian Angel has joined us. He wishes to speak to you about all of this. He knows you are ready to learn."

I feel the tears forming in my eyes as the loving voice speaks, and I recognize it all too well as the voice of Gabriel. "The time has come for you to remember all there is. There are two reasons that I can offer to help you understand. The first reason is that some souls actually believe that they can get away with such deceit. They follow the father of lies, the devil, and do his work. These souls know right from wrong, however, they choose to do wrong. Secondly, there is such a thing as soul merging."

"Soul merging, what does this mean?"

"Soul merging is when another soul moves into a physical body and resides there with the soul owning the physical body. This is very common, and more common than people of the Earth plane realize or understand."

"This is frightening."

"Yes, it can be. Do you not remember a time when you didn't feel like yourself?"

"Yes, now that you ask. I do recall different times when I felt really strange because it seemed as though I was saying things and doing things that seemed out of character for me."

"That's because it was out of character for you. Those were the times when another soul merged with you inside your physical body and took possession. Some of these souls can become quite dominant."

"This is really scary."

"Yes, my dear, it can be scary. This is why there is no such thing as a person having multiple personalities."

"Really?"

"I know that the psychiatric community on the Earth plane has labeled some people as having a diagnosis of multiple personalities, but this is not the true problem. The person does not have different personalities; it just seems that way, because of the different souls inside the one physical body."

"You mean that there can be more than one soul move in and take over another person's physical body?"

"Yes, I mean just that. This is why people on the Earth plane think that a person has multiple personalities. A person having more than one soul inside the physical body knows that even the voice when speaking sounds different. When asked the names, some will give different names and this is because they are different souls. So you see, my dear, the real cure for a person with multiple personalities is to have the souls removed from the physical body, and then to protect the physical body from this happening again."

"How is this done?"

"It takes souls from the higher realms to intervene and to demand the other souls leave, and a protection barrier is placed around the physical body to prevent the other souls returning and inhabiting the body again."

"Who are these other souls that would do such a thing?"

"These are souls from the lower realms who wander the Earth plane trying to find a place to live."

"This must be awful for the person who owns the physical body because that person must hear them, is this right?"

"Yes, this is right. This is why there is no such thing as hallucinations."

Shocked by such a comment, I quickly ask, "There really is no such thing as hallucinations?"

"This is correct, my dear. The soul hearing the voices inside her head, means just that. She is hearing voices inside her head because the other soul or souls are speaking."

"So she is not crazy, as some people put it?"

"This is absolutely correct. These souls are not crazy; nor are they mentally ill. A soul can also experience hearing voices because the soul has the gift of hearing those that cannot be seen and also the soul can travel over to another realm, leaving the physical body behind, and consequently hears other souls talking."

"Wow, this must be true for all hallucinations, for example, the visual and the auditory, visual meaning seeing and auditory meaning hearing."

"Yes, this is correct. However, please keep in mind what I told you earlier in our talk, there is no such thing as hallucinations."

"Yes, of course, now I understand because everything is real."

"Yes, my dear, everything is real. A kindred soul who is a loving soul and one you can trust, would never soul merge unless permission is granted."

"You mean that another soul may soul merge into another soul's physical body, if given permission to do so?"

"This is exactly what it is I am saying. A kindred soul is one that you trust and is a soul friend."

"This is very interesting because a friend of mine, Ken Snow, who I went to high school with, died and shortly after his death, he visited me in a dream. I knew that it wasn't just an ordinary dream. It was an actual visit. Even though after graduation from high school we didn't stay in touch he must have considered me a soul friend, otherwise why would he have chosen to visit me?"

"He does consider you a soul friend and this is why he visited with you."

"I remember he visited a couple of different times and he had nothing of great importance to tell me; he just really came to visit, and to let me know that he was happy to see me. Sometime later, I had met his brother and his brother's wife at the airport. They also went to high school with me. I told them about the visit I had with Ken, and they told me they hadn't received such a visit. I often wondered why he would come to visit me after all those years, and not his own brother and his wife."

"Well, my dear, it certainly seems he considered you a soul friend and one of the reasons he visited you was because he knew he could make contact with you, because of your special abilities. Most likely he visited his brother and his wife but it is just that they did not know it."

"That makes sense."

"Unfortunately, most people living on the Earth plane don't truly understand the real meaning of kindred souls. People living on the Earth plane consider themselves kindred and therefore related because they are blood related. People who think this way are showing they are too grounded in the physical world, and anyone who thinks this way is operating from a lower form of thinking and is displaying lower level thoughts. What most people living here do not realize is that related by blood has very little value. It has no great significant meaning at all. People here on the Earth plane can be very close kindred souls and yet have no blood relation."

"Oh my, Gabriel, I know a lot of people who think this way. They think that being blood related is of the utmost importance. I know of some people here on Earth with this way of thinking and their actions reveal that they are more of a clan than a family and anyone from outside the so-called clan is considered an outsider."

"Yes, and this is very unfortunate."

"This reminds me of a quote by Ralph Waldo Trine in his book entitled: *In Tune With the Infinite: Many people are ensnared by what we term ties of relationship. It is well for us to remember that our true relatives are not necessarily those who are connected by ties of blood. Our truest relatives are those who are nearest akin to us in mind, soul, and spirit.*"

"These are the words of a wise soul speaking."

"Yes, I agree with you."

"And as I said before, these souls who think that physical bonds are of utmost importance are ignorant in their way of thinking and are coming from the lower levels in the spiritual world."

"So what you are saying will also be true for people here on Earth who would never think about adopting a child, and their reason being is that the child is not one of them, meaning that the child doesn't have the parents' blood. Am I right?"

"You are most definitely right, my dear. These souls are ignorant in their way of thinking, for blood ties have very little meaning; for the real value is soul related. In addition, soul related means souls who come from the same or similar levels on the Other Side. Souls who adopt children are highly evolved souls."

"This is all very interesting, Gabriel, and I have to say you have shed a lot of light on this subject for me. Thank you."

"You are most kindly welcome. People on this Earth plane who adopt children do it because they are highly evolved souls and they are kindred souls to the children they adopt. In addition, being kindred souls also means that they are already family, meaning they are a soul family with a strong soul bond connection. And the soul family is what really matters, not necessarily the physical family that one is born into during a particular lifetime."

"A soul family, I don't really understand."

"My dear, you must be familiar with the saying, blood is thicker than water."

"Yes, I am."

"Well, blood may be thicker than water, but the soul is thicker than blood; for the human blood is only of the physical body and therefore the physical world, and that of the physical world perishes and dies. You are all souls living together while living here on the Earth plane and it is very common for you to recognize other souls. Each soul belongs to a group called the soul family. Souls are within a particular soul family to learn soul lessons while living on the Earth plane, for it is within this soul family that a soul has the best advantage to learn and to advance spiritually."

"This is all very thought-provoking."

"Each soul also has a twin soul, soul mate, and kindred souls. Your twin soul, soul mate, friends, family members can also be kindred souls. And of course, all souls are then classified according to where they come from on the Other Side, as either souls of light or souls of darkness."

"Are you telling me I have a twin soul?"

"Yes, my dear, you do."

"And who is this twin soul?"

My Guardian Angel seems to think my question is funny because I hear him laughing. "You know who your twin soul is, and in good time you will meet him."

"Really?"

"Yes, really."

"And where will this meeting take place?"

"It is not for me to say, other than it will be far from your home and it will take place in a large, beautiful building. You will recognize the building by the huge, floor-to-ceiling fireplace as you enter."

"How will I know he is my twin soul?"

"You will know."

"So this must mean that my twin soul is living somewhere here on Earth, is this right?"

"Yes, my dear. One's twin soul may be incarnated in a life on the Earth plane at the same time, as is the case with you."

"So, this must mean that my husband is not my twin soul?"

"Twin souls are not necessarily soul mates; for they can be very unique and different, and not necessarily compatible for one another; for one could be much farther spiritually advanced than the other."

"So if a twin soul is so different, than how will I know him when I meet him?"

"You will know, my dear, for there will be an immediate soul recognition. You will recognize each other even though you both know that it is the first meeting during this lifetime on the Earth plane. One of the most common thoughts during a twin soul meeting for the first time is that one or both have thoughts of marrying the other. So keep in mind, you already know this soul, even though you have never met before in this lifetime. There will be a strong spiritual connection and a strong bond of love, and there will be a deep feeling of affinity. The feelings will be very intense and it will be extremely difficult to resist the love for one another."

"I'm not sure I understand."

"The meeting of a twin soul may occur later in life, after both of you have found soul mates and are already committed."

"Okay, now I understand."

"You can tell twin souls by the way they look. If a twin soul is married, some people mistake them for brother and sister because they look so much alike."

"I know of couples like this! They look so much alike, people tend to think they are brother and sister!"

"Yes, my dear, this is what happens."

"Does this mean I look like my twin soul?"

"Yes, others will see the resemblance. For example, you are short in stature; therefore your twin soul will also be short in stature."

"What are some other characteristics I should look for?"

"You really don't have to look for any because as I said, there will be an instant soul recognition. However, know that he has a beard and is already separated from his wife."

"If he is separated from his wife, then this means that he is married."

"Yes, this is correct. Another commonality of twin souls is that they each know what the other is thinking and it is very common for one to finish the other's sentences."

"I know of couples who do this."

"If you know of couples who do this, my dear, most likely it is because they are twin souls. Twin souls also have a strong empathy bond, meaning that they tend to feel each other's pain, but keep in mind that this can also happen to soul mates and kindred souls."

"I know this to be true, Gabriel. I remember once my husband and I took a trip to Las Vegas. One evening when I was in the hotel room at the Luxor, I sensed a family member was feeling scared. Immediately I went to the phone to call, but then quickly the thought came to me to pray instead. I did and while I was praying, I also thought of the Bible she had in her bedroom that was a form of protection for her, and instantly once my prayer was completed, I felt a peace and calmness and I knew she was safe. When I returned home, sure enough, she told me that the very evening that I thought of her, was the same evening that she experienced danger, but she said, within minutes, the feeling of danger disappeared."

"This is exactly the type of soul bond I am referring to."

"When do I meet my twin soul?"

"It is not for me to say but know that it will be soon, and very sudden and unexpected, and there can be a complete change of plans."

"There will be a complete change of plans? What does this mean?"

"Time will tell all, my dear, but remember I said there can be a complete change of plans, so it does not necessarily mean there will be. But also know that you have been prepared for this meeting, even if you do not remember this."

"Really, I have been prepared to meet my twin soul?"

"Yes, you have."

I am in deep thought trying to figure out how I have been prepared until I switch my thinking and ask, "What is a soul mate?"

"A soul mate is a kindred soul with whom you have a strong love connection, and most likely you have past-life connections. There can be more than one soul mate in one's lifetime."

"I'm not sure I understand."

"My dear, take for example, when a soul mate dies, such as one's husband, then later in life, the widow may find love again with another soul mate."

"Oh yes, of course. I know I have been told what a kindred soul is, but can you explain more?"

"A kindred soul is a soul with whom you feel more of an affinity."

"I'm not sure I understand what you mean, Gabriel."

"A kindred soul is a soul you consider to be a true friend who walks in God's path of love and will never forsake you. It is during a time of crisis when you will understand the true meaning of a friend, for a true friend who is a kindred soul will never let you down and is one who will always be there for you in your time of need. A kindred soul can be a family member of the physical world, but not all family members are necessarily kindred souls, for a kindred soul is one that has a lot in common with you. As the old saying goes, like attracts like, so a soul with the same way of thinking, and therefore with the same type of behaviors as yourself, will be attracted to you. If you are a positive person, then you will find it very difficult to be around people who are negative."

"Oh, this is so true! I experience this myself. There are some people that I find it extremely difficult to be around."

"Yes, my dear, this is because you are a soul of light. However, the souls you are referring to are displaying that they have not advanced very high in the spiritual world, and therefore are souls of darkness. This kind of soul can spend a lifetime on the Earth plane and not advance or evolve spiritually in any way. A soul of darkness can live for years here on the Earth plane and does not learn and grow spiritually as the soul should. Some spend seventy or eighty years here and even longer, and when it is all said and done, they have foolishly wasted away a lifetime. They have squandered away the precious gift of time, which our Creator has bestowed upon them, for they did not learn anything. And if that's not bad enough, some return to a much lower level on the Other Side than where they came from, before they were born here on the Earth plane during this lifetime."

"What do you mean by that?"

"There are sixteen main levels on the Other Side; with each main level having numerous multi-levels. There are eight higher levels and there are eight lower levels."

There is silence because I am deep in thought.

Gabriel continues. "The eighth level is the highest level of all and is represented by the infinity sign, which looks like the number eight turned sideways."

"Yes, I have heard this before. The infinity sign looks like the number 8 turned sideways."

"Yes, this is correct. The number eight also represents the lowest level, because again the number eight represents the infinity sign and means eternity. The lowest level is complete darkness, it is pitch-black; the souls who reside on this level are of the lowest form. One is unable to see anything on this level because there is no light, only darkness. The souls on this lowest level have no garments to cover the soul body, and they display a lot of anger and hatefulness. It is the level that some call hell. Level seven of the lowest levels has some light but is very dim. This area has no windows and is just empty space with walls of a murky, grayish color. The souls from this level are dressed in short sleeved, knee length gowns, and are the same color as the walls. These souls are very, tormented souls who have done a lot of wrong, and until they accept the responsibility for all their wrongs and choose to undo their wrongs, they will not advance to the next level. These souls are like lost souls who move at a very slow pace, as with a shuffle type movement. They move around in this hopeless manner, with their heads down, shuffling and bumping into each other; all the while moaning and groaning."

I now find myself speechless as I am trying to understand all this information. It all seems so incredible to me.

"My dear, it may seem all incredible to you, but that's only because you have allowed yourself to not remember."

Surprised by my Guardian Angel's comment to me because he is able to hear my thoughts, but then very quickly I realize he can do this. "Gabriel, I'm forgetting that you are able to hear my thoughts."

He chuckles as he responds, "That's okay, in time you will remember quite well. It is all in good time."

I listen intently as my Guardian Angel continues to provide me with an extraordinary amount of information about the Other Side.

"As I said, there are sixteen levels in all, with each level having numerous other levels. I will show you with numbers and maybe then you will understand better."

Gabriel then proceeds to show me a representation of the different levels in the spiritual world.

8—7—6—5—4—3—2—1—O—1—2—3—4—5—6—7—8
Higher Levels   **Lower Levels**

As I stare at this configuration in complete awe, I am unable to utter a word. There is silence for quite some time because I have to allow my brain to digest this diagram, which I am seeing in my mind.

The silence is finally broken as my Guardian Angel explains the diagram to me. "My dear, do you see the large circle in the center?"

"Yes, I do."

"This large circle is the center in which all souls return to the spiritual world. The circle represents the point of entrance, which one must travel through on their journey of death."

"Okay."

"While living on the Earth plane, it comes a time for each soul to shed the physical body and to re-enter the spiritual world. When the physical body dies and the soul leaves the physical body and travels to the point of entry, other souls direct the newly arrived soul into which direction he or she must take."

"Gabriel, so you are saying that upon re-entering the spiritual world, other souls give directions as to which level the soul will live?"

"Yes, this is correct. At the point of entrance, either the soul travels to the left, which is the way to the higher levels, the path towards Our Creator; or the soul travels to the right, toward the lower levels, the path to the evil one. If the soul travels to the left, the soul will keep travelling until the soul reaches the level she is supposed to reside, and it is the same for the soul travelling to the right. If the soul travels to the left, the soul will see that with each higher level, there is a change in the quality of light. The closer a soul gets to the highest level; the stronger and brighter the light, and ultimately the closer to our Creator; for the higher the level to God, the higher the level of experiencing love and peace. It is on these higher levels that souls wear any type and color of clothing, they desire. So for example, a soul may wish to wear very casual type of clothing such as jeans and shirt, or she may choose to wear a very elaborate gown. In addition, the higher up the level the soul advances, the main color is white. And it is in these higher levels that souls become angels; who have been adorned with wings, and the higher the advancement for the angel, the larger and brighter the wings become."

"This is incredible!"

"Not really, my dear, for this means that any soul can become an angel."

"I didn't realize this is what you were really saying. This is amazing!"

"Anyone can advance to the highest levels, the same way that anyone can go down to the lowest levels; for it is entirely up to each and every soul. The choice is always there."

It is then I recall a quote from *Prashna Upanishad*, taken from *The Upanishads: The wise see the Lord of Love in the year, Which has two paths, the northern and the southern. Those who observe outward forms of worship And are content with personal pleasures Travel after death by the southern path, The path of the ancestors and of rayi, To the lunar world, and are born again. But those who seek the Self through meditation, self-discipline, wisdom, and faith in God Travel after death by the northern path, The path of prana, to the solar world, Supreme refuge, beyond the reach of fear And free from the cycle of birth and death.* "I now understand. This is the belief of the Hindu religion."

"Yes, my dear, you are correct, and the same goes for a soul who is travelling in the opposite direction and is travelling to the right. The soul will see that with each lower level, there is also a change in the quality of light. The closer one gets to the lowest level, the dimmer the light, and ultimately the closer to the evil one. In addition, the lower the soul travels to the right, the darker the soul becomes, including the garments the soul is permitted to wear. A soul abiding on the lower levels is dressed in all black only; however, the lower the soul travels downward; the least amount of garments the soul wears. As I said before, a soul who finds himself at one of the lowest levels will be dressed only in a short sleeved, knee length, gown. These lost souls wander around as though in a daze, mumbling to themselves and completely self-absorbed, with very little meaning to their life, and the farther down the lower level, the garment gown comes off and there is only a dark existence."

My body is trembling at the thought of such an awful existence. "Gabriel, this sounds so dreadful."

"It is an awful existence, my dear; however, keep in mind that these souls placed themselves on these lower levels by choice. All their evil and hateful ways placed them in this existence, and until they decide to repay their spiritual debts, they will remain there."

"So once the soul pays the spiritual debts then the soul can leave this ghastly place?"

"Yes, this is correct, however, the soul must feel deep remorse and be sincere and has to undo all the terrible wrongs, and then ask for forgiveness from those he has betrayed with hatred and evil thoughts, words and actions. And it is up to the other soul who has been unjustly injured and hurt to grant forgiveness."

"Is forgiveness always granted?"

"No, my dear, not all times, but of course, once a soul who has passed over to the Other Side, realizes that this is where he will spend his time, there is much resistance; for he does not go willingly. And the soul living on these lower levels doesn't have any control over his life while in such a place of torment."

"This is quite understandable. It would seem to me that a lot of people living here on Earth will get a shock of their life, once they die and leave the body, and find themselves having to go to such a horrible place."

"As I said earlier, the infinity sign represents eternity, for there is really no beginning and no end. There is only now. Therefore, there is no such thing as the measurement of time. The measurement of time only exists on the Earth plane. There is nothing measured in time throughout the remainder of the universe."

Once again, I am unable to speak and it seems like minutes pass before I am able to ask, "So, there really is no such thing as time?"

"This is correct. There is no time; for there is only eternity."

In my mind, I find myself repeating the words. "There is no time; for there is only eternity."

My Guardian Angel continues. "And of course at the time of travel, each soul does not have a choice on which level the soul returns because the choice has already been made by the soul, upon completion of the soul's time on the Earth plane."

"So Gabriel, it really is true that each of us living here on Earth decides upon where we return to and live in the spiritual world?"

"Yes, according to the thoughts, words, and actions that one does while living on the Earth plane during a particular lifetime, determines where the soul will reside on the Other Side."

"And so there really is no punishment as such?"

"There is punishment, my dear, but it is only the individual soul that gives out the punishment, because as I said, the spiritual laws are in place and each soul has to abide by the spiritual laws."

"I know of many who have been taught and follow their religious beliefs that God punishes, so what it is you are really saying is that God does not punish."

"Many religious beliefs are false and this is one of them. The spiritual laws are in place and therefore each soul has to take responsibility for his or her actions while living on the Earth plane, and will have to abide by the spiritual laws accordingly. No one punishes a soul, only the soul himself. Souls residing on the lower levels pay a heavy price for their negative, hateful and evil thoughts, words and actions. If a soul thinks and acts in a hateful and evil manner, this is how the soul will arrive on the Other Side. The soul does not automatically change just because he or she has gone through the death process of shedding the physical body. These souls will find themselves among their own; for evil attracts evil. They have their own space to reside, which are the lower levels on the Other Side. In addition, the lower levels on the Other Side, is not Heaven. Unfortunately many do not understand the spiritual laws."

"Do you mean they do not know about the spiritual laws?"

"No, my dear, this is not what I mean at all. All souls are aware of the spiritual laws; it is just that some souls think they can ignore these spiritual laws and therefore get away with the evil they do. They don't truly understand the consequences which they eventually will have to face, once they cross over to the Other Side."

"I cannot help but recall a quote by Plato. *O youth or young man, who fancy that you are neglected by the Gods, know that if you become worse you shall go to the worse souls, or if better to the better, and in every succession of life and death you will do and suffer what like may fitly suffer at the hands of like. This is the justice of heaven.*"

"Plato is a great philosopher, my dear. And as I said, many do not understand the consequences of their actions, and therefore they will have a very high price to pay."

"I think the quote by John Masefield says it all also. *My road shall be the road I made, All that I gave shall be repaid.*"

"John Masefield is another wise soul. He understands that people have to repay their debts."

"Gabriel, it sounds like you are talking about what some people refer to as karma. I know that the Hindu religion refer to karma as the sum total of a person's good deeds and bad deeds throughout the person's lifetime while living on Earth."

"We refer to it as spiritual debt. Each time a soul does wrong, that soul is placing himself into spiritual debt, and all debts have to be paid. No spiritual debt ever goes unpaid. There are always consequences."

"When does the person pay back the debt?"

"This is entirely up to the soul. The free will is always there to undo a wrong. If the soul does not choose to undo the wrong while living on the Earth plane during his lifetime, the soul will have to repay the spiritual debt once he crosses over to the Other Side, the spiritual world. And if the soul still chooses to not pay the spiritual debt, the soul has to live with the consequences for all eternity, or until such time the soul chooses to undo the wrong."

"I know that some refer to this as what goes around comes around. Eventually the hateful thoughts, words and actions will come back."

"Yes, this is exactly what it means. If a soul has made bad choices in the past, it is never too late, for the soul can choose to make a conscious effort to make things right. If the soul chooses to pay the spiritual debt while living on the Earth plane, the soul will be free from spiritual debt. However, if the soul chooses not to pay the spiritual debt while living on the Earth plane, the soul will have to pay it later. No debt ever goes unpaid and the soul will have to answer to God. Every time a soul in the physical world does wrong to another, that soul is also doing wrong to himself or herself for he or she will have to face the consequences of his or her actions eventually. Sometimes the soul has to face the consequences while living on the Earth plane; however, there are also times that a soul has done wrong and thinks he or she has gotten away with it, but my dear, this is far from the truth. Eventually, the soul has to face the consequences of the negative, hateful, and evil thoughts, words or actions. The soul who thinks and believes he or she has gotten away with doing wrong is merely a fool."

"Gabriel, I know some people living on Earth have a lifetime of regrets, and I also know some regrets can cause a lot of guilt."

"Yes, this is definitely true. Are you thinking of anyone in particular?"

"Yes, I do know someone who was driving his car on the highway, and the story that I was told, is that he had pulled out to pass a car, and there was an oncoming car, and consequently there was a collision. During the accident, his child died. I can only imagine the guilt and torment this father has had to endure the rest of his life."

"Yes, however, this soul needs to be reminded that the accident wasn't necessarily his fault; for some things are meant to be, and that it wasn't intentional. The intent of the thoughts, words or actions of the soul is what is taken into account."

"Well, in that type of situation, I know the father's motive was certainly not to ever have his son harmed in any way."

"Yes, my dear, you are right."

"Many years ago, I had a cousin who was killed in a motor vehicle accident by a drunk driver. His name is Don Neil and he had just graduated from university with his Bachelor of Science Degree. He had intended to go on to medical school; however, he was married and had a small child, and instead, took an offer of employment with a pharmaceutical company. Shortly after starting his job, he was on his way to work one morning and the driver of the other vehicle hit my cousin's car, and Don died in the crash. The other driver was not injured but once the police arrived upon the scene of the accident, they discovered that the other driver was intoxicated. Apparently, his wife had given birth hours earlier and he had been celebrating. Unfortunately he chose to drink alcohol, and gotten behind the wheel, and drove his car. So I guess his intent was not to harm another, but he did make the fatal mistake of driving his car while intoxicated."

My cousin, Don, and his baby boy, on his graduation day

"Yes, he made the fatal mistake of driving while intoxicated but again, as you say, his intent was not one of malice. He didn't set out that morning to kill another human being."

"No, but many lives were changed forever that morning."

"Yes, but keep in mind that your cousin Don is still alive."

"So, once the person's time is up on Earth and the person dies, the soul lives on?"

"Yes. As you know, people living on the Earth plane call this death. Nevertheless, as I said before, death only means shedding the physical body because the real person lives on and will never die. Each soul who passes through the veil understands the pain of their loved ones they have left behind."

"They do?"

"Yes, they do. They experience and feel the pain and grief felt by their loved ones, left behind to grieve for their loss. You see, my dear, those left behind on the Earth plane should not really grieve for the death of a loved one, because in essence this is being selfish. Instead, they should rejoice for the loved one, for a life well lived and much accomplished, this is of course, if the loved one lived a fruitful and loving life."

"Amazingly, I have always thought this way."

"The souls who have lived on the Earth plane and have done well in their lifetime have much to celebrate; for it is like a huge graduation and a huge celebration. However, the opposite is true for the souls living on the Earth plane who have let the real things in life pass them by, such as loving others, and contributing in positive, meaningful, and loving ways to help others. These souls will not have a celebration but just the opposite; for these souls did not fulfill a loving life while on the Earth plane."

"Gabriel, this reminds me of one of the greatest movies of all time which is called *Schindler's List*. This is a heart-wrenching movie based on the true story of a German businessman, Oskar Schindler, who lived in Poland during World War 2. He becomes gravely concerned for the Jewish people after witnessing many persecuted by the Nazis under the reign of Adolf Hitler. Oskar Schindler employed many Jewish workers in his factory, knowing that this is the one thing, which prevents these people from the death camps. By the end of the war, Oskar Schindler had lost his entire fortune; however, in doing so, he saved 1,100 innocent people from death."

"Yes, I am aware of this great movie. This movie is part of the spiritual plan to help as many people living on the Earth plane to see the light."

"I can certainly see where people can become spiritually aware and to learn the importance of loving and helping others by watching this movie."

"Yes, my dear, and this is one of the most important spiritual lessons to be learned while living on the Earth plane."

"Yes, I certainly do understand this life lesson. The other thing that I really learned from that movie is a life lesson about material wealth. In the movie, at the end of the war when the allies had taken over, Oskar Schindler is standing by his car ready to leave, when he learns a divine truth. He realizes at that moment that if only he had sold his car to the Nazis, he could have used the money to hire more workers and therefore would have saved more lives. This was a very profound message to me. It was at the very end of this movie that I realized, like Oskar Schindler, if only the financially wealthy people of this world would give up all their desires for their extravagant lifestyles, and instead put their money to saving the lives of many starving and dying children each day, they would be saving many."

"My dear, you have learned well."

"Thank you, Gabriel."

"And not only would these extravagant lifestyle souls save many, they would also be saving themselves."

"Unfortunately, there are many walking this Earth who live, very excessive and wasteful lifestyles, and it is because of this I find it so difficult living here. There are so many with so much, yet so many with so little."

"Yes, but the real truth will be revealed to them when they have to leave their physical body and this physical world behind, and face the consequences of their selfishness and greed."

"Can't the real truth be revealed to them while they live here on Earth?"

"The truth is revealed to people of the Earth plane every minute of every day. There is one and only one main spiritual lesson people of the Earth plane are supposed to learn, and that is how to love and serve. They must learn to love one another, for in order to walk in God's path and to serve God, people of the Earth plane have to learn to love and serve humankind. The more they love and serve, the more they will learn and spiritually grow. To do differently is not doing God's will. They are not fulfilling their spiritual purpose on the Earth plane, and consequently their time on the Earth plane will be considered wasted by our Heavenly Father."

"A person living such a life will actually waste away a full lifetime?"

"Yes, my dear. If people on the Earth plane choose to stay selfish and greedy, and continue to be seduced by the materialistic wealth, power, fame and status, they will continue to create the same type of consequences that they have created in the past, and therefore they are not learning, and will continue to waste a lifetime. Many souls do not reach their full potential or fulfill their life purpose while living on the Earth plane; for they allow themselves to live in a negative, selfish and greedy type of lifestyle and accomplish very little."

"This seems like such a tragedy."

"Yes, my dear, it most certainly is a tragedy and a waste of valuable time. These types of souls must learn that they must give in order to receive. Giving with love will create wealth and abundance for not only them, but for all God's children. However, if they choose to not give or give grudgingly, they will not receive."

"Gabriel, these people living here who are so financially wealthy, how are they going to understand that if they give, they will receive, because they are not giving now and yet they are still receiving. One of the old sayings is that the rich get richer and the poor get poorer."

"Yes, I understand your thinking. However, the financially wealthy souls living on the Earth plane receive more even though they do not need it, but this is because each time they receive more, they are given another chance to make things right and to give."

"So, these financially rich people are given more, and it's only to help them realize that they need to share their wealth and not be greedy, is this correct?"

"Yes, this is correct. Each time they are given more, it just means they are given another chance to make things right and to undo their wrongs, and to give up their selfish ways. It is impossible for a loving soul who comes from the higher realms of the Other Side to accept so much abundance while on the Earth plane and to not give to those who have so much need."

"I must be definitely from the higher realms because as I said before, this is one of the things I find so difficult about living here on Earth."

"Yes, my dear, you are from the higher realms of the Other Side. Keep in mind also, that souls on the Earth plane who have an abundance of material wealth are not truly wealthy; for material wealth of the physical world dies away eventually. However, spiritual wealth lasts for all eternity."

"Gabriel, in order for people to become spiritually wealthy, do they have to give everything away?"

"No, the key word is moderation. Everything must be in moderation. Souls living here on the Earth plane must give of their physical wealth and abundance because it is loving and joyful to do so, and it is a spiritual act of love. And in doing so, they will become spiritually wealthy; for if one is not spiritually wealthy, no matter what physical possessions one has of this world, the person is in essence living in poverty; for he or she is truly poor."

"I never thought of people being in poverty this way."

"Spiritual wealth is to have an abundance of love, peace and harmony, which those of the physical world who are obsessed with money, material possessions and power do not have and will never have until they change their ways. For if they want love, they have to learn to give love, if they want peace, they have to learn to give peace, and if they want harmony, they have to learn to be harmonious with all that is."

"From what you are telling me, Gabriel, am I right to understand that each person who dies, which really means leaving the physical body behind here on Earth and moving over to the Other Side, is still really the same person as when he or she left Earth?"

"This is exactly correct."

"Thank you for explaining this because I know some people believe that the personality of the person changes."

"If you truly think about it, my dear, does this really make any sense? No, it does not. The personality does not change, meaning that the person living here on the Earth plane is exactly the same soul when his or her physical body dies and he or she leaves the physical body behind, and crosses over to the spiritual plane. The soul who has crossed over will have the same issues and problems to deal with as he or she did

221

on the Earth plane. Souls on the Earth plane make the grave mistake of assuming that death alleviates them of all their burdens, which this is false. They have to deal with it all in the spiritual world, just the same as the physical world. But where the soul or person, as you like to say, lives and how he lives, will not necessarily change; for the soul can find himself on the same level as before, which means he didn't move up and neither did he move down."

"This certainly seems as a lifetime wasted."

"Yes, my dear, this is exactly a lifetime wasted. In time, however, the soul may return to the Earth plane for another lifetime. Meaning the soul will still have the same issues and problems to deal with as before, unless the soul learned some of the lessons from the Other Side, however, if he didn't learn, the soul comes back with a new slate so to speak, meaning a new chance to start over and get things right."

"This is all very interesting. Some people, I am sure, assume that a new slate means that all the wrong the person has done is wiped clean. However, this is not really the case, is it?"

"No, it is not the case at all. As I said earlier, a soul who returns for another lifetime returns with a new chance to live another life and to undo all the wrong from the previous life. The soul may have already learned some spiritual lessons while experiencing the life review."

"What is a life review?"

"A life review is simply a review of one's life while the soul lived on the Earth plane. Other souls assist in the life review in a loving and non-judgemental way. The purpose of the life review is not for criticism, but the main purpose is for evaluating the thoughts, words and actions of the soul while he lived on the Earth plane. The soul needs to understand he is responsible for all his thoughts, words and actions, and consequently he will experience the hurt, pain and suffering he has caused others, and to learn from it. It is only by understanding and learning that the soul can then choose to change."

"Gabriel, this makes so much sense to me."

"The newly arrived soul will reflect on the life he had while living on the Earth plane. This reflection allows the soul to review his life in every detail from beginning to end, from the very moment the soul was born up until the very moment the soul took his last breath. The newly arrived soul reflects on his most recent life spent on the Earth plane. He will review his life as though he is watching himself in his own movie, except in this case it is not a movie but the most recent life of the soul. It is during this life review that the soul will see why he made certain choices, and how these choices affected not only his soul, but how these choices affected other souls. He will not only see each event of his life but will also experience each life event."

"I'm not sure I understand. What do you mean he will experience each life event?"

"During the life review, the soul will experience each life event just as it had happened and the soul will experience every emotion. He will see and experience the good and the bad. The soul will not only feel his emotions but also will feel the emotions of others and will feel these emotions the same as others did and with the same amount of intensity. Every time the soul acted in either a positive or a negative manner, acted in a loving or hateful manner, the soul will relive each event, and can then see how he acted in a particular situation, and why. In other words, what were the true motives for the actions? The soul will then see the results of his actions and the harm that he caused others, and will actually experience what the other soul had to go through. The soul will feel and experience the same pain and suffering which he had inflicted on another."

"Are you saying that the person who caused tremendous pain and suffering to someone actually experiences the identical pain and suffering?"

"This is exactly what it is I am saying. When a soul chooses to do wrong, she is choosing to walk in evil ways. And if a soul has lived a terribly evil life while living on the Earth plane and did not abide by the spiritual laws according to God, and through her free will chose to harm others by making them victims of her evil and hateful ways, then that soul will suffer the same consequences. The only one she is truly hurting is herself, for all the harm she has done to another, she has done also to herself. And not only will she suffer the same, but she will continue to suffer until such time she undoes the wrong she has caused; for justice has to be served in order to heal wounds. She then has to seek forgiveness, and forgiveness has to be granted in order for the soul to move forward from all the misery and suffering she has caused."

"One of the things I am unable to forget is the pain and suffering innocent children endured while under the care of the Christian Brothers in our province."

"Yes, my dear, I am all too familiar with these circumstances."

"So you are aware of the Mount Cashel Orphanage scandal in our province?"

"I most certainly am. This was a time when evil prevailed for a very long time and many innocent young souls suffered greatly."

"Yes, this is so true. It is considered Canada's largest sexual abuse scandal, and it is where many innocent children were physically, mentally, emotionally and sexually abused for years under the care of the Christian Brothers of Ireland in Canada."

"Yes, this is correct. These innocent young souls suffered unthinkable acts of cruelty."

"And so are you telling me that these same Christian Brothers who committed these terrible acts and who caused such pain and suffering to these children, will experience the same pain and suffering which they caused these children?"

"Yes indeed, my dear, this is exactly what it is I am telling you."

"So no crime really goes unpunished, even though this is what we may think here on Earth?"

"This is correct. The physical laws are in place, as you know, and there are many times when justice does not seem to prevail; however; even though the physical laws of your Earth plane may not always succeed, be rest assured that the spiritual laws do not fail. There is no crime or evil act which goes without notice and is not dealt with accordingly."

"I cannot help but remember the six year old child, Adam Walsh, from Florida who was abducted and brutally victimized and murdered, and the person the police concluded responsible was already dead by the time the case was solved."

"Yes, I am aware of this case."

"And so you are saying that this person, Ottis Toole, who the police concluded had abducted Adam Walsh, will be punished on the Other Side?"

"Yes, my dear, this is exactly what it is I am saying, and not only am I saying this, but I am also saying that this soul has experienced and is still experiencing the horrendous pain and suffering he had caused not only to the young child Adam Walsh, but also to others. He is experiencing the life that he created. And he will continue to experience and feel the agony and torture of those who suffered at his hands."

There is now only silence between us because I am in deep thought and am unable to speak. After what seems like minutes, I continue. "I would like to quote from the book, *Bringing Adam Home* by Les Standiford with Det. Sgt. Joe Matthews."

"Okay."

I run to the study, pull the book from the shelf, and quickly flip through the pages until I find the quote. After returning to the family room, I proceed to read the quote from Adam Walsh's mother, Reve Walsh, when she stated, ...*we want the cops to clear this case. Until that happens, we will not have peace. It does not matter that Ottis Toole is dead. He died without ever being charge, and as far as John and I are concerned, that is the same thing as going free. Our baby was murdered...* "Gabriel, I want to understand clearly, just because someone like Ottis Toole died without being charged or punished by the physical laws in place here on Earth, in essence this does not really matter. This is because according to the spiritual laws on the Other Side, when Ottis Toole died, he had to face all of his wrong and evil doings, if indeed he committed those terrible crimes. Is this correct?"

"My dear, this is absolutely correct. Those who do evil acts while living on the Earth plane are paying their spiritual debts, one way or another. In addition, those spiritual debts go unpaid until the soul chooses to acknowledge the evil actions and offers an apology to the victim. In addition, even if the soul does choose to be remorseful, and offers an apology and asks for forgiveness, the victim, such as Adam Walsh, does not have to accept the apology or to forgive the other soul. These are the spiritual laws."

"I truly believe that the parents of Adam Walsh would benefit greatly knowing about these spiritual laws and hopefully they can find some solace and peace in their lives."

"They can also have peace knowing that their son is not really gone but waits for them upon their return."

Again, there is silence, for I have to retrieve a tissue to catch the tears streaming down my face.

"Also, please keep in mind that there is always a bigger picture. I know you are aware that the parents of Adam Walsh went on to do great work in regard to missing children."

"Yes, I am. I know that John Walsh, father of Adam Walsh, is recognized by many as a crime fighter, taking into account he is the executive producer and host of the long-standing television program, America's Most Wanted. Also he and his wife Reve dedicated time and effort to make positive changes and as a result, the *1982 Missing Children Act* was passed, and in 1984 there was the establishment of the *National Center for Missing and Exploited Children*, and the national *AMBER Alert Program* in 2003."

"Can you understand when I say there is always a bigger picture, even though at the time it is extremely difficult to see this?"

I know I am having a butterfly moment, as I answer, "Yes, amazingly enough I do understand."

"And so you see, my dear, to get back to the life review which is conducted on the Other Side, it is through this process that hopefully the soul will learn and see how he could have done things differently. If the soul learns and is truly remorseful and sorry for the wrongs he caused, the soul has to receive permission to visit with the other soul he hurt and has caused harm, and then face the soul, and has to explain why he acted toward the individual in such a hateful or evil manner. The soul then has to apologize. Until there is a sincere apology, the soul cannot advance and remains on the same level. After the apology is given, it is then the soul has to ask for forgiveness. However, it is entirely up to the other soul to accept the apology and to extend forgiveness. If forgiveness is granted, the soul is free from the spiritual debt; however, if forgiveness is not granted, the spiritual debt is not paid and still remains a debt until such time it is paid in full; and until the soul receives forgiveness, healing does not occur. This without a doubt is a very painful and humbling experience for the soul to endure."

"So am I correct to say that every act of hatefulness and evil can be forgiven, if the person who has committed these terrible acts owns up to these unspeakable acts of crime, and sincerely apologizes?"

"Yes, you are correct. However, in saying this, they still have to undo their wrongs in order to move out of spiritual debt."

"I'm not sure I understand. They need both forgiveness from those they have wronged and also they need to undo the wrongs which they have caused, is this correct?"

"Yes, this is correct."

"So really, no one gets away with anything while living here on Earth, even though many think they do."

"This is one hundred percent correct, my dear. These souls learn many difficult lessons the hard way, and one of the most difficult lessons for many souls to learn is the lesson of self-love."

"This reminds me of a quote by the Hindu Prince Gautama Siddharta, the founder of Buddhism: *You yourself, as much as anybody in the entire universe, deserve your love and affection.* This quote has great significant meaning."

"Yes, this is so true."

"Would this be why some people here on Earth commit suicide, because they do not love themselves?"

"Yes, it is. It is during the life review that the soul is able to see where different opportunities were given him to love; however, the soul chose not to love, and instead travelled down a path of self-destruction."

"However, Gabriel, I do know of individuals who committed suicide because, as I believe, life was just too difficult."

"Yes, you are right. One of the main reasons for suicide is addiction."

"I'm not sure I understand what it is you mean."

"Addiction of any source is basically being tempted by the evil one, the devil and his followers, and once the soul realizes and understands this, the addiction will be removed from the soul and consequently the physical body; for the soul will no longer be a slave to the evil one."

"Are you saying that any type of addiction is caused by following the devil by being tempted and giving in, and consequently over time, the person finds life too unbearable and therefore ends his life?"

"This is exactly what it is I am saying. Another main reason for suicide is hate. When others do harm to another soul with despicable acts of cruelty, the soul is injured so badly that the soul gives up all hope and feels unworthy, and can spiral down into a depression. And again, please keep in mind that it is the evil one, the devil, who causes the feelings of depression and influences the soul with evil thoughts and darkness. However, if a soul shows self-love, the soul would never do harm to himself, even if the soul is harmed by others."

"I understand. What happens to a person who has committed suicide?"

"The soul is loved my dear, because love conquers all. He must learn to love himself and others. When the soul first comes over, he realizes what he has done and the pain and suffering his actions has caused others. And because of his destructive actions, the soul experiences the same pain and suffering also, and has many regrets, and one of them being that just because he committed suicide, his problems did not disappear and so he still has to deal with it all."

"It sounds as though the person who has committed suicide needs a lot of forgiveness."

"Yes, this is correct. And he needs to forgive himself."

"And the other people still living on Earth must also learn to forgive him also, right?"

"Yes, for if someone in his life chooses to not forgive and holds on to the anger and bitterness, the negative energy of the anger and bitterness will eventually destroy that soul also."

"How does that happen?"

"The negative thoughts of anger and bitterness become real because all thoughts are real, and therefore have power, and with this power, actions will result."

"Thoughts are real because others can hear what it is I am thinking. It's the same as if I were speaking out loud."

"Yes, there is no difference. If you speak your thoughts out loud or if you say your thoughts in your mind, it does not matter, because others can hear, regardless."

"I know that some people believe that if a person commits suicide, that person's soul is punished and goes to hell or some terrible place, so therefore it seems by what you are saying that this does not happen."

"You are right. Some of these false beliefs stem from religious teachings."

"Gabriel, the soul who has committed suicide, is there a special place for this soul to go on the Other Side?"

"Yes, my dear, there is, however, the soul only stays there for a period of time and then the soul returns to the appropriate level where the soul resides. For example, if this soul came from level four when he or she was born onto this Earth plane, the soul could return to level four, or the soul could return to a lower level on level four. Remember I said there are numerous levels within each main level of existence."

"I bet a lot of people don't realize this, otherwise they would reconsider taking their own life."

"Each soul knows this but unfortunately when they come here to the Earth plane, they call themselves people and become too grounded in the physical world and allow their minds to dictate. They choose to lose all sense of who they really are as spiritual beings. They live in the physical world and therefore see themselves as physical beings, and live their lifetime as such; and live, work, and die thinking or believing that is all they are. And of course, this is not true at all."

"I hope I don't sound too cynical, Gabriel, but from what I can see, most people fall into this trap."

"My dear, you don't sound cynical, you are just speaking your observations. Believing is not enough. Many take religion seriously and believe what they think is true; however, they must learn the truth and know what is true. They need to know, not just believe."

"I know this is certainly true for me because I grew up in a religious home where religion was taken seriously and we believed, however, this was not enough for me. I needed to know the truth, and over time the truth was revealed to me, and so now I just don't believe any more, for I know."

"Yes, but many are not like you in their way of thinking. There is nothing wrong with religion, for religion is good, however, religion of itself is not enough."

"And what do you mean by that?"

"To attend regular religious services and to follow the rules of a particular organized religion is not enough. One has to put the religious beliefs into action, and one must understand and acknowledge that some religious beliefs are false."

"So what you are saying is that they need to practice what they preach."

"Yes, my dear, this is exactly what it is I am saying. For example, many religions teach to give to the poor; however, very few followers of religion actually do this. In addition, some religions teach to mainly give to the organized religion, and this is not good. And of course in the end, when all is said and done, these religious followers have done nothing more than belong to a religious group."

"And Gabriel, as you know, there are many different religions here on Earth with many followers, believing in their own beliefs. And so I guess my question to you is, are there many paths to finding God?"

"Yes, there most certainly are many paths to finding our Heavenly Father. However, people of the Earth plane are so close-minded that many think that their way is the only one and true way, and therefore look down upon others for their beliefs. But again, keep in mind, I already said that beliefs are not enough."

"Thank you, Gabriel. All of this makes so much sense to me."

"So you see, my dear, if a soul left the spiritual world from level four, let's say, but then came to this Earth plane and did a lot of wrongs during her lifetime, then when the time comes to return, the soul may find herself on level three rather than level four. The soul has descended downward rather than ascended upward. The levels in the spiritual world are similar to the school system that you have here in the physical world, with a difference, however. The school system here on the Earth plane is structured so that the student can advance to the next grade if he works hard and acquires the knowledge to move ahead. So for example, a child in grade four studies and passes the assignments and examinations and therefore will graduate to grade five. After spending almost a year in grade five, if this child does not work hard and pass all of the assignments and examinations that are required, but instead fails grade five, this child will remain in grade five for another year. In addition, in some cases will eventually move ahead, even though the child still did not pass the required assignments and examinations. This is not so on the Other Side."

"It is not?"

"No, it is not. In fact, the spiritual laws dictate that a soul who has done more wrong than good while living on the Earth plane, will be placed in a lower level of existence. In accordance to how much wrong and evil he or she has done, this will cause the soul to descend lower and lower, and some may find themselves on some of the lowest levels of all. There is a hierarch of levels."

"How low to do levels go?"

"My dear, remember the diagram I showed you earlier."

"Oh yes, I remember."

"The lowest level is also represented by an 8. If you recall, I already told you that the number 8 is the symbol for infinity when the eight is sideways. Infinity means forever more. On the right side of the entrance are the different levels descending until souls travelling in this direction reach the last level, which the infinity sign represents. This signifies the lowest area which some call hell. It is the lowest of all. There is a complete absence of light, which means there is complete darkness. This area represents evil and only souls who choose to not learn their lessons and who keep doing wrong eventually move down to this final level. It is a place of horrendous desolation. Souls who have entered here do not have fully complete forms and have an absolute hopeless demeanor. Agonized cries and screams come from these restless, tormented souls, haunted by their own evil thoughts, words and actions. This area is also inhabited by venomous, grotesque creatures."

I find myself shaking at the thought of such a horrendous place of existence. "This sounds like the end. Is it the end?"

"Yes, my dear. It is the end. It is the last place and it represents evil. However, even these lost souls at the very lowest level can still progress upward, but only if they choose. It is all by choice. Souls on the higher levels can return to the lower levels and assist these lost souls if they choose; however, souls on the lower levels cannot move higher until they have earned it."

"Then why are there even souls who are down in this lowest level if they are able to move out? This doesn't make any sense to me."

"Each soul has been given the gift of free will. Free will means the power to make choices. Free will means free choice. The souls residing in any of the lower levels always have the free will or choice, to move upward and out of such misery. However, if they do not repent their evil thoughts, words, and actions towards other souls, and to undo the wrongs that they have committed, they will not move upward. It is all about choice. These souls need to repent. These souls need to undo their wrongs."

"It all just seems like common sense to me. Why wouldn't souls want to repent and undo their wrongs?"

"There is a very simple explanation, my dear. Souls on these dark, lower levels harbor negative attitudes such as hate, malice, greed, envy, jealousy, control issues and so on."

"So, it seems these souls living in such dark existence choose this because they are not willing to change. Am I right in saying this?"

"You are absolutely right. These lower level souls choose to remain stubborn and therefore ignorant in their way of thinking, and consequently refuse to change for the better."

"I understand this all too well, Gabriel, because I know people who are like this here on Earth."

"Yes, my dear, you are again right."

"Sometimes it may be difficult as to what choice to make in some situations, wouldn't you agree?"

"Yes, I do agree; however, when confronted with a difficult choice, ask your Guardian Souls for guidance and graciously accept their message. You will know what feels right. As a soul, your feelings are your true answers. With love and guidance, your Guardian Souls will support you in your decision, if your decision is out of love. Always follow the advice of your Guardian Souls and make your choice out of love and you will not go wrong."

"I understand."

"When you have made bad choices in the past, make a conscious effort to make things right. Learn to pay your spiritual debt, for when you pay your spiritual debt you will rid yourself of any guilt feelings and you will make amends. If you choose otherwise, you will have to pay it later, as all souls find out when they return to the Other Side. And so it is for these souls who live on the lower levels."

"This lowest area sounds like the same place that some people refer to as hell, as you already mentioned."

"Yes, some refer to this last place as hell or the pit. However, I am also aware that some souls living on the Earth plane don't believe that there is such a place, but they are so wrong."

"And the area on the left side; are souls able to move around?"

"Yes, my dear. For example, if a particular soul resides on level seven, this soul travels to any of the other levels except for level eight. The soul can even travel down to the lower levels, if he chooses. The soul can travel downward but not upward, and the only exception is when a soul from the higher levels grants special permission for a soul to travel to a higher level. Souls on the higher levels can visit other souls on the lower levels, but those souls in the lower levels cannot visit souls on the higher levels."

"So this means that souls on the lower levels are never permitted to visit the higher levels."

"They are not permitted to travel at their own free will; however, exceptions have been made whereby souls from the lower levels have been granted special permission to travel to one of the higher levels, but only while travelling with a higher level soul who has requested such a visit."

"Gabriel, I would like to know which level I belong."

"My dear, you already know this. Do you not remember your wedding day?"

"Yes, of course I do."

"You do remember you wore a long, white wedding gown?"

"Yes."

"Do you remember what your husband and father wore?"

"Yes, both my husband and father wore white tuxedo jackets with the black tuxedo pants."

"And why did they wear the white tuxedo jackets?"

"Because I wanted them both in white like me, I didn't want them wearing all black."

"And why do you think that is?"

"I honestly don't know; all I know is that I wanted them both in white."

"My dear, you do know, it is just that over time, you have allowed yourself to forget your reason."

"Gabriel, you mean that I really do know why?"

"Yes, you most certainly do know. Your soul has all memories stored; to be never forgotten."

"And why did I want my husband and father to wear white tuxedo jackets?"

"As a soul moves up to the higher levels, remember I told you that white is the color of clothing that is worn. You come from the highest level in the spiritual world, and both your father and husband also come from the higher levels, but they do not reside on the highest level as you do. And so, you wanted them both to dress in white because you love them both so much."

Tears form in my eyes as I can visualize both my husband and my father, and how handsome they looked on my wedding day, dressed in their white tuxedo jackets. It now all makes so much sense. At that moment, my husband calls my name, interrupting my talk. "I'm sorry, Gabriel, but I have to go. We will talk later. I have so much to learn from you."

"Yes, my dear, we can talk later."

A year later, my Guardian Angel is true to his word. As I enter the Cree Village Ecolodge, on the small island of Moose Factory in northern Ontario, I get the shock of my life! Two of my friends walk ahead of me, and as we enter the hotel, there is a male that I recognize, but from where I do not know. His head is down, but as I enter, he looks up and as our eyes lock, there is instant recognition! He greets me as I enter, as I also greet him. My friends turn left and head for the restaurant, and as I follow, much to my amazement, there standing in front of me is the most beautiful, huge, floor-to-ceiling fireplace!

Over the next several days, I have the most astonishing conversations with this stranger; a stranger to me but I know him so well. He confides in me that he has been searching for me for seven years! He tells me that he knows without a doubt that I am his twin soul! He says he knew what I looked like and would always look at women who fit my description, hoping that it would be me. It is during our talk he tells me that the very moment he saw me walk through the entrance of the hotel in

Moose Factory, he told himself that I was the woman he was supposed to marry. However, none of this made any sense to me because we were both already married. He confided in me that he was unhappy in his marriage and was separated from his wife.

Left with the memory of such an extraordinary encounter, I wonder why we were supposed to meet at all. What I do know is that our meeting was part of our life plan, and we were supposed to meet, but why? I do not really have the answers other than the reasons are spiritual reasons. It is quite possible we were to meet during this time to help one another learn about love, and that love has no boundaries. I recall the talk I had with my Guardian Angel the previous year, when he said to me, 'Twin souls are not necessarily soul mates; for they can be very unique and different, and not necessarily compatible for one another; for one could be much farther spiritually advanced than the other.' This I believe to be true.

CHAPTER 17

No Need To Say Good-bye; Just Goodnight

I Am Always With You

So be happy in your life and don't you ever fear
For you haven't really lost me as I am still here
I know you cannot see me, nor can you touch
But I'll never leave you as I love you so much.

Margaret Ward
Cupids & Casanovas

Standing in my kitchen looking at the calendar on the wall, I realize that today is April 8. I chuckle to myself because here is my spiritual number eight, staring back at me. It is then I remember, on March 31, just a week earlier, I woke from a dream knowing my dad would soon be leaving me. In my dream, I was with my father and my grandmother, Nan, my father's mother. I recall that it was only the three of us and we were all so very happy to see each other once again and to spend time with one another. However, upon awakening, I knew immediately that my father's time had come to leave this place we call home, and almost instantly, I came to grips with the thought that my grandmother visited my father because she was coming for him, to prepare him to cross over and to take him back to the Other Side. She wanted to reassure him that she would be waiting for him, and I knew it would happen very soon. Now here I am staring at my calendar on the wall and reminiscing about my nan and my dad with a deep sadness in my heart. With this thought,

I can feel the tears in my eyes, and in that instant, I come to grips with the fact that my father knows he is going to die. I feel myself becoming grief-stricken. To shake this unmistakeable sadness, I decide it is a good day to take a walk and so I put on my sneakers, bundle up, and head out the door. It is a nice, crisp spring day with most of the winter's snow gone. I decide to go for a short walk around my neighborhood, which I know will only take me about twenty minutes. As I walk, I enjoy myself immensely for I am determined to focus on the beauty of nature around me in order to alleviate the thoughts of my father being so sick.

After about twenty minutes, as I approach my house, I can see a dark object at the front. It is not a large object, maybe the size of a cat and so I am wondering if it is a stray cat. As I get closer, much to my surprise I realize it is not a cat, but a black crow! I take a deep breath because I immediately get a feeling of sadness. I am well aware that any type of bird can be a sign from my loved ones on the Other Side, and I know the old saying about seeing crows, one for sorrow and two for joy. I take another deep breath because here I am staring at the one, large, black crow that is standing not just in my driveway, and not just any step, but is actually standing on the top step right in front of the door.

I keep walking. I think that the crow is going to fly away once I get closer. Well, much to my disbelief, it does not fly away! It stands there, staring right back at me. I find myself hesitating because I am getting concerned as to whether or not this crow is going to attack me. It does not move; it is just staring at me! I feel terribly uncomfortable. All of a sudden, it comes to me to clap my hands to see if this will frighten the crow, and so I give one clap and it flies off. I approach the front door, put my key in the lock, unlock the door, and walk in. Once inside the foyer, as I am taking off my coat, I can hear my phone ringing. I quickly rush inside to the kitchen and for one brief moment, I hesitate to answer the phone because I know the impending news. With a deep breath, I take the phone. "Hello."

The voice on the other end I recognize immediately as my mother. She is crying hysterically and I am finding it very difficult to understand what it is she is saying to me. Through her sobs of hysteria, I am finally able to hear her words. "He's not breathing. I think he's gone!"

I understand all too well the impact of her words, and my reaction is something I never expected. I am in total shock. I grab a chair to sit down because I feel so weak and the tears start to flow. My father is dead. The numbness I feel and the sense of loss is unbearable. My tears flow like heavy rain. My dad is gone! Finally able to speak, I try to comfort my mother. "Mom, it is Dad's time to go." She is crying hysterically, and I come to realize that she is alone in the house. I am able to utter, "I will call Stan or Ralph and get one of them to go down to be with you."

Through her sobs, she responds, "Okay."

Immediately, I call my cousin, Ralph, the cousin named after my father. In tears, I relay my message to Ralph and he reassures me that he is leaving his house and on his way to be with my mother.

As I once again hang up the receiver of the phone, I slump to the floor in pain. I have experienced sadness in my life, but never to this extent! I have an ache in my heart that words cannot express. I am that small child again; the little girl who wants and needs her dad to make things right; for throughout my childhood and even into my adulthood, my father was my Rock of Gibraltar. However, how can my dad make it right? He is dead. The onslaught of tears reminds me that my life is changing forever. With the tears, comes the onslaught of memories, including regret. My father wanted me to make him his favorite rum raisin cake, like the one I made him and my mother this past Christmas, and I had not gotten around to it, and now it is too late. In my time of misery, I say a silent prayer asking my dad to forgive me.

I know I am experiencing the initial shock of hearing about my father's death, and through my sobs of despair, I manage to get myself off the floor and once again reach for the phone; I need to call my mother to make sure that she is okay. However, I keep getting a busy signal. When I finally do get through, she tells me that Ralph is with her and her neighbors across the street are there, and that the ambulance has just arrived.

I have to call my husband and tell him about my father's death. He says he will leave work and will be home as soon as he can and we will go to the hospital. Upon our arrival at Carbonear General Hospital, we go to the Emergency Department right away. I explain to the nurse that my father arrived by ambulance and I ask if we can see him.

She answers, "Yes, of course," and she escorts us to one of the emergency rooms.

As I enter, I see my father lying on the stretcher and I have to reach into my handbag for some tissues as I walk toward him. My dad is not breathing and not moving, and I know he never will. I kiss him on the forehead and leave the emergency room to allow myself to grieve in private.

Other family members start to arrive, and we all take our turn spending time with our dad and we also help make the arrangements with the people at the funeral home to come and get our father. The time has come for us to leave the hospital because our father is also leaving, but not in the car with us. With heavy hearts, we all return to our small town of Spaniard's Bay to our parents' house.

During this time, I sense a peacefulness coming over me, which I am unable to explain, even though there is so much sorrow. As I sit with my mother, I ask her to tell me how my father died. It seems as though it is very important to me to know everything; why I do not know. All I know is that if my mother wants to talk about it, I am ready to listen.

Through her tears, she says, "I want to talk about it and I want to tell you everything because it seems like such a blessing the way that he went."

I reply, "Okay, Mom."

She starts the story by telling me it was a typical afternoon with my mother and father sitting in their family room and my father enjoying his afternoon drink of Scotch. Since he had gotten older and had become so sick, he had made it a ritual to have one drink of Scotch whiskey in the afternoon. "He was sitting comfortably in his big arm chair, and he closed his eyes. I thought he was going to take a nap and I said to him, Ralph, don't go to sleep. You'll find it too hard to go to sleep tonight. He didn't answer me. I said, Ralph, don't go to sleep. He still didn't answer me and so I went over to see if he was okay." My mother is now sobbing. She wipes away her tears and continues with her story. "I then shook him and called out Ralph, but he still didn't answer me. It was then I realized he was gone. He looked very peaceful."

As I wipe away my tears, I ask, "Mom, did Dad finish his drink?"

"Yes, he had finished it all."

At that moment, I knew my father was completely at peace. I could picture my dad's face with such sweet serenity and calmness. His time had come and he knew he had to go. He slipped away quietly with dignity and grace. My Heavenly Father answered my prayer of request. Just a short time ago, I prayed to God to take my dad because I didn't want him suffering any more. And I asked God to take him in a peaceful and loving way, and now I know that my Heavenly Father has answered my prayers. I found some solace in my grief, and I know my mother did also, knowing that he had gone in such a quiet and peaceful way. I know that my father's religious beliefs had given him an anchor to steady him as he took his last breath, knowing he had to leave, but I know in my heart, the last thing he ever wanted to do was to have to leave us behind.

Faced with the daunting task of having to visit the funeral home with my sister to help with the funeral arrangements and to select a coffin for my father, it seems like a task that no daughter should ever have to do. However, this is life. I find myself holding back the tears as best I can as my sister and I follow the funeral director around as he presents each coffin and talks about the benefits of each one. With heavy hearts, my sister and I choose the coffin we both think is the most suitable. I am starting to feel exhausted as I realize this is one of the most humbling experiences, I have ever had in my lifetime. And I know my sister has to be feeling the same as I do. We return to our parents' house and help finalize the plans for the church service.

I have to help my mother select the clothes my father will be wearing. We both agree on his dark suit, and my mother tells me she has shirts in her cedar chest, which are new. I choose the shirt and tie and I want my father to wear his new shoes.

The next evening after visiting the funeral home, my husband and I stay overnight at my parents' house rather than drive back to our house. My mother insists that my husband and I sleep in my parents' bedroom because it has a queen size bed and we would be more comfortable. I agree, because I am thinking that it may be too difficult for my mother to go to her bedroom, without my father.

As I lay in bed next to my husband, I know he is asleep because I can tell by his breathing. Unfortunately, sleep will not come for me even though I feel so tired and exhausted. My eyes feel sore and heavy and I have a headache. I feel so heart broken. My dad is not here in the house with us; and as I am lying in bed, I can picture him in the coffin at the funeral home, all by himself. The tears are starting to come and I am trying not to cry because I feel I am going to make myself physically sick. As I reach over to grab a tissue from the nightstand, I hear a couple of knocks coming from the corner of the bedroom next to the closet. Instantly I sense a presence in the room and I know it is my father! I quickly spring up in bed to an upright position, as I squeal with excitement. "Dad, don't go giving big, old, hard knocks to frighten the life out of me."

With one of his familiar laughs, he answers, "Okay, my doll."

Now I find I am laughing as well as crying. "Dad, this is really you!"

He replies, "Yes, my doll, it is really Dad."

"Dad, you are not down in the funeral home at all!"

"No, Dad is not down there."

With this comment, we both laugh. I am thrilled to hear my father's voice, knowing he is in the house with us! He is not in the funeral home! As I dry away my tears, I feel such relief, and the feeling of love and peacefulness that has swept over me is so powerful that I realize that my eyes do not feel sore any longer and my headache has disappeared. I ask my father, "Dad, you really are okay?"

"Yes, Dad is really okay. You have nothing to be worried about."

"Dad, you remembered our agreement." Some time ago, my father and I made a pact that if he should die before me, he would come back to let me know that I was right; there really is life after death. Death just means death of the physical body. The real person does not die. My father, even though he was a religious man, did not truly believe that there was life after death. When we would discuss such matters, his comment was that he did not know. Now he has returned to fulfill our agreement, of which we never told anyone.

"Yes, my doll, I most certainly do remember our agreement; and you are absolutely right. I should have listened to you more."

We laugh as I reply, "I'm so glad that at least once in my life I know I am right about something." I retrieve another tissue from the nightstand to dry my tears of joy.

"I want you to get well rested because you know what you have ahead of you tomorrow."

"Yes, Dad, I understand." I know all too well that tomorrow, as a family, we have to face the funeral home once again and then later my father's body is to be cremated. I do not really like the idea of cremation, even though I know it is only the physical body.

My father comments again. "And remember, Dad is here with you in the house. I'm not going anywhere," my father reassures me.

"Okay, Dad."

"Okay, my doll; get a good night's sleep."

"I will. I love you, Dad."

"I love you too, my doll, goodnight."

"Goodnight, Dad."

The next morning, I feel well rested and quite elated as I go about helping my mother get ready for the funeral home and to help her make the funeral arrangements. Visiting hours at the funeral home start at 2 P.M. and so we are busy getting ready to go. As we approach the funeral home, I can see that our car is the only car on the parking lot, but this is understandable because we have arrived early. As I enter the funeral home and walk inside, I can see my father's body lying there, and immediately the child in me reacts. I go close to him, kiss him on the forehead, and say in my mind, "Hello, Dad." I have hardly said the words when I start to cry uncontrollably, and even though the thought going through my mind is that my father is not really lying there and it is only his body, I cannot help it, knowing that my dad is really going to be gone from this Earth. This place we call Earth is no longer his home. I know I should not grieve but I cannot seem to help myself, knowing that he has to leave me. I can now feel arms around me and I look up. It is my daughter, who is standing next to me and comforting me. She too has tears in her eyes as she hugs me. As I take my left hand and rub my father's hair, I say to her, "He was a good father to me."

I know others have arrived and I know they are all standing behind me in a distance in the room, as I spend these precious moments with my dad. I feel I need to be alone and so I walk away. I go to the other room, sit in the big lounge chair, and try to understand my feelings. I think about the night before when my father spoke to me and now I think that maybe it was all a dream. Then I think again, and realize that no, it was not a dream. He really did visit me last night before I fell off to sleep.

It is evening and we get ready to revisit the funeral home because visiting hours start at 7 P.M. Many friends and family members visit and offer their condolences. I know that my father was a very well respected and well-liked man. I remember my friend Ula, after hearing about my father's death, saying to me, "Your father was the salt of the Earth." He was a man many admired. He had such great integrity and honesty. In all my years, I do not recall my father ever lying to me. I realize that not only is there a great bond of love between us, but there is also a great bond of trust. One of the great lessons my father has taught me is that there are people who are true to their word and will never let me down, and of course, one of these people in my life is my dad. He taught me the valuable lesson of trust.

We return to my parents' house and we are all feeling very tired and so we decide to go to bed early. As I lay awake in bed next to my husband, I tell him about Dad's visit the night before. He is not surprised and accepts it as something that is quite normal. I finally fall off to sleep. Sometime in the middle of the night, I wake because I have to use the bathroom. After washing and drying my hands, I reach for the doorknob and swing the bathroom door open; there in front of me is the most brilliant, white light! As I stare at the light, it twinkles. Immediately I know that my father is present. "Dad, is this you?"

The reply is, "Yes, my doll, it is Dad."

"Dad, I am so happy to know that you are okay."

"Yes, Dad is definitely okay."

Before my father died, he suffered from arthritis particularly in his right hip. He had a hip replacement some years earlier, which was quite successful for a long time but during the last five years of his life, he suffered terribly. As I think about this, I say, "Dad, do you have any more pain?"

"No, I don't have any more pain."

"What about your hip, do you have any pain from the arthritis in your hip?"

"No, all the pain is gone."

"Do you still have difficulty breathing?"

"No, I don't have any more problems breathing."

"What about your heart? Are you still experiencing heart failure?"

"My heart is number one, number one."

The pain my father endured during the last five years of his life is now completely gone. My father has no more congestive heart failure, no more difficulty breathing, and no more pain from the arthritis in his hip, and no more medications. My dad is free of pain and suffering! I also know that my father suffered silently knowing that his time was ending and he had to leave his family behind. "Dad, did you find it difficult to leave?"

"If it was up to me I wouldn't have left, but they said I had to go."

"Who are you referring to?"

"There were many, my doll, but it was Nan who said it was my time and I had to go."

"I knew Nan would be waiting for you, Dad."

"Yes, Nan was waiting for me."

"I'm going back to bed now; good-night, Dad."

The light in front of the hall wall shines brighter as he replies, "Good-night, my doll. Get a good night's sleep."

I return to the bedroom and snuggle into bed next to my husband.

The next day my husband, children and I return to our home, which is about an hour's drive away. This is a difficult day for me because my own thoughts on cremation are not positive ones. I do not think I can really explain my feelings, other than I know that it is something that I do not agree with, and it is something that I would not want done. However, if this is my father's wish, then I respect his decision.

I remember standing in our upstairs bathroom in front of the sink, drying my hands, when all of a sudden, I smell the most awful stench of a burning odor. I drop my head, look at my watch and realize that this is the exact time for the cremation of my father's body. While a flood of tears fill my eyes, I drop to the floor and sob.

The next day, we all return to my parents' house. All the family members have gathered and are waiting to go to the church for the funeral service. I am standing in the family room next to a relative seated in the chair, opposite the entranceway to the family room. There are other people in the room, seated and standing. As I am looking at the entranceway of the family room, out into the hallway, a round, brilliant, white light whizzes by! It came from the hallway and entered the family room, passed those seated and standing, and flies by me. I look at the relative seated in the chair next to where I am standing, who looks at me in amazement. He asks, "Did you see that?"

I just nod my head yes, as I look around to see the reaction from others. There is no reaction; it is obvious to me that no one else witnessed this ball of brilliant, white light. At that moment, an unexpected calm sweeps over me and I know all is well; my father is with us. Even if not all the others know, I do.

My son is going to do a reading in the church, so prior to the church service I tell him to speak slowly when he reads the passage from the Holy Bible. "Remember to slow down when you are doing the reading. Do Mom proud."

"Yes, Mom, I will," he replies.

We go to the church and it is time for my son to do his reading. He walks to the front of the church and is taking his place for the reading from the Holy Bible. He starts speaking very quickly, then all of a sudden, he pauses, and starts to speak again but at a much slower pace.

It is later when I have some private time with my son and hug him and say, "You did Mom proud. You did excellent during the reading from the Bible. And I know that you made Pop proud."

My son looks at me and exclaims, "Mom, you're not going to believe what happened while I was doing my reading."

I stare at my son. "What are you talking about? You did everything just right."

"But, Mom, do you remember how I started to read?"

"Well, yes. You started off reading really fast but then you slowed down."

"Yes, I started off really fast, but then I could hear Pop's voice and he whispered to me and said, your mother told you to slow down when you are reading, and to do her proud. And so I slowed down."

With a big smile, I hug and kiss my son. "As I said, I know Pop is proud of you."

Later, as I recall the conversation with my son regarding his reading in the church, I realize that my father attended his own funeral. My dad spoke with me later and explained to me that he could see everything, hear everything and therefore he knew everything that was happening. He could see the actions of everyone involved and how they responded to his death, and he could hear all of their comments.

It is now three months since my father's death and today is his birthday. He would have been eighty-six years old today. I still miss him every day, even though he visits with me quite often. It was just a few days earlier that he had visited me in a dream and this time he brought a visitor with him, my grandmother; but this time it was not his mother, but my mother's mother, Ma. That was the first time that I can recall ever having a visit from this grandmother.

If my father does not visit me in a dream, he comes directly to see me, no matter where I am. He lets me know when he is around for wherever I go he follows me, and blinks a particular light in such a loving and calm way. Whenever I am in the study doing work on the computer, the light behind me blinks, and by the rhythm of the blinking, I know instantly it is my father visiting. I always know it is my dad, for he talks to me and it is always so wonderful to hear his voice. We have such loving conversations. He is so happy now and I know he is not suffering and in pain anymore; for he is gone to a place he loves and is free and living in the most magnificent place ever imagined. He has told me that his time had come to go even though he did not want to leave; however, he assures me that all I have to do is call out to him and he will come. He has told me he will never forsake me and will always be by my side and that he guides me in times of turmoil.

My father has always been a hardworking man and one who believed in commitment and loyalty. He worked very hard in his lifetime and was always able to provide for his family. Many times, his work took him to faraway places. One such time was when he accepted employment in Esker, a remote town in northern Labrador. He worked there as an electrician and stayed for five years, only coming home twice a year, Christmas time and summer vacation. It was during one of his summer vacations at home that I gave him a Bible to take back with him. Looking back now, I realize that even back then, I was spiritual in my way of thinking; and I say spiritual because I know all too well that I was never really a religious person.

During my dad's stay in Esker, my husband graduated from university with his engineering degree and I recall how proud my father was of him. He wrote my husband a letter and in his letter, he told him he regretted not being able to attend his graduation and to watch him walk across the stage to receive his diploma, and that he was very proud of him. My father not only had a very strong work ethic but he also possessed a very strong education ethic. He also missed my graduation from nursing school; however, he certainly let me know how proud he was of my accomplishments also.

Dave and I at his university graduation party

My father was also a very honest person. I remember when I was a small child, he found a man's wallet on his way to the train station. When he looked inside, there was not a name or any contact information, but inside the wallet was $700.00. He turned it over to the gentleman working inside the train station and asked him if he could keep it, and hopefully the rightful owner who had lost it would come back and claim it.

Unfortunately, there were times when others chose to disrespect my father, when he did not deserve it. One such time was when we were vacationing in Florida and we were in a restaurant. The waitress addressed my father as Pops. She looks at my father and says to him, "And what is it I can get for you, Pops?" Appalled by such a belittling comment, I had to bite my tongue. Then there was the time my father had a doctor's appointment. The doctor he was to see that day was a specialist, a cardiologist, and while we were in the waiting room, the doctor came out of his office, and happened to glance in our direction. When he recognized my father, he said loudly for all in the waiting room to hear, "Oh, hello, Pop." Again, I was appalled. My father was not pop to either the waitress or this doctor, and to address my father in such a disrespectful manner was very upsetting. In both circumstances, my father held his head high, even though I know he was insulted, as so was I.

There have been many times in my life that I have been insulted in the presence of others. There were times when the person did not even know her comments were derogatory and insulting, but still, ignorance is not acceptable. I recall a time in the workplace, a colleague of mine from another province made a comment I did not like. She made fun of Newfoundlanders at the airport, travelling with boxes. The Newfoundlanders she was referring to were men and women having to leave their family and home to go elsewhere to find employment. My own father and husband did it more than once over the years, and I myself have travelled to different countries to work. My father was an electrician and when he left Newfoundland to work, he would have luggage but also a box, and in the box were his electrical tools. My husband, being a civil engineer, travelled also with luggage and a box and in his box, would be his computer for his work. It is never right to judge; for not everything is at it seems. I remember my dad many times over the years saying, "There are two sides to a coin," and he is so right.

My father was well liked and loved by many, and especially his family. He always showed much love and treated everyone equally and would never say anything or do anything intentionally to hurt another. He had no problem apologizing if he felt he had said or done something wrong.

Before he died, he made it a point to let me know that he was preparing his will and that he wanted to do everything fairly. He asked me if there was anything in particular that I wanted, and that he wanted everything shared equally, and for one not to have more than the other.

From the moment my father made his presence known to me, I know he is always with me by my side. He has been watching over me, encouraging and nurturing me when I need someone to tell my troubles to, and guiding and helping me in any way that he can. I know he will never forsake me and that he loves me more than words can express.

One of the great lessons that I have learned from my father is that there is no need to fear death. Death means leaving the physical body behind here on Earth, and the real you, which is your soul, travels back to your real home, which is the Other Side. I know if anyone deserves to be in Heaven, it is my dad.

In closing, I wish to convey a message from the Hindu Holy Book: *Bhagavad Gita,* Chapter 2, Verses 13 2 30.

The Self dwells in the house of the body,
Which passes through childhood, youth, and old age.
So passes the Self at the time of death Into another body.
The wise know this truth

CHAPTER 18

Angels In The Night

The Son of man shall send forth his angels,…

The Holy Bible: Matthew 13:41
King James Version

Knowing there are a couple of hours before I have to prepare dinner, I decide to go for a coffee at one of my favorite coffee shops, Tim Horton's, and take one of my books with me to do some leisurely reading. As I sit quietly reading my book, I happen to glance at the doorway as my friend Tex walks in; he notices me and we exchange smiles. He greets me pleasantly as he approaches my table. "It is so great to see you again."

"It's also great to see you again. How have you been doing?"

"I'm hanging in for an old fella like me," he answers as he gives a big grin. "Can I buy you a coffee?"

"Sure, that would be great. Thank you."

He returns with two coffees and as he pulls up a chair to my table, he asks, "Do you have your book finished?'

With a big sigh, I reply, "I wish." We both laugh.

Tex says, "You know, I have been anxious to read it ever since you told me about your book, and especially about the stories you are going to tell."

"Well, you know, Tex, as I mentioned to you before, I do indeed have a lot of stories to tell and I truly believe that there are many others who will be interested in what it is I have to say."

With his eyes wide, he looks at me with great intensity. "I have something to share with you."

"It sounds intriguing," I answer.

We both chuckle as he replies, "It happened last night."

"What happened last night?"

Before Tex continues, he first explains why he feels he can confide in me. "I know I can tell you this because I know you will believe me. There aren't too many people in this world that one can share such stories with."

I chuckle. "Yes, I know all too well. The majority of people are very close-minded."

"You got that right."

"If I told this to some people, they'd think I am ready for the looney bin!" We both roar with laugher.

"I know exactly what you mean."

"Well, you know, really at my age, I shouldn't give a damn."

"What do you mean at your age? You're only a young man, Tex."

We laugh as Tex comments, "Now, Olive, you know I'm no spring chicken."

"Age is only a number, Tex. Some people can be eighty years old and act as though they are forty, and then there are others who are forty and act as though they are eighty."

"Yes, that's true."

"Tex, I believe that attitude is everything." He nods his head in the affirmative as I continue. "Some people are very negative in their thinking and consequently display negative behavior and of course, the other way around is also true. Some people are very positive in their thinking and this shows in their actions also."

"Oh, I know what you are saying is definitely right. I think some people were born negative."

"Well, you know Tex, it's all about choice. God has given each of us the gift of free will and it is up to each one of us how we choose to think or act."

"Oh, I agree with you one hundred percent."

"Unfortunately, some people are so negative. They are chronic complainers, and to them nothing is right in the world. Not only that, but some people are so rude."

"Rude! I know all about arrogance and rudeness."

"You remember when I went to the Middle East, Abu Dhabi?"

"Oh yes, I remember because I missed you."

"Well, one afternoon I went to a fast food restaurant for lunch, and while standing in line to be served, a male comes in, walks up to me and steps right in front of me. He starts to give his order to the person behind the counter, but the young guy serving tells him he has to step back, get in line and wait his turn, because I was already in line and was next to be served. And with that, without uttering a word, he turns around and storms out of the restaurant!"

"Yeah, that's what you would call arrogance and rudeness alright."

"And, of course, I thanked the young guy for being so nice. I remember another time I experienced people who were rude or just plain inconsiderate. I was living in Fort McMurray, Alberta, at the time because my husband had taken a new job there. My son was only a little over a year old, and I was pregnant with my daughter. I remember going into the bank there, or I should say, trying to get in. I found it difficult because I had my son in the stroller and I was unable to hold the heavy door open while trying to push the stroller through the doorway, and would you believe, there were people who went in and out that just did not take the time to offer to help me. And then there were those who were passing by in front of the bank, and they simply watched me struggle to push the stroller, while trying to keep the heavy door open at the same time, without ever walking a few feet to come to my aid."

"Well, you said they were either rude or inconsiderate, and I say they were both."

"I find it incredible how some people can be so nasty."

"I'm a firm believer that some people will never change. They can live to be as old as I am and will leave this world the same way as they came in. When it's all said and done, they made the choice to either open the gates of Heaven or to open the gates of hell."

As I nod my head in agreement, I reply, "Yes, and it's all so sad, don't you think?"

"Well, yes it is and also stupid! As the old saying goes, they're going nowhere fast. Okay, enough about those negative ones, I'll have to tell you about last evening."

As I sit sipping my coffee anxiously waiting for Tex to continue with his story, I answer, "Oh yes, Tex, tell me about last evening."

"Well, you believe in angels, don't you?"

"Yes, I do."

"Do you have any stories in your book about angels?"

"Yes I do. Does this mean you have a story for my book?"

We both chuckle as Tex responds, "You never know."

"Well, Tex, after I hear your story, I might just put it in my book. I have stories about angels, but another one would never hurt."

"What type of stories do you talk about in your book?"

"I talk about real things that happened to me in my lifetime."

"Can you tell me one of your stories, and then I'll tell you mine?"

"Okay. One evening, my husband and I were returning from Spaniard's Bay, after visiting my mother. My father had died the previous April, and it was September, actually, it was September 21, 2003, and it was their wedding anniversary. Therefore, Dave and I thought we would spend the day with my mother so she would not be alone. Later in the evening, we left my mother's house to drive back home. My husband was driving the car and I was in the passenger's seat. I had reclined my seat and was lying back with my eyes closed because I felt tired. I was falling asleep when all of a sudden it was as though someone had woken me up. As I sat up straight, instantly my head turned to the left, and as it did, there on the side, running up the embankment onto the highway, was a moose! I screamed to the top of my lungs, "Dave, stop!" He jammed on the brakes just in time, and the car came to a screeching halt, for the moose crossed the highway just inches in front of our car and continued running over to the other side! We both got such a scare and knew that we had just avoided a terrible accident. If we had hit that moose, I doubt very much that I would be sitting here talking with you now."

"That's quite the story! You and your husband were saved from a near fatal car accident!"

"Yes, we were, and I know there was someone with us in the car, who was watching out for us and who saved us."

"And who do you think it was?"

"It could have been an angel, but I think it was my dad."

"Well, if it was your father, maybe he's an angel."

"I don't know if my father is an angel, Tex, but I do know he is an angel to me. I love my father very much and always will, even though he is not here living on Earth any longer. There have been other things that have happened since my father's death that I truly believe it is my dad, even though I don't always see him."

"Like what?"

"Well, a couple of years after my father had died, all the family were at my sister's house for Christmas, and we were about to exchange our Christmas gifts. Just before my mother was ready to leave, I asked my husband to go to our car and bring in the box so I could give my mother her gifts. He did so, and when he returned, he laid down the box in the living room, directly across from where I was sitting, so I could see the box at all times. Very shortly afterwards, my brother-in-law took the box and brought it out to his car, because my mother was returning home with him and my sister. Later, on Christmas morning, I telephoned my mother to wish her a Merry Christmas and to thank her for our gifts that she had given us. She wished me a Merry Christmas and thanked me for the gifts I had given her. The next comment she made was quite surprising. 'The best gift of all is the angel.' Of course, a bit stunned by this comment, I said, 'Mom, I didn't give you an angel.' She replies, 'I am talking about the white angel that was in the box with the other gifts.' I tell her that must be from someone else. I did not give her a white angel. Her answer is, 'Olive, who else is there to give me this angel? I have all my gifts from all the other girls.' So of course, I was quite adamant about me not giving her the angel, and that it was accidently placed into her box. Well, later I spoke with her again, and she told me that she checked with everyone and no one had given her the white angel for Christmas."

"Well, isn't that remarkable?"

"Yes, it is. I now have this white angel myself. My mother wanted me to have it because she believes it was meant for me."

"And do you believe it was meant for you?"

"I don't know if it was meant for me, but I do believe that the angel came from my father as a Christmas gift."

"Maybe your father was trying to give your mother a message."

"What kind of message?"

"I really don't know, but it must have to do with an angel."

"You could be right, Tex. I do know that it is a beautiful angel and I call her the Christmas Angel."

The Christmas Angel

"That is such a beautiful story. Do you have any more stories to tell?"

With a chuckle, I reply, "Yes I do. I have several such stories."

"How about if you tell me another story, because your stories are really interesting?"

"What about your story?"

"I'm anxious to tell you mine, but I love hearing yours too."

"Well, okay. I attended a conference in Toronto not too long ago and while there, I stayed at one of the bigger chain hotels. One evening, I dropped into the boutique to do some shopping. I was looking at some handbags, which were on the shelves at the back of the boutique. I gradually walked away from the display of handbags and as I was walking away, a handbag suddenly came off the shelf! It literally flew in the air and landed on the floor! I stared at the handbag in disbelief, and then I looked at the sales clerk standing behind the counter. He was also staring at the handbag on the floor, and then turned and looked at me with an expression of shock on his face. He said he had caused the handbag to fall on the floor, however, I knew this was impossible because he was standing behind the counter at the time, quite a distance from the shelf of handbags. In addition, the handbag did not fall on the floor; as I said, it literally flew off the shelf!"

"And who do you suppose caused the handbag to fly off the shelf, if you know the sales clerk didn't do it?"

"Well, are you ready for this?"

"I'm ready for anything."

"I believe it to be someone in the boutique who we couldn't see."

"For sure you don't think it was an angel?"

"No, Tex, an angel wouldn't do such a thing. It was someone with a negative intent."

"And just who do you think it was?"

"I have no idea; however, I do believe it was someone who was quite upset with me."

"Why would someone be upset with you? All you were doing was just browsing around the boutique."

"Oh, that someone was not upset because I was in the boutique browsing; I believe that it was because I had attended the conference."

"You must be joking."

I cannot help but laugh, at the expression on Tex's face. "No, I am definitely not joking. Do you think you're up to hearing any more of my stories?"

"And at my age, I thought I had heard it all! Yes, I am ready for more. It just goes to show that even an old fella like me still has a lot to learn."

Now we are both laughing as I answer, "Okay, one more story and then you have to tell me what happened to you last evening."

"Okay, deal."

"Well, a few years ago, my husband and I took a Caribbean cruise, and we were having a fabulous vacation, really enjoying ourselves. On this particular evening, we were on our way to the dining room, and

I noticed that my husband was not wearing his glasses. Now keep in mind that my husband has worn glasses since his teens because of his poor eyesight. I ask him, 'Where are your glasses?' He looks at me and says, 'I do not need them.' Well, you know my response. 'What do you mean you don't need them?' He answers, 'No really, I do not need them.' So in my mind, I am thinking that he forgot to put them on, which is very unusual because he never forgets, simply because he cannot see without his glasses, or at least, not very well. Therefore, I am thinking that he thinks it will take too long for him to go back to our cabin and get them, and we will be late for dinner. I express my thoughts to him and tell him that we have plenty of time and we will go back and get his glasses. As I start to turn around to head back, he stops me. 'Ol, you are not going to believe this.' My reply is, of course, 'I am not going to believe what?' He replies, 'I do not need my glasses to see because I am able to see without them.' You can well imagine my reaction! He tells me that earlier that evening as we were getting ready for dinner, he noticed a change in his eyesight when he was not wearing his glasses. He was able to see very vividly and clearly, and when he put his glasses on, his vision became blurred! His eyesight was normal with 20/20 vision without him wearing his glasses!" Once again, I laugh because of the look of disbelief and amazement on Tex's face.

As Tex tries to stop laughing long enough to speak, he asks, "Are you serious?"

"Yes, I am quite serious. And his vision remained normal for days, and then at the end of our cruise, his poor eyesight returned and of course he went back to wearing his glasses once again."

"And why do you think that happened?"

"I think it was for my benefit."

"How could it be for your benefit?"

"I believe it was for my benefit, and I guess also for my husband's benefit, and the reasoning being is that I was shown that miracles do happen. It is all in God's hands."

"You know, I think you are absolutely right."

"So now, are you ready to tell your story?"

"I think I would like to hear more of yours. This is all fascinating!"

"And once my book comes out and I tell all these stories, do you think there are going to be some out there who think I'm ready for the psychiatric hospital?"

With a roar of laughter, Tex responds, "What odds if they do. It's only because they don't know any better. Ignorance is definitely not a claim to fame."

Tex has me laughing again. I glance at my watch and realize it is getting late and I will soon have to go. "I'll tell one more story and then you definitely have to tell yours, because I have to go home and cook dinner. I have a hungry man who needs to be fed."

"Okay, we wouldn't want your husband starving to death."

With another chuckle, I proceed to tell my friend another one of my stories. "One Christmas, my daughter went skiing in Corner Brook with her friends. They all travelled by bus, and as you know, it is about an eight to ten hour drive, and maybe even longer, according to the weather and the conditions of the roads. On the evening of their return, it became stormy with high winds and it was snowing heavily. Being the mother that I am, I started to worry. My husband, being the calmer one of the two of us, tried to reassure me that being in a big bus was much safer than even driving in a car during such poor weather conditions, and that our daughter would be fine. Besides, he tells me that he is sure if the weather becomes too stormy, the bus driver will pull over and most likely stop at a hotel for the night.

In the meantime, both my husband and I are on our way to our friends' house to a Christmas party. We are driving in our car, when I become emotional and brake down sobbing. My husband is driving the car, and I am sitting in the front on the passenger's side, and I remember having my head down because I was reaching for my handbag for some tissues, when all of a sudden, my head lifted! It was as though someone was sitting behind me in the back seat of the car, and had put both hands, one on each side of my head, and pulled my head back, and turned it to the left, where I could see the car in the next lane, in front of our car. As I stare at this car, I realize I am not actually staring at the car, but the license plate and the numbers on the license plate are 555. Immediately, a peaceful feeling comes over me and I instantly know that my daughter is going to be okay and would arrive home safely! After arriving at the party, around midnight, I receive a phone call from her, telling me she is at home and safe."

Tex is not laughing anymore and is now teary eyed instead. "That is quite the story! But what did the numbers 555 mean?"

"You'll have to read my book, Tex."

As he dabs his eyes with the back of his hand, he comments, "You better believe I'll be reading your book!"

"Actually, I knew at that moment that the 555 signified that someone from the higher realms was with me and was giving me the message that my daughter would be safe."

"I never knew about numbers like that having meaning."

"They are called soul signs or spiritual signs."

"I'll be watching for them from now on. Got another story?"

"I thought it was going to be your turn next."

"Yeah, after I hear another one from you," Tex replies with a grin.

"Okay, I'll tell you about a time when I was in northern Ontario."

"Boy, you really get around, don't you?"

"Yes, I guess I do. I love travelling. Anyway, as I said, I was in northern Ontario on a small island called Moose Factory. This particular evening, a friend and her husband had a dinner party. Shortly after I arrived, it started to rain very heavily and there was a thunder and lightning storm. Later, when it was time for me to leave, the rain, thunder, and lightning had stopped but it was quite dark outside. Walking by myself, I am approaching my road when the light on the pole above me goes out. Immediately I feel danger around me; however, even though it is very dark, I see this large, beautiful dog walking right beside me! I had never seen this dog around before and I did not know where it had come from, all I knew was that it was walking beside me, as though it was protecting me. I did not feel scared or afraid anymore and I know it was because this dog was with me. This large, gorgeous dog continued to walk beside me all the way down the road to the end where my house was. As I approach my door, it looks up at me with such love and compassion in its eyes. I pat its head, and thank the dog for walking me home and then go inside my house. Shortly after, I go upstairs to get ready for bed, and as I am ready to pull the drapes to my bedroom window, I happen to glance down at my front door. There, to my astonishment, is the same dog, lying across my front doorway as though he is guarding my entrance. I knew that dog was there to protect and keep me safe. The next morning, the dog was gone, and I never did see that dog again."

"Olive, you have such incredible things that happen to you!"

"Yes, I guess I do, but I think many other people have a lot to share but are afraid to because they are scared others will only laugh at them."

"You could be right."

"I have one more story about up north, and then it's your turn."

With a huge grin, and excitement in his voice Tex exclaims, "Wonderful!"

"I had visited Canada's north before but this time it was in the Northwest Territories. I was on a business trip with another colleague, and we stayed at the Grey Goose Lodge, located in a small remote community called Deline, situated on the Great Bear Lake. The lake is famous and known for its world class fishing, and the only way to travel there is by a small aircraft.

"My room was on the back of the hotel and her room was opposite mine, at the front of the hotel. Later that night, I woke up because I could hear drums beating, and people singing and making noises. It was as if there was a pow-wow, which is a traditional native dance, and the noise of the dancing seemed to be coming from the grounds just outside my window. I jumped out of bed and looked outside, but all I could see was darkness. Strangely enough, the singing and drum beating continued for hours, late into the night! The next morning, I asked my colleague if she had heard anything unusual, like a native Indian pow-wow. She said no, she had not heard anything! None of the other guests at breakfast had heard a pow-wow either. However, one guest informed us that it is very common to hear pow-wows in this part of the country, for the word pow-wow means "spiritual leader," and many pow-wows have taken place on these lands for hundreds of years! The native people here believe that their ancestors still come back and perform the traditional, native dance!"

"Olive, you have lived an extraordinary life!"

"Well, I have to admit, my life hasn't been dull by any stretch of the imagination!" I now have Tex laughing. "Tex, while I was in the North West Territories, I had another very unusual experience one night while I was sleeping."

"Was this at the Grey Goose Lodge?"

"No, this was another night when I was staying in Norman Wells. It was late in the night, and I woke because my father was with me."

"What do you mean your father was with you?"

"I mean that I had a visit from my father. My father had died a year earlier, and he visited me while I was in the North West Territories one night."

My friend Tex is laughing once again. "As I said, Olive, you have lived an extraordinary life."

With a chuckle, I reply, "Yes I have."

"Continue with your story. I'm really anxious to know now what it is you are going to tell me."

"My father is present with me, and he shows me a room where there are other people. As he shows me this room, he tells me that I need to know that there is a meeting. As he finishes his sentence, he enters the room."

"How are you able to see this room?" Tex questions with an expression of great curiosity.

"It is as though I am watching a television screen. I am able to see the people, even though I know they are not in the room with me."

"This is astounding!"

"Yes, I know, and I am actually able to see what my father has shown me."

"And your father was with you in your bedroom, and then he left and entered this room?" Tex asks with such bewilderment.

"Yes, this is exactly what happened."

"Okay, continue."

"Well, sitting on a chair sideways to me, is my husband and he is very upset and crying. Sitting in front of my husband, and also sideways to me, is a Guardian Angel, wearing a long beige robe; and standing behind the Guardian Angel is my father. My father is dressed in a grey suede jacket, grey wool pants, and a blue shirt. I can hear the conversation, and the Guardian Angel, who I sense is my husband's Guardian Angel, is telling him he is going to get sick and he is going to cross over. My husband tells the Guardian Angel that he does not want to cross over because he does not want to leave me behind."

With tears in his eyes, my dear friend Tex states, "Olive, your husband has an undying love for you. You are truly blessed."

As I wipe my eyes, my only comment is, "Yes, Tex, I know."

"And so what happens next?" Tex asks with an anxious tone in his voice.

"Well, as I sit in my bed and cry, I can see the Guardian Angel trying to calm my husband down, but to no avail. My husband is very adamant. In no way does he want to leave me and go to the Other Side. There is silence for the longest time. No one is speaking and the only sound heard is my husband sobbing uncontrollably. Eventually, I hear the Guardian Angel say to my husband, 'Your wish has been granted. Go in peace.' It is then my father turns and looks at me, and smiles. Then they all fade away."

"That is quite the story!"

"Yes, it is, isn't it?"

"You got that right."

"Okay, Tex, now it's your turn."

"Okay, I know I won't have any problem telling you my story now, after hearing your amazing stories. Here goes. I had a quiet evening last evening, I guess no different than most of my evenings. I didn't cook anything for dinner; I just opened a tin of soup."

"Was it your usual soup that you like?"

With a chuckle, Tex responds, "You know I love my chicken and rice soup."

"Yes, I know."

"Well, after I ate, I tidied the kitchen and then watched some television. It's always good to keep up on what's going on in the world."

"Yes, this is true. I always like to watch the evening news also but sometimes I find it so depressing."

"Yes, it can be depressing at times, but that's life, isn't it? Don't know why it's got to be this way, but there you go."

"Yes, I'm afraid I don't have answers to all the hatred, turmoil and violence in the world."

"Anyway, on with my story; I am really anxious to see what you think of it all."

"You really have me curious now. I can't imagine what it is you are going to tell me."

"I know you believe in angels, right?"

"I most certainly do."

"Have you seen any angels yourself?"

"No, I can't say that I have, except for the story I just shared with you, and that was like watching a television screen. However, I have heard my Guardian Angel speak to me."

"What if I told you I have seen angels?"

"You mean last evening?"

"Yes, I mean last evening!"

"Last evening you saw angels?"

"Now don't freak out on me." We are both now laughing to the point of near hysteria.

As soon as we both calm down, Tex continues. "Well, as I was saying, last evening was not much different than most evenings for me. I had my soup, tidied up, watched some shows on the television and then I watched the national news; then got ready for bed."

I am now listening very intently, my curiosity piqued. "Yes, go on. You got ready for bed, and then what?"

"I was in bed and was still wide awake. I was just lying in bed. The lamp next to the bed was still on. You know, I like to relax and think about the day before I turn off the light and go to sleep."

"I can understand that. I do the same each night. I like to relax in bed and reflect on the happenings of my day." Tex is now laughing to the point he cannot seem to stop. I sit there, wondering what it was I said that was so funny. "What did I say that was so funny?"

"You didn't say anything."

"Okay, then why are you laughing?"

"I'm just picturing us tonight lying in our beds, reflecting on this day."

He has me laughing again; so much so, I have to get another tissue from my handbag to wipe my eyes. "Tex, I don't know what you are about to tell me, but it sure seems it is out of the ordinary."

"You got that right."

"Okay, are you going to continue? You're lying in your bed and you are wide awake, right?"

"Wide awake, I was no more asleep than what I am right now." He takes another sip of coffee, "I'm just lying there. I was about to turn over and reach for the light to turn it off, when I look over to the corner of the room, and standing there is the most beautiful woman I had ever seen!"

I quickly respond, "A woman in your room?"

"Yes, but that's not the best of it. There was another one next to the window! And then I looked to the left, and there was another one; three altogether!"

"You had three women in your bedroom last evening?"

"Three women, and if you think that's strange, get a load of this. They all looked the same."

"They all looked the same?"

"Identical."

"Identical?"

"Yes, identical. They all had long, curly, blond hair and they were all wearing the same style dress."

I sit and listen in complete awe. "What did their dresses look like?"

"They were dressed in white satin down to the mid-calf of their legs."

"And each dress looked the same?"

"Each dress looked exactly the same."

"Tex, this is absolutely remarkable. Are you sure you weren't dreaming this?"

"Definitely not dreaming, I was wide awake. And they were the most beautiful women I have ever seen. And I've seen a lot of beautiful women in my day, and you're one of them."

Tex has me laughing again as I graciously reply, "Tex, you're too kind. Well, you said they were angels. How do you know that they were angels? Did they say they were angels?"

"No, they didn't say a word. They just went around the room looking at the pictures."

"Did you say anything?"

"Are you kidding me? I think I went into a state of shock!"

Again we are both laughing. "Okay, but how did you know that they were angels?"

He quickly replies, "Because they had wings on their backs."

"Wings on their backs!"

"Yes, wings on their backs! They did not fly but walked around, even though they had wings. As they walked around the room, they looked at each picture in the room. They did not speak one word. They just walked around. They did not look at each other and at that point, they did not even look at me. It was as though they didn't even know I was there, or so I thought."

"And they did know that you were there?"

"Oh yes, they sure knew I was there."

"How do you know they knew you were there?"

"Because after they finished walking around the room and had looked at all the pictures I have, each one looked at me and smiled."

"They smiled at you?"

"Yes, all three of them smiled. These smiles were the most beautiful smiles I have ever seen in my life. I have seen a lot of beautiful smiles in my time, but nothing like this. After they looked at me and smiled, they then faded away."

"Tex, this is truly amazing!"

"You think so?" Now we are both laughing hysterically.

As I compose myself, I respond, "Angels are spiritual messengers from God."

"So you think God sent me these special angels for a reason?"

"It certainly seems that way. Why do you think they visited you?"

"I don't know, maybe because my time is getting short."

"Do you really think maybe that's why they visited you?"

"Who knows? I'll be eighty-one my next birthday. Time is running out for me anyway."

"Tex, this is one of the most beautiful stories I have ever heard. You must feel so blessed to have been given such a visit?"

"I don't know about that."

"Oh, you're not giving yourself credit. I know you are a very loving person and I know you did the best during your lifetime. It sounds to me you are going to a great place once your time is up living here on Earth."

"Well, it's something to look forward to, isn't it?"

"It most certainly is. I sure hope I have the same type of loving, miraculous experience when I am your age."

"Oh, you've got a long time to go yet."

I smile. I look at my watch and realize I am running late. I give my apologies to my dear friend Tex and tell him I will see him later. As I get ready to leave, I say to Tex, "Enjoy your evening. Maybe you'll have more gorgeous women visit."

We both laugh as we say our good-byes.

CHAPTER 19

Two Wrongs Don't Make A Right

"Two wrongs don't make a right."

My father: Ralph Neil

We have received news of a death. After speaking with my husband, I go down to our family room to spend some time by myself. I feel I want some quiet time alone to be able to think things through, as to how I can best help my husband through this ordeal. As I sit in the family room, the lamp on the coffee table next to me starts to get brighter and starts to blink at a very slow pace. Instantly I know it is my father and I immediately start to cry. I find myself sobbing, even though I am trying to control my emotions because I want to be strong for my husband. I am finally able to compose myself, and wipe away my tears. "Hello Dad."

My father replies, "Hello, my doll."

"I guess, Dad, you know what is going on?"

"Yes, Dad knows everything."

I nod my head, as I think to myself, yes of course you do.

"My doll, Dad is here to give you some advice."

"Okay, I could certainly do with your help."

"I know this is not a good time for all of you. And I know that it is worse for Dave, but I want you all to do what is right."

"Okay, Dad. What is it you are saying exactly?"

"I am saying that you and Dave should visit the funeral home. This is what is best for Dave."

"Dad, are you serious?"

"Yes, Dad is very serious. Dave needs to do what is right to do. Just go the one time and you do not have to talk to anyone if you don't want to. If anyone speaks that you do not wish to speak to, just do not speak. Remain silent."

"Well, how am I going to get Dave to go to the funeral home? He says he's not going and he has no intention of doing anything."

"I know, my doll, I know. You need to tell him that I am saying he should go. And tell him that I am saying that after this is all over, he will be able to be at peace once and for all."

"Dave really deserves to be at peace, Dad."

"Yes, he does. You go with him to the funeral home. He will need your strength to deal with this issue. Please tell him he needs to do it for himself."

"You really think this is what is best for Dave?"

"Yes, I do. Dave also needs to go to the church, and you to go with him. You do not have to sit with anyone. Sit in the back of the church. Just attend the church service and don't go to the graveyard for the burial."

There is silence because I am trying to take it all in as to what my father is telling me.

"I know that Dave has been hurt time and time again and I know he doesn't want to do anything or to have any contact with anyone, but tell him he needs to go to the funeral for himself, or he may have regrets."

"Dad, this is what I am afraid may happen and I already said this to him."

"I know you have, my doll, but you need to tell him I am telling him he should go."

"Dad, Dave knows how loving you are, and I know he will realize that you are thinking about us, and you are telling us these things to do because you know what is best for us at this time."

"Yes, my doll, this is right. Tell Dave that you both need to go to the funeral home and to the church, show that you are loving and respectful, and that you are there to do the right thing."

"Well, Dad, I know that Dave has a lot of respect for you, and therefore I am inclined to believe that he will listen to you."

"You both know that I would never do anything to hurt either of you."

The tears are starting to flow again as I realize what my father is telling me is so true. "Okay, Dad, I will talk to Dave again."

"Okay, and remember that Dad is here with you."

"I love you, Dad."

"I love you too, my doll."

I leave the family room and go look for my husband. I find him and tell him we need to talk. He just looks at me and does not respond. I begin by stating, "Dave, we have a visitor." My husband just stares at me and still does not respond. "Dad is here with us." I can see tears filling his eyes, as he looks and smiles at me. I proceed to tell my husband everything that my father has said to me.

My husband is silent. I wait patiently for him to respond because I know he is in deep thought. He finally breaks the silence. "Ol, I know your father knows what's best. If he is saying that I should go, then I will go."

"You mean to the funeral home?"

"Yes, and I will go the church and I will do what your father is saying for me to do. We will sit in the back of the church, away from the others, and then after the church service, we will go home. I trust your father and I know he is concerned, and is telling me to do what he believes to be right."

"Yes, darling, Dad will never steer us wrong."

"I know."

"And as Dad always said, 'Two wrongs don't make a right.' You remember Dad saying this, don't you?"

My husband nods his head. "Yes, that was one of your father's sayings."

Later my husband and I go to the funeral home, even though I know it is extremely difficult for him. We stay only for a short time and then we leave. We will not be returning. At the advice of my loving father, we have decided we will go to the church when the time comes. We will sit in the back of the church, and we will definitely not be going to the gravesite.

When the time came, we took my father's advice and we went to the church and sat in the back. There were not very many people in the church and I know we stuck out like sore thumbs. We sat in the second

---

last seat; there was no one behind us and there were not any people in many rows in front of us or to the sides.

It was very difficult for us to sit through the service but we stuck it out. We did not sing, we did not pray, we did not acknowledge any form of the funeral service. The main thing is that we got through it and then we left the church and returned home.

I feel it is now finally all over and that we can finally be at peace. We walk with God beside us and because He walks with us, I know we can never falter while we walk in His path of righteousness and love, and we have my dear and loving father walking beside us every step of the way also.

After we returned from the church, my husband takes me in his arms and hugs me. With tears in his eyes, he says, "Ol, your father was in the church with us."

I am not surprised. "Dad said he wouldn't leave us."

"Your father was there next to me in the pew. At one point, I didn't think that I could take any more, but then your father spoke to me." Taking a tissue and wiping away his tears, he continues. "He said, 'Dave, I know you are finding this really hard. It will soon be all over.' He got me through it, Ol. He was there for me."

I am speechless. I know this all has great meaning for my husband because he knows he can depend on my father. He is a man of his word. He will never forsake or abandon him, ever. My loving father was there to help my husband through this very difficult time in his life and now it is finally all over.

I decide I will make us some tea, while my husband lights a fire in the fireplace in our living room. After lighting the fire, Dave turns on our stereo and plays some of our favorite instrumental music. I find the tea so soothing, and the crackling of the birch junks and the heat from the fire makes it so relaxing. We are enjoying each other's company as we sit in silence, listening to the beautiful music. It is a very tranquil and peaceful time for us, which I know we will cherish in our hearts forever.

Sometime later, I decide to go to the study, to do some work on the computer. I am sitting at my desk when I realize that the light in the ceiling has gotten much brighter; my concentration from my work is broken. It is then I realize that the light behind me is blinking at a soft and moderate speed. I am not startled or surprised, but in fact, I am lovingly thankful because I know it is my father back to visit. I can feel his presence in the study and I can feel much love. I look at the time on my computer and it is 5:32 P.M. The thought, which comes to me, is that the burial ceremony at the gravesite has ended.

I speak to my father by greeting him. "Hello, Dad."

"Hello, my doll. How are you doing?"

"I'm doing wonderful."

"I am so proud of you and Dave."

Tears are now in my eyes and I feel so emotional. There is silence between us. I finally ask, "How do you think Dave did, Dad?"

"I know it was very hard on Dave, very hard. Although, he was strong. He got through it; that is the main thing. Tell Dave it is all over now. He will finally be at peace. He deserves it. Tell him I am proud of him. I know it took a lot out of him. He will be rewarded in the end."

"He will be rewarded in the end, Dad?"

"Yes, my doll, he most certainly will be, and tell him this for me, okay?"

"Yes, I'll tell him. Dad, how did I do?"

"You did exceptionally well. Dad is very proud of you also. I know it wasn't very easy on you, to go to the church today."

"Dad, I found him so hateful."

"I know you did. His time has come. You have risen above it all. He can never bring you down. You are too far above. You continue to walk with God by your side."

"Dad, you know we would never have done any of this only because of you."

"You know it was all for your own good. Dad would never ask you to do anything if I knew it would do you harm. Dad is here to help you. I will never abandon you. Dad will always walk beside you every step of the way, especially through the hard times."

I now feel overwhelmed with his love and I am crying. "Dad, it is so nice to hear your voice."

"I know, my doll, I know."

"It was so great that you were there with Dave in the church. You helped him so much. Your love means so much."

"Dad loves all of you, all the world."

Now there is silence once again, as I allow the loving words of my father sink into my brain. I find comfort in my thoughts and my feelings. My thoughts are of my dad and I feel so much love from him. I feel so blessed to have a devoted and loving father while I live on this Earth at this time, and to know that he is still with me. He has never really left because he still visits now even more than when he lived here on Earth. I feel so grateful.

The light behind me is still blinking brightly at a moderate rate so I decide to call my husband down to the study.

"Dave," I yell.

"What?" I can hear my husband answer.

"I want you to come down to the study."

As my husband walks in the study, he looks at the blinking light behind me. He then looks at me, and we exchange a smile.

"Dave, you know who is here, don't you?"

"Yes, Ol."

"Dave, are you able to see Dad?"

"Yes, but it is just his face that I can see."

"What does he look like?"

"Your father looks the same except he looks younger. He still has the gray, thick, wavy hair."

I become overwhelmed with what my husband is saying and once again, I become very emotional. "Dad brings us so much love."

"Yes, Ol, I can feel it."

Now the light behind me stops blinking. My father had come to visit us to let us know it is all over. All over, meaning that the others had left the gravesite. He also came to let us know how proud he was of us and how very much he loves us. He also wanted to reinforce to us the fact that he would never abandon or forsake us.

After a short time, I get up from my desk and leave the study, turning off the lights on my way out. Upstairs I find my husband in the kitchen, and as I walk in, he comes to me and hugs me. I now feel so much love and peace. I think back at what my own father had said to me earlier; it is finally all over and Dave can now be at peace. He deserves it.

Because my father's love is so powerful and strong, and he comes from the higher realms on the Other Side, he has the right and the privilege to visit with his loved ones while we remain here on Earth. These types of visits have happened many times since my father died, on April 8, 2003. He is watching over all of us and keeping us safe. He loves all of us very much. With this thought, I come to the realization that my dad has never really left us at all; for he watches over us and is taking care of us at all times and, as he said himself, especially through the hard times.

My father walks with God beside him and therefore he will never falter while he walks in God's path of righteousness and love. I know this is why my father's love is so very strong and powerful. It is so comforting to know that we can never be lead astray. As I think back over all the years when my father lived here on Earth, I realize that I had always found him to be honest. He always spoke the truth. He is an honest and just man with great character and integrity.

When he was my dad living on this Earth, he was always there for us. As I sit here with the loving thoughts of my father, I understand that I do not have to worry about any of us anymore. I take comfort in the fact that I am never alone. Over the years, my father has always been there for my husband, my children and I, and showed his love in so many ways, and just because his body died, does not mean that he is gone from us. He comes around all of us at different times and loves us very, very much. I love my father sincerely, and I love my Heavenly Father for blessing me with His love, and for giving me such a loving and devoted soul, as my dad.

CHAPTER 20

The Blue Butterfly

The butterfly is reminiscent of the soul.

Chinese Folklore

I am very excited because I am taking a cruise; and this is not just any cruise, this is a cruise where I will be spending time with my son. He has made all of the arrangements and has paid for everything for me. I have to fly to San Diego, California for a ten-day Mexican Rivera cruise. The ports of call during the cruise are Cabo San Lucas, Mazatlan, Acapulco, Ixtapa and Puerto Vallarta.

During my cruise, I meet many people and have numerous fabulous experiences; however, there are two experiences, which I shall remember for a long time. It is the day of the Captain's cocktail party and I have made an appointment with a young male in the beauty salon to get my hair done for this special evening. As it turns out, this young person has special psychic abilities, and while he is doing my hair, he tells me to give him a name because he can give me information about this person. I find this all so intriguing and so I start by giving him the name of my husband.

Rudy states, "He loves you with all his heart."

I instantly reply, "Yes, you are so right!"

"Give me another name."

I say my son's name.

He comments, "You are his life."

I smile and think how lucky I am to have such a loving son.

Rudy then says, "Another name."

I say my daughter's name.

He answers, "She also loves you very much and she will never allow anyone to be put down. She will stand up for what she believes to be right and just."

Again, I smile, thinking once again how lucky I am to have such a loving daughter.

Rudy continues. "Your parents loved you very much when you were a child."

Once again, I smile, as I think back on my childhood memories.

Before I leave, Rudy gives me the most beautiful gift; it is a hairpin. While I sit in the chair, he lovingly places the pin in my hair. He smiles at me, wishes me much happiness, and wishes me to have a wonderful evening at the Captain's cocktail party with my son and all the other guests.

After ten glorious days of cruising and visiting the different ports of call, it is time to pack. Like all good things, it must end. The next morning, I am to disembark the cruise ship. My son and I are sitting in the lounge discussing my travel plans back home and he tells me he has arranged for me to stay at a hotel overnight in downtown San Diego because the flights out the day I disembark the ship do not have good connecting times for me to travel. He wants me to have a very comfortable and enjoyable flight back home, and he feels that it is in my best interest for me to travel the following day. However, as I think all of this through, I am inclined to believe that maybe it would be better for me to go directly to the airport, and see if I can get a better flight out of San Diego with better connections to Toronto. With these thoughts, I say to him, "I am thinking that I will go directly to the airport when I disembark."

My son looks at me as he questions my motive. "Mom, why would you do that?"

"Well, because I am thinking the airlines could have a cancellation or a no show for the flight with the good connecting times, and I will be able to fly home tomorrow."

"Mom, there is no need for you to do that."

"I know there is no need, but I think that it wouldn't be necessary for you to spend the extra money for me to stay in a hotel for the night."

My son responds. "I already have it booked for you; it is part of your trip."

"Yes, I know this, but there is no need for you to spend extra money. I have had a wonderful cruise with you and you paid for all my expenses, and it is not necessary to spend more money."

"Mom, money is not an issue. I do not want you going to the airport tomorrow morning, and besides, there is no guarantee that the airlines will have an empty seat. And even if they do, it could be one at the back of the plane or it could be a middle seat, it wouldn't be comfortable for you."

As I give this some thought, I realize what my son is saying is true. "Okay, you are right. I could get to the airport and I am still not guaranteed a seat."

"I want you to get the taxi tomorrow morning and go to the hotel. It is right in downtown San Diego, and you can enjoy the remainder of your trip relaxing, and you can even go shopping at the downtown mall."

"Well, that sounds exciting! Okay, I will do just that."

The next morning, March 28, I hug and kiss my darling son and thank him for such a fabulous vacation and proceed to disembark and get my taxi, which is waiting outside the terminal. I arrive at the hotel, and just as my son said, the hotel is located downtown and just a short distance away from the Horton Plaza Mall. I check in and go directly to my room, and get settled away, unpacking just necessities. I then decide I will take my son up on his suggestion and go shopping.

I head straight downtown in the direction of the Horton Plaza Mall, which is only about a ten-minute walk. It is a large, outdoor type of mall, with many stores and cafes. As I am browsing, I notice one of my favorite café's in the distance, and so I head toward it for a coffee. I go inside, order my coffee and rather than sit inside, I decide to sit at one of the tables outside, because it is such a beautiful day. The table I have chosen is a small, round table with just two chairs. As I pull up a chair at the empty table, I realize it is a perfect place to drink my coffee in the sunshine, while watching and listening to the birds in the trees.

I am sipping my coffee when I notice a male walking in my direction, coming towards me. I am awe struck because of this man's outfit. He is wearing a royal blue jacket, and on his head is a white hat, with three, large royal blue feathers on one side. I watch him as he enters the cafe and in no time at all, he comes out, and much to my surprise, comes directly towards me! He comes to my table and without uttering a word, lays his coffee on the table, pulls out the chair opposite to me, and sits down. He sits back as though we have known each other for years and I have been waiting for him.

Astonished by this man's behavior, I sit and think that this is most odd, and as I glance around, I notice that there are other tables available; however, this stranger chooses to sit with me. I am also thinking that most people, under these circumstances, would ask if it was okay to sit, or to ask if the chair was taken, but not this man; he just sits down as if we were supposed to meet each other. As I sip my coffee, he smiles and looks into my eyes, and instantly I know that even though we have never met, I know him and it certainly seems as though he knows me!

In my lifetime, I have met many people from all lifestyles and from different corners of this place we call Earth, and I find I tend to place people into three categories. The first category I estimate to be approximately 10% of the population living here on Earth, and these souls are the ones that I consider exceptional, and with whom I love to associate. The second category I estimate to be among the 80% of the population. These individuals are the good souls but they are not exceptionally good like the first category. The third category I estimate to be 10%. These are the souls that I thank God for allowing me to be in their presence, because I know it served a purpose for me, however, these are the souls that I wish to never meet again. Now, here I am sitting with this man, knowing that he fits into the first category, which is the exceptional; and I know I am in the presence of a great master!

He starts the conversation. "Gold is on the rise. It went up $10.00 in one day."

I reply, fascinated by his comment, "Yes, I have heard in the news how the stocks in gold are on the rise."

He asks, "Do you have any gold stocks?"

Quite astounded by this man's question, I reply, "No, I don't."

"If you are interested in buying some stock, you should call Monex Company and ask them what you need to do to leverage gold. The number is: 1-800-444-8317."

As I reach for my handbag to retrieve my notebook and pen, I reply, "Thank you so much for this information."

"No problem. It is a quick way to make some fast money."

"Yes, it certainly sounds like it is."

He quickly changes the topic of conversation. "I am writing a movie."

Once again, fascinated by this man's comment, I respond, "How wonderful. It must be very interesting work."

"Yes it is. I enjoy it very much. The name of the movie is Color Money, Blue & Pink."

"It certainly has an intriguing title."

"Do you really think so?"

"Yes, I most certainly do."

"Well, by seeing what you are wearing today, you are confirming to me my movie, Color Money, Blue & Pink, because the top that you are wearing has the colors blue and pink, which are sparkling in the sunlight. You also have the colors blue and pink in your jacket."

Quite amazed at this comment, I look down at the top that I am wearing, and sure enough, I am wearing an off-white top with large colored beads of blue and pink at the neckline, and the beads are glistening in the sun. As I glance at my jacket, I realize what he speaks is correct. I look up and laugh. "This is funny; I am wearing the same colors as the title of your movie."

He laughs also and replies, "I am taking it as a positive sign. Meeting you here today reinforces to me that I am on the right track with this movie, and I need to continue with my writing."

I continue to laugh as I say to this stranger, "Well, I am also taking it as a positive sign, because of what you are wearing."

"And why is that?"

"Because the color royal blue has great significant meaning to me; and your jacket is royal blue and your hat that you are wearing is white with three royal blue feathers sticking up on one side."

"Interesting," is his only comment.

Drawn into this most wonderful conversation with this stranger, I chuckle.

"The color you are referring to as royal blue is also called indigo, and it is a deep rich dark blue. This color indigo symbolizes wisdom, self-mastery and spiritual realization."

"This is quite fascinating."

"Yes it is. And it is also believed that the color indigo is said to increase personal thought and provide profound insights, which therefore allows for instant understanding, which is commonly referred to as intuition and therefore spiritual truth."

"I didn't know this."

"When you have "an instinct," or "a hunch," or "a gut feeling," or you feel "you just know;" this is what is referred to as your intuition. Intuition goes beyond the physical knowing; for it is the spiritual experience of knowing."

"It's all quite interesting, isn't it?"

"It most certainly is interesting."

"Did you know that the color indigo or royal blue as you call it; has a Biblical meaning which symbolizes Heavenly grace?"

"No, I didn't know this."

"It is believed that the Virgin Mary is often depicted wearing this color."

"You seem to know a lot about this color."

"Yes, I guess I do. I also know that this color represents power, importance and wealth. It is a rich color, worn by the wealthy. During the Elizabethan era, only royalty were permitted to wear the color indigo, as sanctioned by English laws."

"I can certainly understand this because it is such a rich and vibrant color."

"Apparently, the name indigo comes from the indigo plants which make the dye. It was quite expensive because it had to be imported from India."

"You seem to have such a wealth of knowledge."

He smiles and asks, "And why is the color indigo of such significance to you?"

"I really don't know. All I know is that the color means a lot to me. It is as though I am drawn to this color, and I love it because I know it is of great importance."

"I find what you are saying to be extremely enchanting."

"I am curious as to why you are wearing a jacket which is royal blue and a white hat with three royal blue feathers."

"I don't know if I can give you any real explanation, other than this is me."

"Hmm," I respond. "I am also curious as to why you chose to sit at my table."

"Again, I don't have an explanation, other than it just came quite natural for me to join you."

"Would I be correct in saying that you take it upon yourself to sit with strangers on a regular basis, especially if the strangers are female?"

We both laugh. He answers, "No, you wouldn't be correct. Actually this is very unusual behavior for me."

"Really?" I question.

"Yes, really."

"Well, don't you think it is time for us to introduce ourselves?"

With a chuckle, he responds, "I'm Adam."

"It is very nice to meet you, Adam. I'm Olive."

"And it a pleasure to meet you, Olive. Tell me, why were you called the name Olive?"

"I really don't know."

"That name has special meaning for you."

"It does?"

"Yes it does, even if you don't remember."

"Well, what I do remember is that I have always felt I had been privileged by being given the name Olive. Why I have these feelings I really don't know, and over the years, these feelings have become stronger and stronger. It is as though, as my life started to unfold, I began to understand more and more. I can only describe it as pieces of a huge puzzle. Bits and pieces of information started to come to me, and I have been trying to make sense of it all. I know my name is different and not very common."

"Yes, it is different, and especially for you."

"Oh my, I now remember many years ago when my aunt told me I have a special name."

"Your name is very special."

"I know other people are captivated by my name. One such time was when I was celebrating my birthday with my husband in a restaurant, back home. During the evening, I received a gift from the couple at the next table. They had ordered a wonderful dessert and had it delivered to me as a birthday gift. They were complete strangers, yet they took it upon themselves to be so considerate and loving. We later joined them at their table and we found out that they were tourists from the United States, visiting Newfoundland for the first time. They introduced themselves as Minnie and Rod, and then my husband introduced us. I remember Minnie looking at Rod with an expression of surprise on her face. It was then she looked at me and told me that she loves my name, and so much so, that she had already decided that should she ever have a girl, she was going to call her Olive. She also told me that she feels so much love from the name, that when she says the name Olive, it sounds like, "I love you." Quite the story, don't you think?"

"That is quite the story."

"Yes, it is, isn't it? After this couple returned to the United States, I sent them an email and I told them that our meeting in the restaurant on my birthday was no coincidence, and that there is no such thing as a coincidence in life. We were meant to meet and that I believed that God had sent them to me on my birthday, as a gift."

The evening of my birthday

284

"That is such a beautiful story and I do believe that there is a message in there; not just for them, but for you also."

"Yes, I do believe you are right in saying that. I find that people search me out and one of the reasons is because of my name."

"I'm not surprised because the name Olive is a spiritual name."

"Oh my, I remember another time when someone else I met told me the very same thing as you are saying. She also said my name is a spiritual name."

Adam's facial expression changes to an expression of curiosity. "And when did this happen?"

"Some years ago, I was visiting Canada's North West Territories, and one of the communities I visited was Fort Good Hope. I met the most charming person there; she called herself the Four Winds Woman. As we chatted, I remember asking her why I was there in Fort Good Hope, and why did I have to meet her. Her answer was quite amazing; she said it was planned for me to meet her, and that I was to be part of the healing movement. She said that there is a strong belief down south that the healing is going to take place from the north."

"What healing was she referring to?"

"I asked her the same question and she told me the healing of the people of all nations."

"She sounds like a very spiritual person."

"Yes, I know she is."

"Is she aboriginal?"

"Yes she is. She is from the north, the North West Territories."

"I thought so."

I continue my story. "She talked about the Medicine Wheel and actually drew a picture of it for me. In the picture of the Medicine Wheel or the Wheel of Life, as some people call it, she explains to me that the North represents mental; the South represents emotion; the West represents physical; and the East represents spiritual." I can sense that Adam is quite mesmerized by my story of the Four Winds Woman.

"I can tell by what you are saying that this person, who calls herself the Four Winds Woman, is a very special and very spiritual individual."

"Yes, Adam, I know you are right. Before my conversation ended with her, she said to me, remember your name. And of course, you can well imagine my reaction to such a comment." With both of us laughing, I continue my story. "She told me my name has special meaning and that it is a spiritual name, and that the reason I was given this name is that when I look at a person I don't see the outside. What I see is the goodness, the place where the goodness is."

"I certainly agree with her understanding of your name. She is right. The name Olive does have very superior meaning."

"Well, I do know that the olive branch means peace."

"Yes, you are right. The olive branch is a symbol of peace and good will. We learn this from the Bible, where the dove returns to Noah after the flood, and in its beak it has an olive leaf."

"Yes, I remember. The story of Noah is in the Holy Bible in Genesis."

"According to Christian belief, after the crucifixion of Jesus, he wandered for 40 days and 40 nights on the Mount of Olives, before he ascended to Heaven."

"Yes, I'm familiar with the story of Jesus on the Mount of Olives."

"Olives also represent peace from a practical sense because many years of peace are required to grow olive trees, and then it takes several years to produce the olive fruit. The olive tree is considered the tree of life, and it represents abundance, glory, peace, power, unity and healing."

"You seem to have acquired a lot of knowledge regarding the word olive."

Adam chuckles as he continues. "The Greeks consider the olive tree "the daughter of the sun," and "the blessed one." And do you know that the oldest olive tree in the world is supposed to be over 1000 years old?"

"No, I do not know this about the olive tree. This is all incredible. I do know a beautiful poem called, *The Olive Tree*. Would you like to hear it?"

"Yes, of course. You have memorized this poem, have you?"

With a grin, I reply, "No, my memory is not that great. I have a copy of this poem in my handbag. The poem is written by Elizabeth Mason and is taken from a selection of poetry in the book, *Thoughts & Reflections For Throughout the Year*.

The Olive Tree

Above me, a myriad of precious jewels are ripening in the sun,
inviting me to stay and fix my silent gaze upon.
I close my eyes and speak to my creator through my prayers,
His holy presence capturing all worries, doubts and cares."

"You are right, Olive. This is a beautiful poem indeed."

"Yes it is, isn't it?"

"Do you know that the name Olive has a spiritual meaning?"

"It does?"

"Yes, it does. The olive represents all that is good, such as love. In both the Christian faith and the Jewish faith, the olive is recognized to possess special qualities, and is associated with peace and love."

"I do know that it was the oil from the olive, with which priests and kings were anointed and lamps were lit."

"Yes, I do remember reading that. And I also know that the olive has great meaning to many people."

As I find myself deep in thought, I respond, "You could be absolutely right."

"In the Hebrew scriptures, the olive represents a very powerful symbol, and this is because the oil from the olive gives light and brightness in the world. The olive tree is supposed to remind us that while living life here on Earth, our light should burn constantly."

"I find all of this so interesting."

"It is interesting, isn't it?"

"Is this the origin of the belief that light means love?"

"It could very well be. It certainly makes a whole lot of sense. As I already said, the olive represents light and love."

"And therefore it makes sense that darkness represents hate."

"It certainly does make sense, doesn't it?"

"Yes, it does."

"Many believe that the olive also means victory."

"Really?"

"Yes, do you not remember that olive wreaths are worn during the Olympic Games to represent victory?"

"Oh yes, you are absolutely right."

"So, your name Olive is not a coincidence. You were given this name for a very exclusive reason."

"Well, I know that there is no such thing as a coincidence. I know that life here on Earth is all planned and orchestrated, far beyond even my comprehension."

"Yes, I agree with you. However, most people think their life is all about coincidences."

With this comment, we both laugh.

"People living here on Earth have been given gifts, and one of the gifts is the gift of free will or choice. People who come here to Earth during this time have their life plan already in place whether they realize this or not. However, many times throughout one's life, the person can change his or her life plan and choose not to follow it. It is during these times that the person falls by the wayside, so to speak, and veers off in the wrong direction."

"I know about the gift of free will because it has happened to me so many times when I have changed my mind about something that I know I was supposed to do."

"So, are you talking about times when you made a lot of bad choices?"

"There were times when I have made wrong choices; I wouldn't call them bad choices."

"Whatever choices you have made on your life journey, know that you always did your best. Don't be too harsh on yourself. You must always treat yourself with kindness."

"Yes, you are absolutely right. There were times when I didn't necessarily make wrong choices but times when I changed my mind. I will give you a couple of examples. I have a friend John who makes predictions about things that will happen or are supposed to happen. He told me about a cruise I was going to take, and sure enough, this was true because I had planned to take a cruise, but later I changed my mind and cancelled my cruise. Then another time John told me I was going on a trip to a country where there was beautiful scenery, and he could see me horseback riding. Sure enough, this was true again, because I had a trip planned for Dominican Republic. One of the things I intended doing during my vacation was to go horseback riding, but I didn't go because I thought it would be too hot and I couldn't bear the thought of a horse carrying me on its back in such heat. And so I veered off my path because of free will."

"Free will means you can change your mind and consequently your plans about anything, either the positive or the negative."

"You are referring to people, who for example, get caught up in negative behaviors."

"Yes, there are many examples, such as physical assault and murder." Adam quickly changes the topic. "You know, you are an angel."

I cannot help but chuckle, as I exclaim, "You can't be serious?"

"Yes, I am quite serious. You always knew that you are an angel, even when you were a child."

Shocked by such a comment, I react by laughing. "Adam, I can't help but laugh. I certainly don't consider myself an angel!"

Adam replies, "There is a saying, always welcome a stranger, because you may be meeting an angel in disguise. And I am saying that you are an angel."

Still laughing at this stranger's comment, I respond, "And I certainly don't remember knowing that I was an angel when I was a child. What I do remember is that I always knew and felt that I was very different from everyone else, especially those in my family."

"How is that?"

"I was just different. I do not even look like anyone in my family. I look and act different. I'm just different."

"How many are there in your family?"

"I grew up with four sisters, no brothers. I am the middle child, so I have two older sisters and two younger sisters. I do not look like any of them, not even my parents. Now that I have gotten older, I think I have become more different. It is as though I have nothing in common with them anymore, and really, I guess I never did. I consider my personality quite unlike any of theirs. The only one that I can say that I resemble is my father. I have been told that I am like my father because he was spiritual and so am I."

"Well, I certainly know that to be true of you."

With tears starting to well in my eyes, I answer, "Actually it is very interesting, because since my father's death, I have come to realize just how much I am like him."

I am starting to become emotional as I think about my dad, and I sense that Adam realizes this as he changes the topic. "I know you are married because you have already mentioned your husband, but do you have other family?"

"I am very fortunate because God has blessed me with the most loving husband and two beautiful children."

"I can see that everyone in your family is healthy. You have no concern there."

"This is wonderful to know."

"You must choose your friends wisely."

"Anyone can be my friend, if they so choose. I like all people and I respect the differences of all people. It does not matter to me if the person is black or white, tall or short, male or female, married or single, homosexual or heterosexual, rich or poor, religious or not; as I said, I respect all people. I know that God made us all and we are all His children."

"I can tell by what you are saying that you are a very, very spiritual person and very loving."

"Yes, I am."

"So, are you also religious?"

"I am a Christian, of the Anglican faith and I respect the Christian religion; however, I am more spiritual than religious. There is a difference you know."

"Yes, of course there is. One can be religious without being spiritual, and one can be spiritual without being religious. Unfortunately, there are many people in this world that consider themselves religious just because they are a member of a particular organized religion and attend their service of worship regularly; however, this does not mean that they are also spiritual, and therefore they may not have any idea about spirituality. They don't realize that without spirituality, religion has very little meaning."

"Yes, Adam, you are absolutely right. To know God is to be spiritual. If a person is not spiritual, he or she does not know God. They may think or believe they know God because they profess to be of a particular religion and as you say, routinely attend their ritual weekly religious service; however, this does not necessarily mean they know God, our Creator of all."

"I've met these kinds of people. They are everywhere."

"They do not walk in God's path of righteousness and love. They claim to be religious and loving; however, their negative and hateful attitudes and behaviors tell a different story. They are not following a loving God; they have chosen to follow the evil one. They know the difference between right and wrong, good and bad, love and hate. Yet, they choose to go about living their lives in turmoil, and then they claim to be good and righteous because they are religious. Worse still are those such as some priests who have abused little, innocent children, and who claim they represent God and preach to others, but in actual fact do the workings of the evil one."

"It's all about choice. One can choose to be religious and not be spiritual and one can choose to be spiritual and not be religious."

"Yes, this is true and one can also choose to be both religious and spiritual."

"And one can choose to be loving or hateful or to choose to follow our Creator or the evil one, which most people in the western world refer to as the devil."

"Some also refer to him as Satan, as is stated in Muslim writings. *For Satan is to man an avowed enemy.* The Holy Qur'an, Al-Isra, Surah 17: 53."

"Yes, and he is also referred to as Satan in the Holy Bible."

"Yes, you are right. Many times throughout the Bible he is called Satan."

"Well, whether one calls him the evil one, the devil, or Satan, it all means the same thing."

I nod my head in agreement, as I continue. "One has to be spiritual to truly know God and it is the responsibility of each person to travel the road of a spiritual journey. I remember the writings by Kahlil Gibran, in *The Prophet*: *Your daily life is your temple and your religion. Whenever you enter into it take with you your all.* One does not have to be in a building to worship God."

"I agree with you completely, Olive, and of course I agree with Gibran, the famous Lebanese artist, philosopher and writer. His great works are known throughout the world."

"Spirituality is a journey of knowledge, and of course the more knowledge one has, the more understanding and wisdom; whereas religion is a journey of faith. While every follower of each religion of this world believes his religion is the one and true religion, in reality the only true religion is knowing that there is only one God, and that one God represents love; for love is the essence of all, and therefore the one and true religion is the religion of love."

"I couldn't have said it better myself, Olive."

"Does this mean you are spiritual or religious or both?"

"I would have to say I am both, but like you I am more spiritual, and I do consider myself a Buddhist."

"So, you follow the practice of Buddhism?"

"Yes, I do."

"Buddhism began in India, didn't it?"

"Yes, it did. The founder of Buddhism is Siddhartha Gautama."

"What is it about the practice and teachings of Buddhism that has drawn you to this particular religion?"

"Well, as I see it, Buddhism is more than a religion. It embraces a philosophy and philosophy means love of wisdom. Buddhism teaches the importance of wisdom and consequently understanding, which in turn teaches one to live a moral life. This leads to true happiness and one can achieve this by being mindful at all times of one's thoughts, words and actions. The Buddha, Siddhartha Gautama, was born into a royal family and was, of course, financially wealthy; however, at a very young age, he realized that living a life of luxury doesn't necessarily bring happiness. He spent the remainder of his life teaching others the principles of Buddhism, which mainly consists of the 'Four Noble Truths.' It is within these truths that one should strive for peace and love."

"I have heard of the 'Four Noble Truths,' and I know they are of great significance to anyone who follows Buddhism."

"Yes, this is correct."

"Would you explain to me the 'Four Noble Truths,' because I would like to know the importance of these truths?"

"Well, I will give you a brief explanation of each one. The first noble truth is that life is about suffering. The second noble truth is that expectations cause suffering. The third noble truth is that suffering can be conquered and the fourth noble truth is that one must follow the Noble 8-fold Path."

"What is the Noble 8-fold Path?"

"Basically, the Noble 8-fold Path is about leading a moral life."

"I can understand, Adam, why you say you are a Buddhist, because you are very wise."

With a chuckle, Adam replies, "Thank you, Olive. True wisdom is not about believing, as other religions of the world teach, but about understanding. It is only when one understands himself, that he can then understand others."

"All of this makes so much sense to me."

"The other thing I really like about Buddhism is that it teaches one to search for the truth himself and consequently to take responsibility for his own actions."

"These are very powerful teachings."

Adam changes the subject. "I am able to tell that Phoenix, Arizona is an important place to you."

I chuckle. "It is?"

"Yes, it is. Have you ever been there?"

"No, I haven't but it's funny that you should say this, because it is one of the places that I wish to visit."

"Phoenix, Arizona is a spiritual land. Arizona has a lot of Aboriginal people there."

"Maybe this is why I am drawn to this place."

"I can also tell that Australia is important to you."

Again, I chuckle because Adam is right. "It's funny you should say this because I consider Australia to be a spiritual land. I do not know if it really is; I just feel it is, and I want to visit it someday. And for some unknown reason, my son has an unquenchable thirst to visit Australia, of all the places in the world. And he wants me to go with him."

"Australia is a spiritual land; and what about Mexico?"

"What about Mexico?"

"Is this a place where you would like to visit also?"

"I have already visited Mexico. I love Mexico."

"That's because Mexico is also considered to be sacred land. The Aztec gods lived in Mexico. Actually, the Aztecs were a Mesoamerican tribe who inhabited the land in what we refer to now as Mexico. The Aztec religious mythology is very rich and has a large variety of gods and goddesses. I can see that you are drawn to the spiritual lands here on Earth."

"I love to travel and I have been fortunate that I have been given many opportunities to travel in my life."

"I can also see that Montreal has great value to you. Have you been to Montreal?"

"Yes, many times. I love Montreal. In fact, I also love Quebec City and Paris. There is something about the French people, which I truly admire. I love everything about the French people; the way they dress, the French food, the French language, the French accent, the French culture, I love everything about them. I think the French are a very classy people and I admire them."

"There must be a special reason why you are drawn to the French people so much."

"Yes, I think so and I do have my theory."

"Well, let's hear it."

"When I was a child, I read about many places in this world, and for some unknown reason, I was attracted to Paris. I always had this driving, burning desire to go to Paris. It seemed to me to be the most spectacular city in the world. So my one and only dream as a child was that someday I would visit Paris."

"And did you?"

"Yes! The first year my husband and I were married, we went to Europe for vacation, and of course, Paris was on our list. I remember arriving in Paris for the first time, and I felt awe struck, for everything seemed so familiar to me. I felt as though I had lived there before. Everywhere I went, I gazed in wonderment. The feeling was mesmerizing. I felt extremely comfortable with the people and their culture. As I said earlier, I love everything about the French people. I felt as though I was accustomed to the French way of life, as if I had just returned home. What was amazing is that I felt I knew my way around. Everything seemed familiar to me, even speaking in the French language; it felt very normal to me. It was like a déjà vu."

"Well, I know you have a theory, and now I have one also. I am thinking that my theory is the same as yours. You lived a former life in Paris."

We both laugh again as I answer. "Adam, I think you are right. I do believe in reincarnation, and my theory is that I did live a previous life in Paris. It must have been a very rewarding and beautiful life for me, because I love Paris and the French people so much."

Adam says, "My theory is the same as yours."

"Isn't life amazing at times?"

"It sure is, Olive. I can tell that you enjoy travelling and meeting people."

"Yes, I most certainly do. If I didn't come here today in San Diego, I never would have met you."

"Well, I think we both know that this meeting was certainly meant to be. This was already planned out for us; all we had to do was to follow."

"Yes, and strangely enough, I wasn't going to follow."

"And why is that?"

"Because I have just been on a cruise and I thought it would be better for me to go directly to the airport, but my son insisted and was quite adamant that I check into the hotel he has booked for me, and enjoy the remainder of my trip here in San Diego. He even suggested that I go shopping here at this mall."

With a chuckle, Adam responds, "As I said, this meeting was already planned; all we had to do was follow."

"Adam, we are sitting here talking to each other as though we have known each other all our lives."

"This is definitely a sign that we are kindred souls."

"Yes, I definitely agree; there is no doubt in my mind, but I would like your definition of what a kindred soul is."

"A kindred soul is you."

We are now laughing hysterically to the point that I have to retrieve a tissue from my handbag to wipe away tears. Finally, I am able to speak again. "Yes, I know I am your kindred soul. From the moment you sat down, I knew we were very comfortable in each other's presence and we started talking as though we have known each other for years. But we both know that we have never met before."

"We both know we have never met before in this lifetime, and therefore it had to have been in a previous lifetime on Earth, or we know each other from the Other Side before we came here this time, or both."

"Yes Adam, I completely agree, we are kindred souls. We have met before today."

Adam changes the topic. "You have one more time here on Earth."

I am astounded at this comment, even though I remember my Guardian Angel telling me the same thing. "I do?"

"Yes, you do. You have to come back just one more time and then your work is complete. I can tell that you are advancing very quickly."

"Well, I believe that one should try and accomplish as much as one can during a lifetime. I know that most people squander most of their time away and live here on this Earth for years and years, and after it is all said and done, don't learn anything. I think it is so sad. People get caught up in material things and don't understand who they really are and why they are really here."

"And why do you think people really come here?"

"We all come here for a lifetime to learn and to grow spiritually as much as we can. Don't you agree with this?"

"Yes, of course I do. I just wanted to hear what you had to say. The majority of people living on this Earth become influenced by witchcraft."

"What do you mean by witchcraft?"

"Witchcraft is the movement of darkness."

"And the movement of darkness is following the evil one, the devil."

"You got that right."

"What I find with a lot of people is that they don't understand the real meaning of witchcraft."

"How is that?" he questions.

"Some people don't understand that they use witchcraft in their everyday encounters. For example, when a person thinks undesirable thoughts of someone, this is witchcraft. They are practicing witchcraft each time they use phrases like, "Drop dead!" or "Go to hell!" or any other hateful expression or comment. They are thinking negative and hateful thoughts, and consequently are following the ways of the evil one, the devil. They are doing his work and are actually one of his followers."

"I never looked at things this way before, but you are absolutely right."

"Some people think that if a person can heal, this is witchcraft and it is evil."

Adam is now laughing as he nods his head, agreeing with me. "And how bizarre is that!"

"I know. How anyone in his or her right mind can think or believe that someone who can actually heal and help others is doing evil is beyond my understanding."

"It's beyond my understanding also. If people believed that the person caused the illness, then this makes sense to believe it is witchcraft and evil; however, to think or believe otherwise is ridiculous."

"I had a conversation with a young man once, who told me that when he was younger he went to a person in the community who made his warts disappear. Now that he is older and as he puts it, has become religious, and thinks he is wiser, he considers this to have been evil. To this day, I cannot understand any logic to this way of thinking. I truly do not comprehend how someone can consider a person evil, if that person is doing God's work to heal. It is God's work to heal because it definitely is not the devil's work. The evil one does not heal. The more logical way of thinking is if he thought the person in the small town gave him the warts; then I can see him thinking this is evil."

"Well, I think I understand that way of thinking. You mentioned that this young person said he became religious. Well, there's your answer."

"I'm not sure I understand what you mean."

"Some people take religious beliefs to the extreme and soak up every word in the Bible as though it is the gospel truth. And I am assuming this young male is a Christian."

"Yes, he is."

"History tells us of the leaders of organized religion and of organized politics who have resorted to manipulate and twist the truth to their own advantage. And it was all done to control people in their way of thinking."

"Yes, this is true."

"The Bible has been translated so many times that I do not think anyone really knows the beliefs of the original version. For example, the earlier readings from the Bible included reincarnation; it was once a part of the Christian belief. However, you will not find anything about reincarnation now. There are many other examples that I can use. Then you have to take into account the interpretation of the words in the Bible. One person can read a sentence or passage and interpret it one way and then another person can read the same sentence or passage and interpret it a completely different way."

"Oh yes, Adam, you are absolutely right. I know there are passages in the Bible that religious leaders preach as truth, which I certainly do not agree with as being the truth from God. A teacher back in my province, Newfoundland and Labrador, shared his story about how he was abused by the Christian Brothers as a small child, while he lived at the Mount Cashel Orphanage in St. John's. He recalls one such time when Brother Murphy beat him with a paddle, and then took him in his arms and sexually assaulted him. Afterwards, this Christian Brother said to him, 'Always remember that God said, whomever I love, I chastise.'"

"You've hit the nail right on the head, Olive. Just goes to show those evil minded people will interpret even quotes from the Bible as they see fit."

"Yes, you are absolutely right. And then you have these religious leaders preaching to people on a daily basis, telling them how they should think."

"These religious leaders who preach what they believe to be true are really using a form of brain washing, don't you think so?"

"I certainly consider it to be brain washing and it is wrong. A friend told me that while she was attending mass at her Roman Catholic Church, the priest preached about how gay marriage is wrong. This may be his opinion but I consider this a form of brain washing, considering this priest was preaching this during the church service and it shouldn't be allowed."

"I totally agree." Adam continues, "Well, if you recall the story in the Bible about Jesus, he was a healer, and you know what happened to him."

"Yes, I most certainly do."

"Anyone who is a Christian knows that our Lord Jesus was crucified on the cross. And what did he really do to deserve such hatefulness and evil? He didn't do anything wrong, only everything right. All our Lord Jesus did was good. He went throughout the lands healing the sick wherever he would go, and he showed love and respect for all people, and yet because some people considered Him to be evil, he was murdered and died a horrible death."

"He endured horrendous pain and suffering, and all because he was a healer, and healed the sick."

"You are a healer."

"I am?"

"Yes, you are. You know this but you just don't believe you are."

"It's very interesting you are saying this, Adam, because some years ago I was told I am a healer, and yes, you are right. I guess I don't really believe I have the gift to heal."

"And why is it you don't believe you have the gift to heal?"

"I guess it's because I figure I am like most other people."

"You are not like most other people, and you know what I am saying is true."

"Yes, Adam, I know you are right. I know I am not like most other people. And actually it was just last year I was told to visit someone who was diagnosed with a serious illness."

"And who told you to visit and why?"

"I was told by my Guardian Angel that I needed to visit this person who was a patient in the hospital, and to offer her prayers of healing."

"And did you?"

"I did, but very reluctantly."

"And why is that?"

"Because I really didn't know her that well. And also I thought that most likely others would think I was crazy, including her."

"And did they?"

With a chuckle, I answer, "Yes, I'm pretty sure they did."

"Did she get well?"

"Yes, she did."

"So I am right. You are a healer."

"At the time, I didn't want to go to the hospital to visit her because as I said, she was almost a stranger to me. I resisted for days until finally I gave in because I thought it was the right thing to do, and Gabriel kept telling me I should go. I remember sitting with her by her bedside and talking to her and offering my prayers of healing, and when I finished praying, I knew she was going to get well again. I remember telling her this, but I think I scared her."

"Well, you may have scared her but you helped her to heal."

"All I know is that she did get well, and she was discharged from the hospital. It was some time later, she saw me downtown and she walked right by me as though she didn't know me."

Now Adam is roaring with laughter. "Well, I guess you were right. You scared the daylights out of her with your visit and your prayers."

Laughing also, I reply, "Yes, I was right. She must think I am crazy."

"And I also bet she is a religious person, am I right?"

"Yes, Adam, you are absolutely right."

"See what religion does to some people? You actually helped her with your visit and your prayers of healing, but instead of being grateful, it seems this person is just the opposite."

"I just think it is lack of knowing any better."

"Oh, you got that right. However, I just think it is absolutely mindboggling how someone could be so blind."

"Well, if you think that is mindboggling, Adam, I know some individuals who attend religious services on a regular basis, and think themselves as good people, yet I know this is far from the truth. These types of people are very hypocritical."

"I certainly know for a fact that what you are saying is true. Some people have the weird notion that just because they follow a particular religion, and go to church every Sunday, they think they are good people, and of course we all know for some people, this is not true. All we have to do is look back on the history of child abuse within the different religious faiths."

"Yes, unfortunately you are right. We have a terrible history of abuse of young children, all covered up for years under the umbrella of religion. In the house of God, many crimes have been committed; however, it is in the name of the evil one, the devil, which the crimes occur. There was a story in our local newspaper, *The Telegram,* dated Saturday, May 18, 2002, a special report written by Bonnie Belec. The title of this report, as I recall, was *Waiting for Closure: Vatican's quick response to U.S. sex scandal involving clergy angers victims and others in Newfoundland.* Ms. Belec tells the story of a man named Keith, who was a victim of evil. A priest had sexually abused Keith when he was an altar boy in the Roman Catholic Church in his small hometown. The report recalls how Keith remembers the reaction to the people in the small town where the sexual abuse took place. He said the people were panic-stricken for years after a priest claimed to have put a spell on their town. I hope that over time, these people in this small community understand that if there is anyone who has cast an evil spell over the people, it is the evil one, the devil. It is definitely not God.

"It is the devil that represents hate and evil; not God; for God represents love and all that is good and righteous. Love is the opposite of hate and they cannot coexist, for if you love, it is impossible for you to hate at the same time. In addition, if you are serving God, you are automatically rejecting the evil one. However, in the case of the priest who sexually abused Keith when he was a small child, he chose not to live in God's love, even though he wore the religious garments and had the religious title. Instead, he chose to live and follow the way of the devil. He was a hypocrite through and through. And then when the child told of the sexual abuse and the people in the small town tried to unravel the truth, this priest acted in a very malicious, hateful and evil way by saying he put a spell on the people."

"These hateful acts are done with conscious malice. These types of individuals are fully aware of their malicious intent and it is nothing short of evil."

"I wholeheartedly agree with you, Adam. Any form of abuse to a child is hateful and evil. Dereck O'Brien, who was a victim of child abuse while living in foster homes and later at the Mount Cashel Orphanage, wrote a book, entitled, *Suffer Little Children*. He tells of the horrendous abuse and suffering he had to endure as a small child when he lived in a foster home. He wrote about daily beatings, and the awful way he and other children under the foster mother's care were treated. He writes many accounts in his book. In one such account, he tells when she forced him to sit in an icy cold bath and held him there, even though he was screaming. She then took him out, drained the tub, filled it with scalding hot water, and then forced him into the tub again."

"These are horrendous stories of child abuse!"

"Yes, Adam, you are right. He writes in his book that sometimes she would leave the punishment to her husband. He was just as cruel as her. On one occasion, he tells how this man made him pull down his clothes and then he hit him with the buckle of his belt. At the time, Dereck says he was only six years old."

"These are such heart-wrenching stories, Olive."

"Yes they are. It is sickening to know that such people were allowed to take in foster children."

"And where were the social workers?"

"Wherever they were, they certainly weren't doing a very good job."

"It's disgraceful that innocent children would have to suffer such cruelty."

"A person who commits such horrendous, horrifying acts such as physical abuse is not only being disrespectful and hateful towards the child, but to God, our Creator. And it is my belief that when one directs hate by projecting hateful behaviors towards others, in actual fact, the person is also projecting the hatefulness towards himself, and will no doubt, will have to pay for all the pain and suffering."

"Olive, I couldn't agree with you more. As I said before, you are so wise. As it states in the Bible, in Proverbs I think, it is better to have wisdom and understanding than gold and silver."

Nodding my head in agreement, I continue. "No debt ever goes unpaid. These priests have to answer to God. They have to learn the valuable lesson that what goes around comes around, and as my Aunt Elsie would always say, 'The wheel is always turning.' Eventually, their hateful actions will come back to haunt them for they chose a road that leads them to spiritual debt. The person who has accumulated spiritual debts, will eventually become spiritually bankrupt and is indeed poor and living in spiritual poverty, and until all spiritual debts are paid, the soul will not be free."

"The time has come for change. The year 2012 is the year for the beginning of transformation."

"Do you really believe this?"

"Yes, I do," Adam reaffirms.

"Why do you think it is the year 2012?"

"I know that the time is coming for great change, and the year 2012 is the beginning."

"Then would I be correct to say that numbers have significant meaning for you?"

"Yes, they do. I can tell that the numbers six, seven and eight are special to you."

"You are remarkable. The numbers six and eight are very special to me."

"The number seven is special to you also, it is just you don't understand what the number seven represents."

"No, I don't. What does the number seven represent?"

"The number seven means you clearly have it, you have clarity, meaning you are psychic. In addition, the number eight means infinity and prosperity and it means for the children. The number six means balance."

"The numbers six and eight have been with me my whole life."

"What do you mean when you say the numbers six and eight have been with you your whole life?"

"Well, I'll give you some examples. I was born on September 16, I got engaged on September 16, my wedding day was on April 28, God gave me my son on May 8, God gave me my daughter on October 6, and the list is endless."

"That is truly astonishing!"

"As I said, the numbers six and eight have been with me my whole life, even the places where I have lived have always been with the numbers six or eight."

"Are you serious?"

"Yes, I am very serious. I will share a story with you about the house I am living in now. Before my husband and I bought this house, we lived at 60 Perlin Street, so there is my number six. At the time, we transferred our children to another school in another city because we thought the school that our children were supposed to go to was too old, and we heard that there were many problems in that particular school. We did not feel that it was in the best interests of our children and so we moved."

"Why did you move?"

"In order for our children to go into another school, we had to live in the area, and so we set out to buy another house. We looked at many houses but for some unknown reason, I kept going back to one particular house, and finally I convinced my husband that this was the house for us. In the long run, we put in an offer on the house, not knowing the owner because he kept his name anonymous, and it wasn't until after the sale went through, we found out that the owner was my cousin, Ralph Neil, and the house was on 18 Fleet Street!"

"So there's your number eight."

"Yes, but the story gets better."

With a chuckle, and a tone of suspense in his voice, Adam encourages me to continue. "Okay, you really have my attention now."

"Well, as I said, Ralph Neil is my cousin and apparently he was given the name Ralph because he is called after my father, who is Ralph Neil. So you can imagine how surprised I was to hear that my cousin Ralph owned the house."

"And you didn't know it was your cousin's house at the time?"

"No, not until after the sale had gone through. My cousin was already living in another house and had built this new house for his wife, but his wife had taken seriously ill and so they never did move into the new house. And there's more."

"More?"

"Yes, more!"

"Earlier in my life, I knew I had a Guardian Soul watching over me and protecting me, and this Guardian Soul is my Uncle Edward; and my Uncle Edward is Edward Neil, who is Ralph Neil's father!"

"You can't be serious?"

"I'm quite serious!"

"This is all quite remarkable! So really if you think about it, from a physical point of view, that house was built for your cousin's wife; however, if you look at it from a spiritual point of view the house was built for you!"

"Yes, I agree with you."

"You are truly a soul coming from the much higher levels on the Other Side and you are psychic, it's just that you don't realize how psychic you are and what special abilities you have been given."

"But aren't we all psychic?"

"Yes we are, because we are all souls, but there are different levels of being psychic just as there are different levels of being smart. It all depends on how each of us uses our souls or our brains."

"I guess I don't realize my full potential."

"No, you don't but you will. It is all coming in good time. This is why the number six has great meaning for you. You have to understand that living life here on Earth is a process. It takes time to learn and to grow and in order for you to do your best and to accomplish what it is you are to do during this lifetime, you have to find balance. As I said, the number six represents balance. You have to find balance in all that you do; you have to find balance in your life."

"This makes so much sense to me. Adam, you are a genius."

We both laugh again as Adam says, "I wouldn't go that far."

"I can certainly identify with the number eight because I feel this is my number; this is the number that represents me."

"Yes, it is. This is because the number eight represents infinity. The number eight sideways is the sign which means infinity and infinity means endless or limitless, such as unlimited energy, excellence, or knowledge; as in the infinity of God."

"The infinity of God, meaning that once we reach the level of where God resides, it means unlimited and forever more, is this correct?"

"Yes, this is correct. And I can see that the butterfly is going to have great significance for you because the butterfly also represents you."

"It does?"

"Yes, you can be compared to the butterfly and the blue butterfly at that, because you are like the beautiful blue butterfly."

Again, Adam has me laughing, and now I have him laughing.

"I predict a transformation taking place with you, the same transformation as with the blue butterfly when it is only a caterpillar and then in time, it becomes the magnificent blue butterfly."

"It all sounds so marvelous."

"The time is coming when you have to spread your wings and fly; you will become the true person that you are meant to be in this lifetime. I can see where you have much work to do. You are going to help many people."

"Strangely enough, Adam, I feel what you are telling me to be true. I don't think I told you but I am writing a book."

"You are?"

"Yes, and I have been told that this is one of my great spiritual works which I am supposed to accomplish during this lifetime, and in writing this book, I also have been told that I will be helping a lot of people."

"And who told you these things?"

"My Guardian Angel has told me these things," I quickly reply.

"Well, you are absolutely right. You have great work to do in this lifetime. This is your life's mission. You have a lot of important work to do and you will be helping many."

"Yes Adam, it certainly seems that way."

"You have been singled out because of your greatness. You are a very wise soul."

"Thank you, Adam. I'm not sure you are one hundred percent right, even though I have been told this before," I respond with a chuckle. "However, what I do know is that my main goal living life here on this Earth is to do God's will and to abide by Him. Everything I do on a daily basis I do with God in mind. Even in my prayers. Every night I ask God to help me to walk in His path of righteousness and love and to do His will. Also when I pray for others, I always ask for God's help and blessings according to His will."

"As I said, you are a very wise soul."

"Well, I just feel to do otherwise is being selfish."

"I totally agree with you, Olive. Most people that I encounter tell me they go to God only in times of trouble and ask for His help according to their needs and desires, never according to the will of God. I find it interesting that people of this Earth in their arrogance think they are in control. The audacity of the human race to presume they are the master of their fate is simply foolish. And as I said earlier, you are a very wise soul indeed."

"I also know that this is true of you, Adam. You are also very wise."

"Thank you, Olive. I am not sure I am as wise as you are but what I do know is that I seem to have a lot more knowledge about things in this life that most people do not even consider. Most people think they are the masters of their own fate; little do they know that they are being so naive. It is God who is the master of all and who orchestrates all."

I glance at my watch and notice how quickly the time has gone. I say to my newfound friend, "Oh my, Adam, I think it is time for me to return to my hotel."

As Adam pushes back his chair, he says, "It has been such a pleasure spending time with you."

"And it has been such a pleasure spending time with you also. I really enjoyed our talk."

We hug and as I start to walk away, Adam states, "Keep safe, but then I know you will be safe because you have someone watching out for you."

I smile and respond, "You keep safe also, but then I know you will be safe because you also have someone watching out for you."

As I continue to walk away, I put up my right hand in a gesture, by curving the palm of my right hand, allowing my thumb to touch my middle finger, and I smile at him.

He returns the smile. "That sign means teach."

"It does? I don't even know why I did that."

"You are clearly telling me that I need to teach others."

"I am?"

"Yes, you are. As I said, you are very wise. Peace and love be with you."

I reply, "Thank you, Adam. Peace and love be with you also."

Leaving Adam and walking away, I am thinking that this has been the most bizarre, yet incredible meeting I think I have ever had in my life. I feel as though I have known Adam for a lifetime, and that I just happened to run into him in downtown San Diego, at a cafe. I have heard of the term kindred souls and for sure, Adam has to be one of mine. As I reflect, I realize that as soon as I saw Adam, there was an instant familiarity. Who would ever believe such an encounter? I can hardly believe it myself! With this thought, I laugh aloud and think life is so superb at times!

Walking back to my hotel, I suddenly stop and look into a jewelry store window. Much to my surprise, there in the window is a large, royal blue butterfly! I then look in the next window and again there is another large, royal blue butterfly! I can hardly believe my eyes. As I stand on the sidewalk in downtown San Diego and stare at these beautiful blue butterflies, I hear a loving voice speak to me. The loving voice gives me a message that the blue butterfly is a spiritual symbol for personal growth and spiritual rebirth because of its transformation from a caterpillar that crawls on the ground to a beautiful, magnificent butterfly that spreads its wings and flies freely. I get the most fantastic feeling of peace and love as I receive the thought that I have done well, and it is the time for transformation. I need to spread my wings and fly!

As I continue to walk back to my hotel, my mind is swirling with these thoughts and all the comments that my newfound friend, Adam, had to say to me. I will cherish this encounter forever.

The next morning, I leave my hotel and head for the airport. My flights back home to Newfoundland are long but I do not mind because I love travelling and I love meeting people. When I finally arrive at St. John's airport, my husband is there to greet me. He is so happy to see me, as I am to see him. We hug and head for the carousel to retrieve my bags.

During the drive back to our house, my husband asks, "What is it you would like to do for the remainder of the week?"

With a yawn, I reply, "With the way I feel right now, I just want to relax."

"I have a suggestion for tomorrow evening."

"What is it?"

"How about we rent out a movie and spend a quiet evening at home?"

"That sounds perfect. After you get off work tomorrow, we can go to the movie store and see what we would like to rent."

"Okay, after we have dinner, we can both go get a movie."

"Perfect."

The next evening after dinner, my husband and I head for the movie store to rent a movie. As we enter, I head in one direction of the store, as Dave heads in the opposite direction. For some unknown reason to me, I head directly down one of the aisles in the store that has the older versions of movies. As I look back on this, I realize this is so out of character for me because I always go to the section where the latest movies are stacked on the shelves on the walls. However, not this time. This evening, I find myself headed towards the older movies, and as I find myself standing in the aisle, and looking at the movies on the shelves, I can hardly believe my eyes! There staring back at me is a picture of the most marvelous blue butterfly, and the words read, *The Blue Butterfly*! I am astonished! Reaching for the DVD, I read the heading that says the only way to catch a miracle is to believe in the blue butterfly. I keep reading to find out that the movie is about the true story of a young boy, who has brain cancer and has only a short time to live. This child's one and only dream in life is to catch a blue butterfly. I take the DVD to show my husband, and he is as dumbfounded as I am, because I had already shared with him the meeting I had with my newfound friend, Adam, in San Diego, and Adam comparing me to the beautiful blue butterfly. We take the movie to the checkout counter and head home to watch one of the most awe-inspiring movies we have ever seen.

The movie is inspired by the real life story of David Merenger, who was born on August 16, 1981, in Coteau du Lac, Quebec, Canada. At the young age of six, he was diagnosed with terminal brain cancer. The doctors had given up all hope, and the small child was expected to live only months. David had but one dream, and that dream was to catch the most beautiful butterfly on Earth, the legendary Blue Morpho... the Mariposa Azul, a magnificent blue butterfly found only in the rain forests of Central and South America. This young child believes that if he can catch the beautiful blue butterfly, it would be able to reveal to him the mystery of life, because it is magical and has all the answers to life. In 1988, the Children's Wish Foundation offers David a trip to Mexico. David, accompanied on this special trip by an accomplished entomologist from Montreal, Quebec, Mr. George Brossard, has the opportunity to make his dream come true. During the trip, David does indeed catch the beautiful blue butterfly and his lifelong dream becomes a reality. Upon his return to Canada, a miracle happens! David's cancer goes into remission. Years later, David, now a grown man, travels to schools and hospitals, sharing his extraordinary story about the magnificent blue butterfly.

The legendary belief of the tribal people of Central and South America is that the blue butterfly is a magical creature, and it can give you the answers to the mysteries of the world just by looking at it. These native people believe that when you do see this fantastic butterfly, you must offer it your dreams because it will take your dreams to the Great Spirit, and your life will change forever.

It was on April 6, 2008, that my life had been transformed, for I saw this magical creature for the very first time! After seeing this magnificent blue butterfly myself, I believe wholeheartedly that the legend of the tribal people of Central and South America regarding the blue butterfly is true! I know my dreams are gone to the Great Spirit and I truly understand, for the first time in my life, the mysteries of the world.

CHAPTER 21

Unexpected Visitors

"What more do you want, o soul!
And what else do you search for outside, ….

St John of the Cross
Dark Night of the Soul

Years later, I am sitting in the living room of my condominium in
Ontario, when my Guardian Angel speaks to me. "My dear, there
are others who wish to speak to you."

"There are?"

"Yes, my dear. Your father is here and the Noseworthys are in the
distance."

I am not surprised to know that my father is here to visit me, but
I am certainly surprised to know that the Noseworthys want to speak
with me. There is very little I want to say to the Noseworthys, and yet
here they are, requesting to visit me. I can now see them in the distance.
It is the same as when I watch something on television; I can see the
people on the television screen, yet I know they are not really in the
room with me. They are not present in the room because I know they
need permission to visit with me. My husband's father, mother and sister
are all waiting to speak to me, and the three of them all look the same
before they died, the only difference being that they are all dressed in
black and their hair is black.

I can now sense my father's presence as he asks, "How are you,
my doll?"

"I'm doing okay, Dad, but I am somewhat surprised and concerned that you are here to speak with me; knowing that the Noseworthys are in the distance."

"They want to talk to you."

"I know it must be important if you allowed them to come with you."

"Yes, it is important."

"Okay, Dad. I will speak to Mr. Noseworthy."

"Okay, my doll."

"Mr. Noseworthy, I have been told that you wish to speak with me."

There is silence for a moment and then Mr. Noseworthy speaks. "I want you to forgive me. I have done a lot of wrong and I want to make things right for David's sake. In order to do this, I need your forgiveness. And I need you to talk to David for me."

There is only silence. The silence is finally broken as he says, "I need your blessings. I did a lot of wrong and I am not very proud of myself."

Again, there is silence.

"I am very sorry. I have to try and make things right."

Once again, there is silence. I can now see Mrs. Noseworthy move forward and immediately I recall the other times she visited with me. The first time was a few days after her death, and I was standing in my kitchen in front of the sink when I felt a presence with me. As I turned around, there was my husband's mother looking at me. She did not speak and neither did I.

With concern in my voice, I ask, "Mrs. Noseworthy, do you want to say anything to me?"

"Yes, I would like to speak. I want to thank you for taking care of David. We are all very proud of you. You have sacrificed a lot in order to help David. We all know this. You have stayed by his side and you have never let him down."

I can feel the tears well in my eyes as her words pierce my heart. I know all too well the memories of the past and I cannot help but become emotional. It occurs to me that she must be referring to my husband's car accident and the full year it took for his complete recovery, and then later him becoming very ill and being admitted to the hospital. I was in Ontario at the time and I took the first flight back home. A week later, he returned to Ontario with me, under my care and responsibility. It was some time later that he was diagnosed with diabetes. I reply with a simple, "Thank you." As I wipe away my tears, I am able to see Mrs. Noseworthy step back and her daughter Doreen, steps forward. I ask, "Doreen, do you wish to speak?"

"Yes," she answers.

"What do you wish to say to me?"

"I want to let you know that I am truly sorry for everything and for all of the wrong that I have caused both you and David. I realize this was all wrong of me and I acted in very mean ways towards you for many years. I am very sorry. I know I have done a lot of wrong."

"Yes, you did do a lot of wrong. I know you wished me harm and you wished that Dave would leave me. You truly wanted our marriage to end. You caused a lot of trouble. You showed no respect for me and consequently showed no respect or love for your brother, and he is not just a brother to you, he is your twin brother."

"I was very foolish and I have to admit that I was jealous of you."

"Well, your jealousy caused many problems."

"I realize now how wrong I have been and I am very sorry. You are David's wife and you did not get the respect that you deserved. I am very sorry for all that happened in the past. I need your forgiveness."

"It has almost been twenty years, so why are you only coming now?" She does not answer. After what seems like minutes, the silence is broken as I continue. "I know you have been given permission to come to me and speak and I understand that this is part of your own spiritual journey, asking for forgiveness; for asking for forgiveness is an opportunity to let old wounds heal. However, please understand the wounds go very deep. Even after Billy's death, an individual came to me and said, 'Of all the terrible things I've heard about you over the years, I realize now they are not true.' She still does not answer. "You acted in malicious ways in most of your dealings with us. Even after you were diagnosed with cancer, you kept it all shrouded in secrecy from Dave. Later when you knew you were dying, you still did not contact him. You have hurt Dave very deeply. You should never have treated him with such cruelty and disrespect." Again, there is silence between us as I think everything through. I am finally able to respond, "I do forgive you. I wish you peace.

I also forgive you, Mr. Noseworthy. I do hope for Dave's sake he is able to forgive both of you also."

There is only silence. They do not answer.

My father now speaks. "My doll, you have to get yourself prepared. The time is short. You know Dad would never tell you anything to hurt you. Dad is here to help you."

"Dad, what is it you are really telling me?"

"Dave's time is coming to an end. He has to come over here where I am. Dad will be here to meet him."

With this comment, I can feel myself becoming very emotional. "When is this time coming?"

"This is not for me to say, but you need to be strong and you need to get ready."

"So Dad, this is really why the Noseworthys wanted to visit with me. They know that Dave's time is coming to cross over."

"Yes, you are right. They know they have done a lot of wrong and they want to make things right. They know that Dave will not have anything to do with them because of the way they have treated you over the years. This is why they requested to visit with you because they know they need your forgiveness, as well as Dave's."

"I'm not sure they are going to get Dave's, Dad."

"I know, my doll, I know."

"Okay, Dad. This is somewhat of a shock to me because I thought Dave was doing really well now."

"Dave is doing well, but as you know, he's not supposed to be living on Earth at this time. You know he has been granted extra time."

"Yes, I know this and you know that I am truly grateful to God each day for the extra time God has given me with him."

"Yes, we all know this and we know you are doing your best."

"Dad, I don't want to be selfish; it's just that I am finding it so difficult to let go."

"I know, my doll, I know."

"If Dave was suffering, it would be different. But he is not in any pain at all, and he is doing really well."

"Yes, Dad knows this. But you know what Dad is telling you is for your own good."

"I know, Dad. You are here to help me."

"Yes, Dad is here to help you. You have to do your best. I know this is not easy but you have to be strong. Next thing you will get yourself down and that's no good."

As I wipe away my tears, I understand what my father is saying to me is true and I know I have to listen to him, but I feel as though I am in a state of shock.

My father speaks again. "You have to get prepared because this is going to happen. Dave has been here with you longer than he is supposed to be."

As his words echo in my ears, I cry uncontrollably. I now hear my Guardian Angel speaking to me. "My dear, you have to get ready. You need to listen to what your father is telling you. You know that he knows best."

"Yes, Gabriel, I know Dad only wants what is best for me. What are your thoughts?"

"I am concerned you are not going to be strong enough and you are going to make yourself sick."

I feel so distraught and as I wipe away my tears, I feel a headache coming on.

My father speaks again. "My doll, you know Dad loves you very much. You know this. I do not want anything to happen to you. You need to take care of yourself. You will end up getting sick and that is no good. Do not allow yourself to get down. You can rise above all of this. You have gone through hard times before and you came out of it on top. Do it again this time."

"Yes, Dad, I know, but this time it is different."

"Yes, I know this time is different but you will always have Dave with you, he just won't be in his physical body."

I know what my father is telling me is to help me but I cannot seem to accept what it is I am supposed to face. The only thought that is going through my mind is that Dave has to leave me.

"This is all for your own good. You have to believe this."

"Dad, how can this be for my own good?"

"Just believe what Dad is telling you. It will make you stronger. This is all in your control. You can control all of this. You know you have choices. Do not allow yourself to get down. You can rise above all of this."

"I don't think I am strong enough to handle this."

"You are very strong and you have been very strong in the past, and there is no reason why you can't be strong again."

"Should I get ready and go home?"

"This is not for me to say. You have to decide what is best to do."

"I am scared. I know it really feels like an impossible task. I feel so weak. Dad, I can't deny my feelings."

"The time is coming and you need to be better than you are. I thought you would be stronger than this. You are surprising me. You seem to have changed."

I whisper through my tears, "I know, Dad. I guess I have changed. I'm not sure I can handle this news."

"This is all for your own good. You have to believe this. And you know you will always have Dave with you, because he loves you so much."

I am now crying uncontrollably, and as I reach for a tissue, I blurt out, "I feel I need to go home."

"Okay, my doll. You need to do what is right for you. If you feel you should be home with Dave, then get ready and go home. I know Dave needs you and you need to be with him."

"Dad, I am feeling so down?"

"Dad knows you've been through a lot and you are still going through hard times but it is to make you stronger and better."

My Guardian Angel speaks. "You have to help yourself. You have to put yourself first. If you can't take care of yourself, you're not going to be any good for anyone else."

"Am I able to go home?"

"This is not part of the plan. We all have to do what is best for you. This is what is supposed to happen. You have to travel in sorrow. You need to do what our Heavenly Father has planned for you. He knows best. This is the plan that is in place. You are supposed to be where you are."

My father speaks again. "You seem to think that things have changed but this is not the case. I want you to be strong for Dad and Dave needs you to be strong."

"I just feel I will be so lonely. I will miss Dave too much. I don't want to be left alone."

My Guardian Angel speaks again. "You know you have your children. They will take care of you."

"I know, Gabriel, but you know it is not the same."

My father answers, "I know, my doll, I know."

"I feel I can't handle this. My mind cannot seem to rest."

Gabriel responds, "The time is coming and you need to be better than you are. We are all concerned for you. You need to listen to your father. What he is saying is true. Dave is called to return Home, and as you know, he was granted extra time but now his time is up. It is all coming to an end for him. You also need to keep in mind that if you find it too difficult to let him go in peace and love, this will make it more difficult for Dave. He is finding it extremely difficult as it is. You have to let him go. The time is right. You have to move on and there are many things which you are supposed to accomplish while living here on Earth."

"Can't I accomplish those things with Dave by my side?"

"My dear, this is not part of the plan, and no, not really. Dave has other things which he must work on and he is not supposed to live here on Earth any longer than necessary."

My father speaks again. "My doll, everything is going to work out, you will see. Do not be afraid. Dad will always be here for you. You know this."

"Yes, Dad, I do know this but I am feeling so scared. I really don't know if I can handle this."

"Time is cutting very short. You know that Dave's time is up. He has to come over here where I am and you know I will take care of him."

There is now only silence. I am deep in thought trying to understand that I need to be able to handle this situation; however, I am lost for words, and can only utter, "Dad, I just want to be with Dave when his time comes. He needs me and I need to be with him."

"You do what you feel is best to do. I do know that Dave needs you and he would want you to be with him."

Gabriel answers. "Yes, my dear, if this is what you want to do. God has granted your wish for you to return home, and you will be able to stay there. You will not be alone. You will have both your children with you."

"Thank you, Gabriel. Thank you, dear God."

"You are most kindly welcome, my dear."

With this comment, I break down in uncontrollable sobs. I find myself crouched on the floor, leaning on my sofa. I just cannot seem to handle this news very well. I know I have to be strong, as my father is telling me, but I just cannot seem to do this, no matter how hard I try. As I sit on the floor, I start to pray to God to give me the strength that I need. I beg Him to help me to be stronger than I am, but it seems as though I am supposed to deal with my emotions on my own, without any help from anyone. The only thought that is coming to me now is that I really do not know if I am going to get through all of this. I pray to my Heavenly Father to help me and to give my husband more time and to allow him to stay with me; for I fear I am not strong enough to let him go.

All that day and into the evening and night, I cry. I do not know where all the tears are coming from, but they keep coming. I feel physically sick. I have a headache, and I am feeling weak to the point of exhaustion. I honestly do not know how I am going to do this. I thought I would be much stronger than I am but I am not.

All of a sudden, the light in the room is changing to an unbelievable brightness, which I have never seen before, and coming from the brightness is the most loving voice, which I recognize instantly. *"My child, do not despair for I have granted your wish."* The brightness slowly fades away but the love and peace remains. With my tears of joy, I say a silent prayer of gratitude to my Heavenly Father.

CHAPTER 22

Love Never Dies

Love is the law of God.
You live that you may learn to love.
You love that you may learn to live.
No other lesson is required of man.

Mikhail Naimy
Book of Mirdad

We had a fabulous vacation, spending a week in Fort Lauderdale and then the remainder of our time onboard the beautiful cruise ship, the Carnival Destiny. My husband wanted to take me on a cruise for my birthday and so we boarded the ship on September 16, and now our fabulous cruise has ended, and we are on our way back home.

Before boarding the plane at Miami airport, I purchased a book at the bookstore, entitled, *Heaven Is Real*, by Don Piper and Cecil Murphey. As we fly over Miami on our way to Toronto, I pull out my book, turn on my reading light and settle comfortably into my seat. As I focus on the words on the pages, the brightness of my reading light interrupts me. I look up and, to my amazement, my reading light overhead has become exceptionally bright and is now blinking! I glance at my husband next to me to see if he has noticed my reading light. His attention is on his tiny television screen in front of him, and he is too absorbed in his television show; he hasn't noticed. I look around to see if there are other lights blinking and there aren't. I know all too well what this means. I am excited because I know it must be my father visiting me. Instantly I know my father is with me because I can sense his presence. I want to remember every detail of the conversation I am about to have with my dad, and so I take my pen and turn to the last pages of my book, and start to write as I smile. Speaking without saying the words out loud, I ask, "Dad, are you here?"

I hear my father's all-too-familiar, loving voice, as he answers, "Yes, my doll."

With excitement, I can barely contain myself as I say in my mind, "How are you, Dad?"

"Very good, very good."

I am now able to see him and with tears in his eyes and a quiver in his voice, he says, "You're doing exceptionally well. I am very proud of you. I know you are doing your best."

"I've made some mistakes, Dad."

"Just a few, not many; don't be too hard on yourself. Don't forget what you've been told. Always treat yourself with kindness."

"Okay, I will be better with myself."

"Yes, my doll, you need to be. You don't realize who you really are."

I am somewhat taken by surprise by my father's comments to me, and in particular, curious as to why he seems so emotional. I am wondering what has transpired to trigger such a visit. I am unable to respond and there is only silence between us. I reach down and retrieve a tissue from my handbag, to wipe away the tears that have popped into my eyes. I know all too well how loving my father is towards me, and he has sparked tears of joy in me.

The silence is finally broken as my father speaks again and this time with much conviction in his voice. "I want you to know it was a great honor for me to be your father while I lived on Earth, and that it is still a great honor to still be your father. I love you very much. You make Dad very proud."

I become distracted because I am able to see my dad wipe away his tears, and now I lose my focus, because I too have to wipe my eyes. After what seems like minutes, I am able to compose myself.

He continues. "You have to be strong; for everything is going to change for you."

Taken aback by this comment, I think back to just a few days earlier when I had found a bruised area on the upper thigh of my left leg, while aboard the cruise ship. Since discovering the area, I have been worried. With this thought, I question, "Dad, are you talking about the area on my leg?"

"Yes, but don't be concerned because it will all work out."

It seems to me that his voice has become more saddened. "Are there other issues?"

He answers, "Yes, my doll. I will not talk about my other concerns now but know that Dad will always be by your side. You have to be strong. Others will look down upon you. This makes Dad very sad but this is who they are. I want you to hold your head up high and never be afraid. God walks with you and so do I. Always remember you are never alone. Do not be scared and do not be afraid. Do Dad proud. It is because of you I have learned so much and I am still learning."

As I continue to wipe away my tears, I ask, "Dad, what do you mean you have learned so much from me and that you are still learning?"

"Dad has many regrets. I'm not proud of how I handled many situations when I was living on Earth."

There is silence. I am finally able to speak. "Dad, I know you did your best."

I can see my father wiping his eyes again. "Dad is really sorry for a lot of things. I should have known better."

I completely understand my father's feelings and know all too well what it is he means. "It is okay, Dad, I do understand. I know you didn't understand a lot of what was going on and I now realize that you do."

With a deeply saddened voice, he says, "Dad is very sorry, very sorry."

"You have nothing to be sorry for, Dad. I know you would have done some things differently and would have reacted differently in many situations over the years, if you had known what it is you know now."

"Yes, my doll. I just want you to know that I would never have done or said anything to intentionally hurt you."

"I know this, Dad. This is why I don't feel you have anything to apologize for."

"Okay, but you see now what I mean when I said I have learned so much from you, and that I am still learning."

"Yes, I understand."

"Dad sees everything, hears everything and knows everything."

Once again, there is silence and I have to retrieve more tissues from my handbag. I am finally able to speak again as I ask, "Dad, do you really see everything and hear everything?"

"Yes, my doll, I certainly do. Dad knows everything."

I find myself crying more as I listen intently to my father's words to me.

"You have great work to do."

"I have great work to do, Dad?"

"Yes, you most certainly do. You have much to accomplish."

I wipe away my tears once again; as I listen intently to every word, my dad is speaking to me.

My father states, "You have been prepared. All your life has been a preparation for the spiritual work that you will do. All the travelling you have done in your lifetime, and all the travelling that you are still doing and will still do, is all part of your learning and preparation for what is to come. Everything is now in place for you; just follow."

"Dad, is this concerning my book?"

"Yes."

As I dab my eyes with my tissue and try to compose myself as best I can, my father continues to speak to me with such conviction and love.

"The work you have to do is more than just your book."

"I have to do more?"

"Yes. Also, know that you have more hardships to go through. However, know that you will be rewarded in the end. You have many roads to go down and you have a very bright future. Always remember, Dad walks by your side. You are never alone. Dad comes around you often. Do not ever think you are left alone because you're not. Do not feel as though you have been abandoned because this is far from the truth. Dad knows all too well, what has been done. I am very disappointed and hurt by it all. If I were alive on Earth, I would give a piece of my mind."

Immediately I know what my father is referring to, and because I have become so emotional, I am unable to respond.

"Don't let yourself down by allowing others to pull you down."

My father loves me with all his soul and will never intentionally do anything to hurt me. He loves me dearly and stands by me. I have to retrieve more tissues from my handbag because the tears keep flowing. Again, I glance at my husband to see if he has noticed me crying and he has not.

My father continues. "I am so proud of you. We are all very proud of you."

"When you say we, Dad, who do you mean?"

"I mean all the others over here who love you."

"Oh!" I exclaim.

"Dad wants nothing but the best for you. You have made Dad very happy. I can finally be at peace. I do not have to worry about you anymore. You deserve everything and more. Put everything else behind you. You did not deserve any of it. Put it all behind you."

As I wipe away my tears, I come to the realization that my father was not at peace and I didn't realize this.

He continues. "Don't underestimate your abilities and who you really are. The main thing is to focus on who you really are and the work that you have to do. You are loved more than you realize. I love you with all my heart and soul and so continue to make Dad proud."

"I will, Dad."

"Dad is going now. Always remember, just call out to me and I will hear you and come. I will be back later. Bye for now, my doll."

"Okay, I love you, Dad."

"I love you too, my doll," he softly and lovingly responds as he wipes away his tears, and fades into the distance and can no longer be seen.

As I sit quietly in my seat reflecting on everything my dad has said to me, I realize that I have learned so much from my father over the years, and I continue to learn. He is teaching me to move on and to move through the hurt. His incredible insight I find amazing!

It is at this moment, I notice my reading light dims, and there is no more blinking. I know that my father has left but the strong bond of love he has for me remains.

Months later, on Sunday, June 19, my father visits with me again. It was after I had signed his Father's Day card and kissed it and placed it on the hall table, that I immediately felt the presence of my dad with me. The tears gently fill my eyes as I hear the familiar, loving voice of my dad, knowing that he had just finished reading his Father's Day card. I express my love by saying, "Happy Father's Day, Dad."

"Thank you, my doll. I want you to enjoy yourself today for me." With a laugh, he says, "And tell Dave to have a drink of Scotch for me."

With a chuckle, I reply, "I will, Dad."

My father continues to visit with me as each year goes by, and especially during the difficult times in my life.

My sister has been quite sick and I am concerned about her health. She was diagnosed with cancer of the bladder and was admitted to hospital for surgery. Although the surgery went as planned and was successful, she experienced complications afterwards, and then she had a stroke. We were all devastated and very concerned. I ask my father, "Dad, how is Shirley doing? Is she going to be okay?"

"She's going to pull through. It's been granted."

As I wipe the tears of joy streaming down my face, I respond, "This is wonderful news. We all have been so worried."

"Yes, I know. Dad comes around you often, so don't ever think you're left alone because you're not."

Minutes have elapsed because I have become very emotional, and am unable to respond. Eventually I compose myself and ask, "How are you, Dad?"

"Very good, very good."

I chuckle, knowing this was always his answer whenever I asked him the same question when he lived here on Earth. My thoughts go back to my sister. One day while I visited my sister in the hospital, after her surgery, we shared the most astounding conversation. I was sitting by her bedside while she was sleeping; she woke and looked at me, and told me she had been speaking to our grandmother, my father's mother. I asked her what our grandmother said to her and before she could reply, she dozed off again. Shortly after she opened her eyes and this time, she tells me she had been talking to our uncle, Uncle Stan. I want to know whether she really did meet our grandmother and uncle, so I ask my dad. "Did Shirley really meet with Nan?"

"Yes, my doll, she really met Nan."

"Did she really meet Uncle Stan also?"

"Yes, she met Uncle Stan too."

"Dad, she said Uncle Stan is getting a new truck. Is this true?"

"Yes, he's getting a new truck. We got everything over here, more than you can imagine."

My thoughts now go to me and I ask, "How am I doing, Dad?"

"You're doing exceptionally well, my doll. We're all very proud of you. We know you are doing your best."

"Yes, Dad, this is true. I really am trying my best."

"You don't realize who you really are."

"I don't?"

"No, you don't. Just know that Dad knows who you are. And keep writing your book."

"Will my book be successful?"

"Yes, it will be very successful. You're going to do a lot of good in the world and you're going to help a lot of people. You will help many. You're doing exceptionally well. Dad is extremely proud of you."

"I'm so very proud of you also, Dad."

"Thank you, my doll. I have to go now but I'll be back."

"Okay, Dad. I love you."

"I love you too, my doll."

I can feel my father's presence leave the room. As I sit and reflect, I learn another very important life lesson; and that is my father's love for me will never die; and neither will my love for him. My father has given me the most cherished gift of all; a gift that ties me to him for all eternity, and that is the gift of undying love.

I have many cherished memories of my dad. He was a wonderful, kind, and loving father to me and remains so to this day. He always treated everyone equally and would never do anything intentionally to hurt another, especially his children and grandchildren. He never lied or used deceit in any manner, for he always did what was right and just to do. If he gave one a candy bar, he made sure he had the same for the others.

When I was a young child growing up, I remember my father having to go away to work and he only came home on the weekends. Every Friday evening as he approached our house, he would toot the horn of his car to let us know he was home. When he entered the house he always carried with him a small paper bag, and inside the bag would be candy bars and chewing gum.

Before my father died, he let me know that he was going to make his will and he asked me if there was anything in particular, that I would like to have. He also let me know that everything he has, he wants shared out equally and he did not want one to have more than the other; for he wanted all of his daughters to be treated the same. My father was a hardworking man and one who provided for his family all his life. He invested in mutual funds with Investors Group; invested wisely, and had done extremely well over the years. One of my favorite memories of my father was when I would visit on the weekends. Every Saturday morning, my dad and I would check the newspaper to see how his mutual funds were doing. I recall always having a good laugh with him, because fortunately for him, the mutual funds he had invested in were doing extremely well, for it was a time when the market was having a bull run, and was at an all-time high for many years.

Of all my years with my father, I can honestly say that he has never let me down. We had our differences but he would say what was on his mind and I would always say what was on my mind, but in the end, if he thought he had said or done something wrong, he always apologized to me. The echo of his apologies I can still hear in my mind to this day, for he would say, "My doll, I'm sorry." Those simple words had such an enormous impact on me as a child and as an adult.

Another valuable life lesson I have learned is that I had to experience the death of my father; for the loss of my father in this physical world is an experience that helps me grow, and I know when it is my time to cross over, my dad will be waiting for me with open arms. I still buy a card for him every Christmas and every Father's Day, for I know he will visit, and he still visits me every September 16, the day of my birthday, without fail. He has never forgotten. He also visits during other times of the year, unexpectedly. One such time was when I took a cruise with my son aboard the cruise ship, the Carnival Destiny. After dinner, we were in the theater ready to watch the show, when I knew my dad was sitting next to me. He told me to look around at the grandeur of the theatre, and the exquisite colors and extraordinary, beautiful décor and told me this is what to expect when I leave Earth and return Home. I became very emotional and started to cry, but of course, they were tears of joy.

Not too long ago, I had the privilege to attend an amazing seminar in Toronto, with psychiatrist, Dr. Brian Weiss. Dr. Weiss' reputation preceded him, for his credentials are quite impressive, having graduated from Columbia University and Yale Medical School. As well as being former Chairman of Psychiatry at Mount Sinai Medical Center in Miami, Florida, he has become known throughout the world as a past-life expert, and is the author of several books, including the bestseller *Many Lives, Many Masters*.

During this seminar, Dr. Weiss began his demonstration of hypnosis and past-life regression, by starting with relaxation exercises which continued into hypnosis. It was during this hypnosis state, I was regressed slowly back through my childhood and was told to go to an enjoyable childhood memory, leaving it up to me which happy memory I wanted to recall. As I drifted further, I could feel myself slipping deeper and deeper into a very relaxed state. Suddenly and with absolute clarity, I found myself in the arms of my father while we were both in the water on a beautiful, hot summer's day, and he was teaching me how to swim. I had both of my arms around his neck, hanging on for dear life, for I was terrified of deep water. I was laughing and screaming at the same time as my father would try to put me into the water, reassuring me all the while that he would not let me go. I was aware of every moment; even as I slowly let my grip around my dad's neck loosen, he held me in his arms and lowered me into the water then told me to kick my legs and move my arms. The experience of reliving that beautiful, hot summer's day with my father was incredible.

After enjoying my time swimming with my dad, Dr. Weiss told me to go back to when I was in my mother's womb. I was fully conscious and experiencing being in my mother's womb as if it was actually happening. While in the womb, I could see my mother and father, and I could feel their joy regarding my mother's pregnancy. In addition, I could actually hear them speak. I knew they were excited about having another baby and I knew that they loved me even though I had not even been born.

After experiencing being in my mother's womb, Dr. Weiss instructed me to go to a past-life, either one of my choosing. To my surprise, I started to experience a past-life! I could see myself riding on horseback wearing a long, black cloak with a hood and I had long, reddish, curly hair that was pinned and hanging down my back. Without any doubt in my mind, I knew immediately that I was Joan of Arc in that lifetime! Born on January 6, 1412, in a small French village, Joan was the youngest daughter of five children. She was known to have been very religious and a healer, and wanted only to do right by God. At an early age, she claimed she was able to see and speak to saints and angels, including Archangel Michael and the Angel Gabriel. She convinced the king of her honor by giving him details of a prayer he had made to God, days before.

During the war, Joan knew she was called by God to save the French people from the English, and so she entered Orleans, and after nine days, on May 8, freedom was upon the city. She disguised herself by dressing as a man when she travelled with the soldiers, as a form of protection from the male soldiers. She referred to herself as the 'virgin,' explaining that it was God's will, and was later nicknamed 'the maiden' or 'the virgin,' but unfortunately, she was later charged with cross-dressing. Later, after being abandoned by the king and his soldiers, Joan of Arc was put on trial because she was claimed to have 'magical powers' which many believed to be associated with witchcraft. She was condemned as a witch and a heretic, which meant she did not follow the rules of the Roman Catholic Church, and was therefore condemned to death. As she wept, she addressed her accusers for condemning her to die; however, she forgave them for their actions and asked them to pray for her. Tied to a pillar high above the crowd of people, she asked for a cross, and one English soldier made a small one out of wood and gave the cross to her. The flames took over her body and she burnt at the stake in Rouen's Market Square. Her head then dropped and the end had come.

Twenty-five years after the execution, an Inquisitorial court ruled that Joan of Arc had been wrongfully accused and sentenced to death by a corrupt court, which had ruled with "malice." She became a martyr and in 1920, the Church of Rome officially declared her a saint. Over time, she has become known throughout the world as a patron saint of France. On January 6, 2012, Joan of Arc celebrated her 600th birthday!

Dr. Weiss instructed me to go to another past-life and during this lifetime, I was once again a female, and this time I was a healer also, and I helped many people. As the scenes unraveled, I knew I was living in Saudi Arabia, and that my mission on Earth was to heal others, and teach people how to heal themselves, and especially teach them that most of their sickness, they caused themselves. I also was to teach them about God. Some people I knew were atheist, not believing that there really is a God; and some people believed but not in our loving God, for they chose to do evil and follow the evil one. There were also people who believed but only on the surface. They went through the motions of belonging to a particular organized religion, yet were corrupt in their way of thinking and acting. It was really a mockery, for what they preached, they did not practice. Even though I was healing the sick and wounded, many considered me a witch, and the traditional Sharia Law, sentenced me to be stoned to death.

I became aware of my present day fear of public speaking and immediately knew why I had this strong phobia in my present lifetime. I was in a square facing a huge crowd of very angry people, who were there to witness my death. This long forgotten life trauma played out once again, as I stood before my accusers, knowing that I am innocent. However, with exceptional clarity, as my accusers throw the stones, and as the roar of anger from the people in the crowd becomes louder, I witness myself floating out of my body and I watch from above, looking down on the tormented souls who thought they were doing right. I can also see many standing in great sorrow, knowing that I did not deserve such cruelty; and all because I helped heal the sick, many of whom were children and the elderly. So once again, I die a horrific death.

As the death scene continues, I realize that my fear of those evil ones has disappeared and that my phobia of public speaking in this lifetime is because of the cause of my death in this past-lifetime, as well as the previous lifetime in France. It is at this moment I realize that even though the angry, hateful people are still throwing stones at my poor, battered body, they are not harming me. I am up above them, watching everything unfold, realizing that little do they know that they are not getting rid of me as they think; I am still with them.

My phobia of public speaking has disappeared and I know I am back once again to face these same people. I know without a doubt that these same people, who had stoned my physical body to death and who had burnt me at the stake, so many years ago, are now here in this lifetime and I have faced them once again. However, this time, their anger and hate cannot cause me harm, for I have learned that I am stronger and wiser than ever. The fear they had tried to instill in me does not exist any longer. I know that part of my life plan in this lifetime is to not only heal and teach others to heal, but it is also to teach life lessons, for I have learned that negative experiences from past-lifetimes can be healed also and I am back again to do God's work!

Soul Signs

Imagine if you told a family living in abject poverty that there
was a treasure of gold under the dirt floor of their shanty.
In the same way, we are not aware of the treasure of our
spiritual nature, hidden by our own ignorance and delusion.

First Teaching
Gautama Buddha
Founder of Buddhism

Soul signs are a symbolic language used as a form of communication and a way for souls on the Other Side to make contact and to let us know that they are around. They are spiritual signs to guide and protect us, as a way of letting us know that we are following our chosen life plan while living here on Earth. As people living here, the more open we are to this form of communication, the more we will experience soul signs in our everyday life.

Soul signs can also let us know that we are not alone and that we are guided and directed each day. I know I have my Heavenly Father in Heaven watching over me, and I know also I have my Guardian Angel, Gabriel, and my Guardian Souls, Aunt Mildred and Uncle Edward, guiding and protecting me every minute of every day. I also know I have my Uncle Stan and my father who have now passed over to the Other Side but who have never really left me, and have shown me repeatedly that I am never alone and that I am loved and protected, more than I ever realized.

Soul signs can be recognized in various ways; however, one of the most common is the manipulation of electricity. An electrical appliance turning on and off at different times for no apparent reason, such as a radio, television, and computer, is a very common soul sign. My Uncle Stan would get my attention by turning my computer back on as I would be leaving my study. After I finish working on my computer in the afternoons, I am in the habit of shutting it down, but sometimes I would be leaving my study when I would hear my computer come back on. Sure enough when I walked over to my computer, it would be on! Words, phrases or sentences can appear on the computer screen, which has happened to me. There was one time I was typing on my keyboard and had finished a number of sentences, when right before my eyes another sentence appeared, which was a message for me!

Both my uncle and my father manipulate the lights in the different rooms when they come and visit with me, and they each have their own style of manipulation. Souls on the Other Side try to be subtle when sending soul signs, and this is because they do not want to frighten us. My Uncle Stan usually blinks the lights in the bathroom while I am in front of the mirror and he blinks the lights in our basement. My father has blinked the lights in the different rooms of my house such as the study, the laundry room, and the side door off my laundry room. He also blinks the lights at different times when I travel, for example, while staying at the Fairmont Hotel one evening, and another time in the hallway at the hotel in Dominican Republic. No matter where I go, I know there is always someone with me. This has become quite evident when photos are taken.

Downtown, Las Vegas—The soul orb is to the right side of my feet

Christmas Eve in my house—The soul orb is to
the top, left side of my Christmas Tree

Both my uncle and father have also gotten my attention while I have been in stores shopping. One such time was when I was far away from home and living in Saudi Arabia. It is April 26, 2007, and I go shopping at the Dhahran Mall in Al-Khobar. This is a huge mall with many stores. I am standing in one of the stores looking at clothing on a rack, when the light directly above me starts to blink. I look up at the light, which is blinking very softly and regularly. Immediately I know my father is with me! My dad starts to speak to me using telepathy. "I'm very proud of you and this is just the beginning of great things to come for you." With tears in my eyes, I am unable to answer because I feel so emotional. The light above stops blinking and I know my father will always be there for me, even in Saudi Arabia!

Another time while I was out shopping, I bought a figurine of an angel. Even though I bought the angel myself, I knew it was really a gift from my father because he was with me in the store. I had gone to the hair salon earlier in the day and for some unknown reason to me, I decided to have my hair styled in a different way than usual. Rather than have my hair combed on the left side, I chose to have it combed in the middle. Much to my astonishment, the angel had the exact same hairstyle; it was the same length as mine, the same color and parted in the middle. I know my dad impressed upon me to buy the angel, which looked like me. I call her the Olive Angel.

The Olive Angel

Birds, like robin red breasts, blue jays, and crows, can represent soul signs. My wonderful friend, Marilyn Maddigan, shared a story with me when she experienced a soul sign.

Marilyn owns two dogs, which she cherishes with all her heart, one of which she had fostered but had decided to adopt. This particular dog, Sasha, suffered from anxiety and separation anxiety in particular, as she had been in several different foster homes before Marilyn took her. It was on a sunny afternoon and Marilyn decides to take Sasha for a walk. Sasha had on her leash and they both head out the door and go down the stairs. As they start their walk, Marilyn loses her footing but manages to catch herself before falling face first onto the ground. However, as she falls, she loses her grip on Sasha's leash and her dog takes off running! Marilyn quickly runs back into her house and grabs her cell phone; unfortunately when she returns outside, Sasha is nowhere to be seen. Marilyn has no idea where Sasha is, or which direction she took. At that moment she starts to feel panicky. She tries to calm down, all the while repeating to herself, "I'll find her. I'll find her." As she speaks these words, a real sense of peace and calmness comes over her and instantly she knows everything would work out, because she believes her guardian angels are with her. Marilyn runs down the street calling Sasha's name, however, Sasha is nowhere to be seen. She then stops running and says aloud, "I need help. Please give me a sign if I am going in the wrong direction to find Sasha." She continues walking, when suddenly out of nowhere comes this huge group of crows; the number of crows is so large, she has never witnessed so many crows at one time, ever, flying through the sky! There is at least forty crows! As Marilyn stares at the crows in amazement, all of a sudden, the crows stop in mid-air, turn around, and fly in the opposite direction. She realizes this is the sign she asked for just minutes earlier. She instantly turns around and goes in the opposite direction. As she approaches the top of the incline, she sees Sasha running into her neighbors' back yard. Marilyn quickly turns the corner of the house, to find that the yard is fenced in and Sasha doesn't have anywhere to go. It is at that moment, Marilyn grabs the end of her beloved dog's leash!

Your Guardian Souls or Guardian Angels can also send you soul signs with such things as white feathers, ladybugs, numbers, songs, phrases, photos, and of course butterflies. One day while shopping in Saudi Arabia, everywhere I went I saw beautiful butterflies! In one store, there was a beautiful blue butterfly pin, which I bought as a gift to myself, and later, a young salesperson gave me a blue butterfly for my cell phone as a gift! It is very common also to see photos moved in a different place or moved in a different direction, such as lying flat down.

Some souls try to get our attention by making knocking sounds, which my Uncle Abel did in my parents' house one evening. We were all sitting in the family room and across the hallway from the family room came a knocking sound on the wall in the dining room. Upon investigation, there was nothing, which could have contributed to the knocking sound, but immediately I could sense it was my uncle. At the time, my aunt, who is my uncle's wife, was visiting.

Souls can also impress us with a particular song on the radio, for example, the song, "In Dreams" by Roy Orbison tells me that my father is reminding me that I had a visit with him the night before while I was sleeping and dreaming. My father's favorite song is "Now I'm 64" and when I hear this song playing, I immediately sense my father's presence. One such time was on New Year's Eve 2011, when my husband and I were driving to Woodstock Colonial Inn for the New Year's Eve Gala. My dad's favorite song started to play on the radio, and instantly I knew he was with us in the car. There are times when I may just start humming this song to myself, and immediately I know my father is with me. Another song that gets my attention is the song, "Save Your Love" by Renee and Renato. I dedicated this song to my dad on Father's Day in June 2012, because when I heard it, I knew right away it was a special song for my father, and it was my gift to him. Now this song just comes to my mind at different times, for no apparent reason, other than my dad letting me know he is thinking of me or he has come to visit with me.

Other ways souls or our loved ones try to get our attention is by impressing us with a particular scent such as a perfume or the odor of a certain brand of cigarettes or cigars, if they smoked during their life on Earth.

Feathers are also a common soul sign. There was one such time my dear friend Lisa experienced seeing feathers in her pathway. One morning she was walking to the bus stop to catch the bus to Newcastle, when she saw two feathers in front of her. She picked up the two feathers and as she did, she wondered to herself, if she would see another one because she recalled that everything seems to happen in threes. Then suddenly when she looked in the direction where the bus comes, she could see a white feather falling from the sky. It landed about 10 feet away from her! She found this quite amazing, to watch this feather literally fall from the sky to the ground, with no wind whatsoever or bird in sight! She says that whenever she sees a feather, she always thinks of me because until she met me, she never knew the significance of feathers or even noticed them.

My wonderful friend Christine found a white feather with a gray tip. She knew about feathers being soul signs, so she asked me what the meaning of this feather meant. I told her the white feather means love, but because the tip of the feather is gray, this signifies that the sender recognizes she is going through somewhat of a difficult time in her life, but it will only last for a short time, and he was sending her love. If the tip of the white feather had been black, this would indicate that her troublesome time is extremely difficult. If the feather had been black, with a white tip, this would mean a deeply troubled time in her life, and it would last for quite some time.

I too have experienced feathers in my life, knowing they were soul signs sent to me. One such time was when my husband and I were about ready to embark a cruise ship in San Pedro, California, when right in front of me, on the ground, was a beautiful blue feather. Later, while aboard the cruise ship, we were at dinner with another couple and I was sharing with them the story of the blue feather. I could tell our friends were somewhat skeptical; however, after we were leaving the dining room, again, right in front of me, was another beautiful blue feather! They just looked at me with such an expression of bewilderment on their faces that I could not help but laugh.

A particular word, thought, sound, smell, color, or object can suddenly pop into your mind. It is common for most people to ignore these soul signs by pushing them out of their consciousness and concentrating on their world around them. It is also common for the soul sign to reappear in your mind. It can be very vivid; however, if you are not spiritually aware, once again you will dismiss the important spiritual information that a loved one is sending to you. If your loving soul is persistent, the sign will most likely appear to you again. If you choose not be become spiritually aware, unfortunately you are choosing to ignore vital information which is of utmost significance to you.

Soul signs are also soul symbols which when worn are a powerful form of protection. For example, I wear my cross around my neck when I feel I need protection to visit certain people or places. I also keep my Bible on my nightstand, which I know is a form of protection throughout the night while I sleep. Before I went to Saudi Arabia, my husband and I took a Caribbean Cruise. One evening during dinner, one of the guests aboard the ship asked me why I would ever consider going to Saudi Arabia to live. I really could not understand his question and told him so. He very quickly pointed out that, as a Christian, I could not bring my Bible or any other Christian symbol, such as a cross, into this Muslim country. I was very swift to reply. "I can make a cross out of anything, no matter where I am in the world." I did just that and, after I arrived in Saudi Arabia I made a cross out of toothpicks, and kept it in my living room on my shelf.

My wooden cross made out of toothpicks

Signs are also seen with the different numbers that keep showing up in your life, whether you see them on license plates, on clocks, or any other place. A dear and loving friend of mine, Trisha Wakat Shafer, was going through a very difficult time in her life, and consequently made the bad decision to drink and drive. The police arrested her for a DWI, drinking while intoxicated, and she became so devastated that she decided she would stop fighting for custody of her children, because she felt so ashamed and like a complete failure. However, that night she woke up at exactly 3:16 in the morning, and instantly the verse from the Holy Bible, 1 John 3:16 came to her mind. *Hereby perceive we the love of God, because he laid down his life for us:* It was then she saw a small beam of light in her bedroom, and she describes it as "a lamp at my feet." That Sunday, she went to church and during the service, the passage read from the Holy Bible was, 1 John 3:16. She now knows that when things get hard and she feels the world is against her, God lets her know she is not alone and gives her confirmation with the passage, 1 John 3:16. She gives thanks to our Lord Jesus, knowing that all things work together for His glory and His timing.

A similar experience happened to me with the numbers 444. Some years ago, I woke up at exactly 4:44 in the morning. This went on for three consecutive mornings, at exactly the same time each morning. I knew instinctively that there were angels around me, and I could feel their love. The angels spoke to me each morning and told me that the numbers 444 are spiritual signs from God and the numbers 444 mean that the angels are around me, especially my Guardian Angel, and that God's love is with me. A kindred soul, who I had met at a spiritual conference some years earlier, first introduced me to the numbers 444. She told me about the importance of the numbers 444 and offered me her book to read, called *The Messengers* by Julia Ingram and G. W. Hardin. At the time, she also gave me a soul message. "When you see the numbers 444, ask for a miracle."

Ever since that time, I see the numbers 444 very frequently in my life and as soon as I see them, the feeling comes over me that I am doing well; I am on the right track, that I am following my life plan and fulfilling my life journey to the best of my ability during this lifetime. I have this feeling because I know it is a message for me from the angels. At that time, I also ask for a miracle. The number 1111 has great significance and spiritual importance also. My son tells me that whenever I see this number 1111, I should always make a wish.

The number 57 also has critical meaning to me in my life. When I see the number 57, I feel some sense of change is going to take place. Sometimes this can mean a warning, beware, caution, disappointment, or the feeling that there will be conflict or that danger is near, for it represents change. Change is either positive or negative, and can always foster spiritual growth.

I know that the number 8 represents me as a soul. I also know that the number 6 and the number 8 represent soul signs to me that tell me that I am following my spiritual life plan while living here on Earth. The numbers 6 and 8 can be together to form the number 68 or they can be separate, with just the number 6 or just the number 8. The numbers 6 and 8 can also go in combination with the numbers: 0, 1, 2, or 3. The numbers 6 and 8 have been with me all my life, and they go with me wherever I go, and are associated with anyone who has important and close ties to me.

Examples of my soul signs presented to me during my life, in the form of either the number 6 or the number 8, are as follows:

- My birth—September 16

- My Grandfather dies—October 8

- The day I got engaged to be married—September 16

- My sister's wedding day, I was her maid of honor—July 8

- My wedding day—April 28

- God gave me my beautiful baby boy—May 8

- God gave me my beautiful baby girl—October 6

- My sister's wedding day, I was master of ceremonies—March 18

- My beloved dog Tippy dies—October 28

- My Uncle Stan dies—July 26

- My first contact with my Guardian Soul, Uncle Edward—February 28

- A bird comes to my bedroom window chirping—April 16
- My husband's tragic car accident—May 8
- One blue jay in my garden—May 18
- My husband returns home from the hospital—June 6
- I go to Corner Brook after my husband's car accident—October 28
- My husband's first day returning to work on "ease back"—January 28
- One robin red breast in our garden—February 8
- My husband drives his car for the first time since his car accident—May 8
- One black crow on my door step, facing me as I approach my house—April 8
- My father's death—April 8
- While in the North West Territories, sleeping during the night, I wake because I had a visit from my father who gave me a very important message—April 16
- My father visits me in my apartment in Saudi Arabia—January 26
- Seven Angels visit me in my apartment in Saudi Arabia—January 28
- My Uncle Stan and my dad visit me in my apartment in Saudi Arabia—January 28
- I finish reading the complete Bible—October 8
- I meet Adam in San Diego—March 28
- I see the blue butterfly for the first time—April 6
- I find a beautiful butterfly in our house—August 26
- My son tells me I should make a wish when I see the numbers 1111—December 6
- My daughter's wedding day—October 16
- My beautiful dog, Katie, would have died—December 16
- Joan of Arc's birth—January 6

The following is a list of the different places where I lived for any permanent length of time, after leaving my parents' house, and living on my own:

- Room # 628, Nurses' Residence, Grace General Hospital
- Lot # 6, Gail Place
- 8 Kilbride Ave.
- 8 LaManche Place
- 60 Perlin St.
- 18 Fleet St.

Soul signs have become an everyday occurrence for me, for without them I would feel lost in this faraway land we call Earth. Soul signs let me know that I am guided and protected every minute of every day, by my Heavenly Father, my Guardian Angel, Gabriel, my other six angels, my Guardian Souls, Aunt Mildred and Uncle Edward, as well as my Uncle Stan and my dad, while I continue my travels on this life journey, for this lifetime.

Epilogue

Simply put,
there is more power in knowledge
and awareness than ignorance.

James Van Praagh
Ghosts Among Us

One of my spiritual purposes during this lifetime on Earth is to write this book, *Secrets of My Soul*. All my life I have been hungry for knowledge, but not just any type of knowledge, it had to be spiritual knowledge. Now as I look back over my life, I have come to understand that this was all part of my learning process in preparation for me writing this book, and singled out for a special mission while on my life journey. God has prepared me to serve Him and I will strive to do so with excellence, for I possess a deep love that has such an impact on my devotion to complete these writings. If I am able to help at least one person, then I know I have accomplished my spiritual mission.

This book has been one of the most challenging experiences of my life, for I have been working on this manuscript for about twelve years, and I always questioned myself as to why it is taking me so long to complete. Then one day, a loving voice speaks to me and tells me that the time is right; for I will complete my manuscript in the year 2012; for the year 2012, is the year for the beginning of transformation, and that my book will be available to all, in the year 2013, a time for new beginnings!

Because the year 2012, is the year for the beginning of transformation, I would like to share with you a discussion I had with a friend of mine in May 2012, where he tells me about the most remarkable meeting he had with his guardian spirits several years ago while driving home on the highway. He said the event was so dramatic it left him crying. The guardian spirits, as he calls them, tells him that he has to make his own way, he is responsible for his actions, and he must accept the consequences on Earth for the pain he causes here. They offer no comfort, only for him to know that no matter what happens, they would always be with him, and not only in the good times, but also the bad times. They do not help or intervene, but watch out for the safety of his soul. Everything else they said was up to him.

I too received very powerful spiritual messages while living in Saudi Arabia. I had been to the Middle East before and because of life circumstances, thought I would never go back again. Then things just started to fall into place without any effort; it was like pieces of a jigsaw puzzle automatically fitting into place, and I knew I was on the right path. I knew that if I was not on the right path, I would experience roadblocks all along the way, and I could either travel the path or veer off it and do something completely different. Instead, I chose to travel the path presented to me because there was no doubt in my mind that God had orchestrated the events in my life, and that everything was perfect, including the timing.

It is January 26, 2008. I am sitting in my apartment, in Al-Khobar, Saudi Arabia, when the song "You Never Walk Alone" comes on the radio. After the song finishes playing, my father appears in my apartment, and this time, I am able to see him. He speaks to me. "You have to get prepared and you will not be alone. I will be with you. I will leave now but I will be back. And if you need me, all you have to do is call out to me and I will hear you, and come." He then slowly fades away.

Two evenings later, on January 28, 2008, while relaxing on my sofa, in my apartment, once again in Al-Khobar, Saudi Arabia, seven angels appear, and one of them is Gabriel! The seven angels are all male and they are all dressed in long, floor length, white robes, with long sleeves, a hood, and a white rope belt, tied at the waist, hanging down the left side. I do not become alarmed, for I know instantly that they are very loving, and besides, my father and my Uncle Stan are with them! Only one speaks by using telepathy and he says to me, "We have come to speak with you." Also using telepathy, I question, "Who are you?" The same male speaks, again not speaking the words aloud, but speaking using telepathy. "We are angels. We will continue to be with you on this journey and aid you in your spiritual accomplishments. You have been given free will which is a gift from God, and it is through your free will whether or not you will choose to forge ahead, and tell your secrets to the world." It is at this moment that I know that my trip to Saudi Arabia has been for far greater reasons than employment. I answer, also using telepathy. "I will forge ahead and tell my secrets to the world. But won't there be many who will not believe what it is I have to say?" The same male angel replies, "There will be many but that means they will choose to live in darkness; for they too have been bestowed upon them the gift of free will. Yet, remember, there will be many who will listen to what you have to say, and you will help many." He then fades out of sight, as well as the other angels and my uncle and dad.

Later that night, I have the most wonderful dream, except it did not seem like a dream; for it seemed I was actually there. I was in this huge room, decorated with such magnificent furnishings. With me were many others, however, the others were mostly males dressed in tuxedos. One of the males is my father, and he too is wearing the white dinner jacket with the black tuxedo pants, the same he wore the day of my wedding. I too am dressed in formal attire, wearing a long, white flowing gown, with long, pointed, v-shaped sleeves, and a v-shaped neckline, with a long, v-shaped back, all embroidered with diamonds. The diamonds sparkle beyond anything I had ever seen on Earth. I remember my father giving me such a loving compliment, telling me how beautiful and radiant I look. He then takes my hand and guides me to a long, floor length mirror, where I look at myself. My hair is blond, and pinned up with not a hair out of place. As I look at myself in the mirror, I express to my father, "Dad, these can't be real diamonds." He gives a big smile. "Yes, they are real diamonds, and you deserve each one of them."

One of my big fears while writing this book is whether many would believe what it is I have to say. In February 2010, I attended my first writers' conference in San Francisco, California, and as I started my pitch with the recall of events of that December 28 night, when I met my Heavenly Father, a flood of memories swept over me, and I collapse in a torrent of tears. Nina, who is listening to my pitch, looks at me with compassion and love in her eyes. When I ask the question, "Do you believe what I am telling you to be true?" She simply responds, "Yes."

A year later, in February 2011, I take a trip to San Diego, California and while there, I meet the most remarkable woman, Alicia Marion. I know instantly she is a messenger from God. As she sits, she tells me she is, and has come to meet with me. Sitting in silence and awe, she gives me very powerful, spiritual messages. "I have been told to tell you, be so much kinder to yourself. Show yourself great, great gentleness. They do not judge you and therefore you can do no wrong ever. You cannot make a mistake. You do journeys. Do not take anything seriously, as nothing is real for you. Only see the good things. Make a list of silly things and laugh. Change what you remember as pain. All the things in your life that you remember that give you great pain and anguish, yes they happened, now erase everything. In addition, replace all the sadness with memories of all the good things that have happened to you. And, remember that the depth of the pain is always equal to the abundance of love experienced. Also, once you know you are powerful, you can no longer pretend that you are not, for you are at the threshold of the vortex, and you are about to enter. And He says to you, 'My child, I do not take, for I receive.'"

It is two years later, on July 2013, when I meet with an Indian Chief who gives me more powerful spiritual messages. This Indian Chief is wearing the traditional Indian headpiece with blue and white feathers, and by just being in his company, I know I am in the presence of a great master. He speaks to me. "You will awaken the dead. The people walking the Earth are wearing blindfolds and they are the walking dead because they are very foolish people. They are not powerful like you. There will be a time of healing for all people of all nations. You have started the healings and you must continue. There is great work to be done. Don't ever feel like you are alone, because you aren't. With your help, we can move mountains. The people of the Earth have been living in darkness too long. There is a great gift bestowed upon you. You will save many souls, lost souls who are trying to find their way in the darkness. The more they try to get away from the darkness, the darker they become. A lot of healing needs to take place and the time has come. Go in peace."

I choose to walk in God's path of righteousness and love and to make a full commitment to God to love and to serve, and to do His will. It is God's will and I will humbly serve. I now find myself with a new inner peace. I choose to live in peace, harmony and love, and you can choose the same also; it is your choice.

Conclusion

My philosophy of life is similar to that of the fifteenth-century Jewish philosopher, Joseph Albo, whose belief is that we must not think that something is impossible, simply because our mind does not understand it. If your mind does not understand, you can teach it to understand, and to know what is real. I have spent a lifetime searching for the truth and I do not have to search anymore, and neither do you. If you too are a "doubting Thomas," challenge yourself to learn the truth. The moment I *knew* the truth, the name "doubting Thomas" disappeared from me, and so if you too consider yourself a "doubting Thomas," search for the truth and remove the name from you forever. My purpose in writing this book is not to convince anyone of anything; however, my purpose is to challenge you, the reader, to seek the truth, and to *know* what is real.

The more knowledge you obtain, the more you learn and grow, and I know this is true for me. You are honoring your soul and God by obtaining knowledge and therefore knowing the truth. Knowledge provides intelligence, which in turn speaks the spiritual truth. There is a difference between believing and knowing, for to know speaks the spiritual truth and in turn, the spiritual truth gives you power. This spiritual truth will set you free. You will experience the feeling of becoming a free soul. Because you have chosen to learn the spiritual truth and to grow spiritually, you will elevate yourself to a higher spiritual level, closer to God. When it is your time to leave Earth, you will have made the choice where it is you will return to. Make the choice to return to our Home, which is Heaven.

I once read that we all have a map in a tiny suitcase, called a heart, and along with the map, we have a compass, called the mind. Use your heart, mind and soul, to explore and search for the truth, for the truth awaits you, and the truth will set you free.

In closing, I offer you a Native American Prayer by Yellow Hawk, Sioux Chief:

Oh Great Spirit,

Make me ever ready to come to You,
with clean hands and straight eyes,
so when life fades as a fading sunset,
my spirit may come to You without shame.

We are all God's children, so this means that you are my brother or sister. God loves you, and therefore I do also. Choose love over hate. Choose to walk with peace and love in your heart for the remainder of your short visit here on this Earth. Choose to be a loving soul. I wish you love, peace, and happiness and I bless you with my love, and may God bless you with His.

If you would like to share your own personal, spiritual experience you may have had, I would love to hear from you. Please contact me by e-mail at:

oliveneilnoseworthy@hotmail.com

The Olive Angel Foundation

God grant me the serenity
to accept the things I cannot change;
courage to change the things I can;
and wisdom to know the difference.

Reinhold Niebuhr

In 2008, I moved to Hamilton, Ontario to live and to work and while there, I questioned in my mind why I considered moving to a smaller city. It really did not make any sense to me, but I knew there must be a bigger reason for me being in Hamilton, much bigger than I could understand. I also knew that everything would be revealed to me in God's time, and not in mine.

God's time started almost immediately. I remember walking down the sidewalk on King Street one sunny afternoon, and as I passed by a store window, I could not help but notice a poster in the window of a young male who had gone missing. The poster read that on February 22, 2006 in Hamilton, Ontario, Canada, William (Billy) Mason was last seen in the area of 917 Main Street East.

Then not even a year later, while still living in Hamilton, on April 8, 2009 in Woodstock, Ontario, Canada, eight-year-old Victoria (Tori) Stafford went missing. The news alert stated that Victoria was last seen being escorted from her school grounds at Oliver Stephens Public School by an unknown female.

Later I was to learn about Jessie Foster. Jessie, 22 years old, was recruited in Calgary, Canada, to work in Las Vegas, U.S.A. For ten months after Jessie moved to Las Vegas, family members would hear from her almost daily either by e-mail, phone or text message. Then on March 28, 2006, all contact stopped. The belief is that Jessie may have fallen victim to an international human trafficking ring. Human trafficking is the abuse and exploitation of humans, in particular children and young males and females, for the purposes of sexual pleasure.

Jessie Foster—Missing, March 28, 2006

Here were my spiritual numbers staring back at me! It was as though a light bulb had gone off in my head because I instantly knew at that moment that helping to find missing children was also part of my spiritual work! God has given me special abilities and the message I received was that I was to use these special abilities to help bring these missing children home and to help bring closure. I also received a message that I would tell the world that these predators have to stop because they will never get away with these hateful crimes, for someone is always watching and they will have a very high price to pay.

When a child or a loved one goes missing, it has to be one of the most heart wrenching and devastating things that can happen to the missing child or missing adult; and for the family members and loved ones left behind to search and grieve. It is the belief of many that human trafficking is the fastest growing criminal industry in the world, and that millions of people live in modern-day slavery, including children.

The dedicated individuals making up the Olive Angels span throughout the world, and commit their time and abilities to help determine the circumstances and whereabouts of the missing child or missing adult, and to reunite them with their searching families and loved ones.

Founded in June 2010, the Olive Angel Foundation, a non-profit organization, is for these missing children, missing adults, and their families and loved ones.

A portion of the proceeds of this book entitled, *Secrets of My Soul*, goes to the Olive Angel Foundation.

To learn more about this important work, and for further information regarding me, please visit:

www.oliveneilnoseworthy.com
www.facebook.com/oliveneilnoseworthy
www.twitter.com/secretsofsoul
www.linkedin.com

Lightning Source UK Ltd.
Milton Keynes UK
UKOW03f144100914

238306UK00001BA/54/P